76489

S0-BRG-704

Music on My Mind

THE MEMOIRS OF

AN AMERICAN PIANIST

by *Willie the Lion Smith*

with GEORGE HOEFER

DA CAPO PRESS • NEW YORK • 1975

Library of Congress Cataloging in Publication Data

Smith, Willie, 1897-1973.
  Music on my mind.

  (The Roots of jazz)
  Reprint of the 1st ed., 1964, published by Doubleday,
Garden City, N.Y.
  Includes bibliographies, a discography, and index.
  1. Musicians—Correspondence, reminiscences, etc.
2. Jazz music. I. Hoefer, George. II. Title.
ML417.S675A3   1975   786.1'092'4 [B]   74-23406
ISBN 0-306-70684-9

Published by Da Capo Press, Inc.
A Subsidiary of Plenum Publishing Corporation
227 West 17th Street, New York, N.Y. 10011

MUSIC ON MY MIND

Music on My Mind

THE MEMOIRS OF

AN AMERICAN PIANIST

by *Willie the Lion Smith*

with GEORGE HOEFER

FOREWORD BY

DUKE ELLINGTON

Doubleday & Company, Inc., Garden City, New York, 1964

LIBRARY OF CONGRESS CATALOG CARD NUMBER 64-13840
COPYRIGHT © 1964 BY WILLIE SMITH AND GEORGE HOEFER
ALL RIGHTS RESERVED
PRINTED IN THE UNITED STATES OF AMERICA
FIRST EDITION

To Silvertop, better known as Jane

ACKNOWLEDGMENTS

They tell me that if you get somebody to write your book for you there's something funny about it. Well, let's have none of that. Nobody wrote this book for me but this book wouldn't *be* if George Hoefer hadn't put the words down on paper. But almost all the words he got from me. You ask *anybody* if anybody ever said anything for the Lion. They're lucky if they get to say it with him.

I owe thanks also to Dr. and Mrs. Arthur Logan. The doctor, one of the world's best men, is co-director of the upper Manhattan medical group and he is responsible for keeping a good many good musicians alive. His beautiful wife, Marian, once worked at Doubleday and she brought me together with the publishers.

And, of course, those cosmic influences had a lot to do with it. The Lion, a Sagittarian, has an affinity for those born under the sign of Leo. My two August-born colleagues, George Hoefer and Sam Vaughan, were sent to me by the spirits because sympathetic planets are in all our houses.

Yeah, the Lion roars when the vibrations are right!

FOREWORD

My name is Edward Kennedy Ellington; also Duke Ellington.
Before I left Washington, D.C., to come to New York I spent
all my time listening to piano players: Doc Perry, Lester
Dishman, Louis Brown, Turner Layton, Gertie Wells, Clarence
Bowser, Sticky Mack, Blind Johnny, Cliff Jackson, Claude
Hopkins, Phil Wurd, Caroline Thornton from Washington,
Luckey Roberts from New York, Eubie Blake from Baltimore,
Joe Rochester, Harvey Brooks from Philadelphia—and all the
others who passed through Washington. So you see that makes
me an eligible dilettante. Eligible also to speak about another
piano player, to play him an introduction:

THE LION

The Lion—Willie the Lion—Willie the Lion Smith—what a
wealth of subject tingle! Would that I were sufficiently prolific
to expound on the endless excitement and adventure of my
first meeting and total exposure to this melodic, harmonic
kaleidoscope.

Sonny Greer and I were real tight buddies and, naturally,
night creatures. Our first night out in New York we got all
dressed up and went down to the Capitol Palace. Greer had
always told me that he and the Lion were real buddy-buddies
and that we would not have to worry about anything where

spending money was concerned (we had none); so down the steps of the Capitol Palace we start.

My first impression of the Lion—even before I saw him—was the thing I felt as I walked down those steps. A strange thing. A square-type fellow might say, "This joint is jumping," but to those who had become acclimatized—the tempo was the lope —actually everything and everybody seemed to be doing whatever they were doing in the tempo the Lion's group was laying down. The walls and furniture seemed to lean understandingly —one of the strangest and greatest sensations I ever had. The waiters served in that tempo; everybody who had to walk in, out, or around the place walked with a beat.

Downstairs, Sonny took the lead waving at people, people I know he did not know, but some of them figured, I suppose, "Well, maybe I know that cat from someplace," and waved back, and some even invited us for a drink, which of course we always accepted. When Greer got to the Lion (incidentally the Lion was from Newark and Greer from Long Branch) Greer ups and says, "Hey, Lion, you remember me, Jersey-boy Sonny Greer"—he then proceeded to rattle off a few names of hustlers, pimps, etc.—from Long Branch.

"I want you to meet the Duke," says Sonny. "He is just a yearling, you know. Hey, Duke, come on over, shake hands with Willie Smith the Lion, my man."

The Lion extends his hand and says, "Glad to meet you, kid," —and, looking over his shoulder—"Sit in there for me for a couple of numbers. D-flat. As one of those Western piano plonkers just fell in, I want him to take the stool so I can crush him later," he adds.

This is the great thing about the Lion: a gladiator at heart. Anybody who had a reputation as a piano player had to prove it right there and then by sitting down to the piano and displaying his artistic wares. And when a cat thought that he was something special, he usually fell into that trap (or, you might say, into the jaws of the Lion) and he always came out with his reputation all skinned up, covered with the lacerations of humiliation, because before he got through too many stanzas the Lion was standing over him, cigar blazing.

Like if the cat was weak with the left hand, the Lion would say, "What's the matter, are you a cripple?" Or, "When did you break your left arm?" Or, "Get up. I will show you how it is supposed to go."

The Lion has been the greatest influence on most of the great piano players who have been exposed to his fire, his harmonic lavishness, his stride—what a luxury. Fats Waller, James P. Johnson, Count Basie, Donald Lambert, Joe Turner, Sam Ervis, and of course I swam in it. Most of it still clings—agreeably. Even the great Art Tatum, as great as he was—and I know he was the greatest—showed strong patterns of Willie Smithisms after being exposed to the Lion. I have never heard anybody accompany a singer like the Lion (they used to sing twenty or thirty choruses, each one different), and every supporting phrase that Willie played fit like a glove and drove her into her next melodic statement.

I love him—he is wonderful. I can't think of anything good enough to say about the Lion, Willie the Lion, Willie the Lion Smith.

EDITOR'S NOTE

Willie the Lion Smith is a pianist, a composer, a gunner, a rabbi, a Harlem oral historian and raconteur, and a patron of other jazz musicians.

No book can capture a man completely, and Willie the Lion's is not an exception. Missing from these pages is the sound of his voice: a grainy but gentle tone with an occasional friendly growl, a soft whisper, a deep chuckle. Music, as he says, is on his mind and it is in his talk, too.

He stammered as a child but he seldom stammers now. When he does, it is either because he has received a momentary setback in his durable conviction that life and all the people in it are beautiful, or because he does it on purpose at the piano. "I have played in a stammering way at times," he said in one session as we worked on the book, "looking for another strain. I call that 'searching.'"

A word about the history that follows. Willie's Boswell, George Hoefer, has made every effort to add reliable historical information in "Interludes" added to Willie's account. The author's own sense of history is immense; he seems to have known, almost from the start, that he was a part of something big. But the Lion's memory is not infallible. He can swing from a telling set of notes on the protocol of the Harlem night club to a perfectly outrageous or impossible story told winningly. Whatever contradictions or omissions there may be we

have not attempted to sort out or set straight. The facts, important as they are, and too much buffing up of the material seemed
less vital than to stay with the Lion's version of what he saw
and what he did.

He is, as everyone who knows him and as the reader will
soon discover, not without ego and not without humility. For
him jazz did not begin downriver somewhere, and he has seen
more than one ragtime or show-business legend in dishabille.
He can put a man down or build him up and with some men
he does both. The result is that his ideas on life are delivered,
as he remarked in another connection, with an effect "a little
like cursing, a little like praying." But he does everything his
way. "Always tell the truth," the Lion teaches, "it's going to
cross you again. You got to pass my house to get to yours."

The Lion can say, unblinkingly, "I played a little Chopin, the
last thirty-two bars of which I rewrote," because that is the way
he thinks, that is the way it was, and that is his truth. Timme
Rosenkrantz quoted him on the First World War. "It was a
tough war," said Willie, "and I'm proud and happy that I won
it."

There is at least one other thing missing too, of course:
Willie's piano. Some of the talking part of his performances
shows here, but music is its own medium. If you can find the
Lion's records, play them before or as you read. They may say
more than he has said here, or less, but they will certainly be in
harmony.

They are almost all gone now—Fats, Bechet, James P., Jelly
Roll, the men who figure in these pages and in Willie's memory.
But Willie the Lion, bless him, is very much with us. "I can't
sleep half the time," Willie once said to me, "because I've got
music on my mind." Who would have it otherwise?

SSV

CONTENTS

MUSIC ON MY MIND

1

Music on My Mind

I wake each morning and first start yawning
Then hum a beautiful tune as a vocation.
It's my line
I've got music on my mind.*

The Lion is here. Full name: William Henry Joseph Bonaparte Bertholoff Smith. Quite a name. Takes in French and Jewish. What I'm going to tell you is all the true facts.

First, the Lion has always had music on his mind.

My mother used to say, "Willie, you've got a real truth to tell the people and you've got a God-given right to scream it at them. But you must remember—that sometimes the screaming won't do any good."

She spoke the truth. This world is full of chirpers, belchers, and flips from the funny papers who like to go out on the town. I learned to go home when my antennae picked up vibrations from the off-key kids and the whisky tenors. You might as well try making love to each member of a girl quartet at the same time as to try playing your music when the vibrations are

* From *Music on My Mind* by Willie the Lion Smith, with lyrics by Lillian Ross.

wrong. The Lion knows. He was born under Saturn, the get-it-the-hard-way planet.

A man's music comes from his heart and soul, flavored by the spiritual inspirations derived from the stars and his environment. When those bad vibrations reach you, you've either got to dominate them or give them silent treatment. I've learned it is better to duck than to hurry yourself out of this world by thinking you can roll with the punches. Loud people are like a bad drink of whisky—you either fight them or join them. Either way, it's a bad idea.

One night, Barney Josephson invited me down to his Café Society Downtown to entertain his customers. I was happy to help old Barney out, but when I walked in, ready to make my usual announcement, "The Lion is here!" a wave of hostile vibrations met me head on. The room was full of jabbering voices and the piano in the corner was hidden under a pile of mink coats. That crowd was there to be heard, not to listen.

My only announcement that night was quiet—"The Lion's here, but this ain't his lair." I went back home and called Josephson on the phone. "I only roar when the feeling is right," I informed him. "You need a cocktail-hour piano player."

An experienced performer just can't afford to have his reputation hurt, and that is what happens when you try to buck the current. There are and have been too many musicians allowing themselves to be pushed around like a herd of cattle.

Now what I'm going to tell you about the music business is all the true facts, because music has occupied my mind for a lifetime. I am climaxing sixty-five years on the scene. It has been a good life and no one in the music line has enjoyed it any more than I have. But there have been rough spots. That is what this book is all about—the good and the bad.

I've played it all, barrel house, ragtime, blues, Dixieland, boogiewoogie, swing, bebop, bop—even the classics. It doesn't make any difference what names the writers and the music critics want to paste on—it's all music and it's all an expression from the soul of a human being.

What they call jazz is just the music of people's emotions. It comes from wherever there have been colored people gathered together during the last hundred years. You'd think from reading the jazz books, most of them written by non-playing, so-called critics, that all the jazz and all the musicians came from New Orleans. They'd have you believing that if a musician had not been born down in those swamps, down in the Delta country, he had no business trying to play jazz.

Well, I'll tell you. All the different forms can be traced back to Negro church music, and the Negroes have worshiped God for centuries, whether they lived in Africa, the southern United States, or in the New York City area. You can still hear some of the older styles of jazz playing, the old rocks, stomps, and ring shouts right in the churches of Harlem today.

Sure it made a difference where a musician was born. Various parts of the country had their own particular styles. When those of us around New York, Baltimore, and down as far as Georgia got a good romp-down going, we called it a slow-drag. We'd tell each other, "Now I'm really going to get in the alley." This meant we were going to tell the folks what it was all about, just like a blood and thunder Baptist preacher sounding off. What they called a carving contest was when we would try to see who could decorate a well-known melody with the best variations.

The writers who make up titles for the ways of playing music have called our piano style here on the eastern seaboard Harlem Stride Piano. I'm not very sure I know what they are talking about. I do know how we played here in the East. A good pianist had to be able to play with both hands, performing in perfect unison. It was like learning to walk correctly. Some people just lope along, others walk like they are crippled, while a good walker goes forth with balance and dignity. We had such control that we could play a different song with each hand at the same time. I could play "The Double Eagle March" with my left hand as my right hand was beating out "Home, Sweet Home." A good many modern jazz pianists tinkle with their left hand while their right is going nowhere. They play lame.

Those of us who played in the old-fashioned saloons before Prohibition had to be two-fisted ticklers. We had to be because those saloon owners wanted to hear that piano going all night long. I learned to move the piano with my left, so I could handle the drinks (bought for me by the customers) with my right hand without missing a note.

Yes sir, you can take my word for it, there was a lot of jazz played and sung in other places besides New Orleans in the early days. I first heard the blues sung while I was still a barefoot boy out of New Jersey. It was up around Haverstraw, New York, where they had around thirty-five brickyards. The yards employed Negroes to load and unload the millions of bricks, and when you got anywhere near to that town, you could hear the workers chanting and singing. Many of the songs you heard had things in them you read about in the Bible, or were familiar melodies from the church songs. They sang them in the style that is known as spiritual, or blues, today.

Another thing—all the jazz bands on river boats were not making it up and down the Mississippi, either. There were jazz bands on the boats going up and down the Hudson River. I can recall, as a boy, seeing and hearing bands on the boats with white and Negro musicians playing together. That was something you didn't see on the Mississippi!

The other jazz books? They all have to mention Willie the Lion, because when they came here, they didn't know what street they lived on.

It all goes to prove that music does not stem from any single race, creed, or locality. It comes from a mixture of all these things. As does the Lion.

GOSHEN

My correct, complete name, as I said, is William Henry
Joseph Bonaparte Bertholoff Smith. My mother and grandmother, who had Mohawk Indian blood, selected the names
to represent all the important things in my heritage. The Joseph
came from the Bible, Bonaparte from my French ancestors;
Bertholoff was my real father's last name, and Smith, added
when I was three years old, applied to the name of my stepfather. The William and Henry were added for spiritual balance. They insisted on listing me as plain William H. Smith
when I went into the Army in 1917, but by the time I was dis-
charged in 1919 I had acquired "the Lion," by which I am called
the world over.

It was 1949 before I ever had a chance to see my full name
in print. At that time I was preparing a world tour to play
concerts for the Europeans and Africans. In order to get a
passport, it was necessary to produce a birth certificate. I had
to make a special trip to my birthplace, up in Goshen, New
York, to get the needed vital statistics. Sure enough, they dug
up records in the Orange County Courthouse, and my name
was registered just like my mother, Ida Oliver, had said it should
be. Every one of my names appeared in their proper order,
with the exception of Smith, and, as I said, that was added when
my mother remarried.

According to the birth certificate, I came into the world on
November 25, 1897. My mother had told me it was November
23. It doesn't make any difference, because, using either date,
I was born under Sagittarius, the ninth sign of the zodiac, which
indicates that the Lion is philosophical, religious, and inspirational. My life has been guided by the cosmic laws taught to
me by my mother. She had Spanish and Negro blood, in

addition to her Mohawk, and it was to her that I owe my musical feeling and my volcano-like temper.

I was destined to inherit my mother's psychic powers. She had been born with a veil of skin over her eyes and had an unusual insight into spiritual matters as well as being able to tell what was going to happen in the future. She taught me to watch out for favorable vibrations and to seek out people and situations where I would be most relaxed. For that reason, I have spent most of my life in New York City where the things that appeal to me have happened. This town is the center of it, of big-time show business, of everything. I would rather be a fly on a lamppost in Harlem than a millionaire anywhere else.

Sagittarians all search for the vibrations that will give them the peace of mind they need to succeed. Many other famous and successful people were born under the sign of Sagittarius, the Archer. My sign mates include Sir Winston Churchill, Frank Sinatra, Mark Twain, General Charles de Gaulle, Adam Clayton Powell, Jr., Sammy Davis, Jr., Jean Sibelius, Fred Astaire, and Archie Moore.

I was born in a sportin' man's town. The village of Goshen, up in the Hudson valley above New York, was noted for Historic Park, the oldest horse-racing track in the country. My father, Frank Bertholoff, was a light-skinned playboy who loved his liquor, girls, and gambling. He never did get around to holding down a regular job and my mother worked as a domestic for the Hitchcock family in their mansion. (One of the boys from that wealthy family later became an international polo star.) When my daddy insisted on running around with other women, my mother finally blew her cork and ran him out of the house. That made it necessary for my mother to support me and my two older brothers, as well as to help Granny now and then. But you just can't have romance without finance, and she got tired of giving my old man the loot to spend on his chicks and his betting at the track. I was two years old when Frank Bertholoff got his walking papers.

I can't remember what my father looked like in real life but my mother kept a snapshot of him that she would show me from time to time. He was a handsome man, sharp and smart-looking. My mother told me he was a great dresser and always cut quite a figure with the ladies. She used to say that I favored him in the way I walked, talked, and acted. I must have inherited his concern about wanting to always look good for the opposite sex. A good appearance is good for the mind and soul; it gives a man the dignity to conduct his affairs in the proper manner.

Less than a year after my father had been booted out, he became seriously ill and returned to our house to ask for forgiveness. He begged my mother on bended knees to take him back. It was too late. She had fallen in love with a young master mechanic named John Smith, who had originally lived in Paterson, New Jersey.

Frank Bertholoff passed away in 1901 and left my mother free to marry Smith. My stepfather-to-be was unhappy working in a Goshen garage and went back to Jersey, looking for a job. The marriage took place when he began work driving a wagon for a pork-packing plant in the city of Newark.

Ann Oliver, my mother's mother, had eyes for the big town and wanted us all to move to Greenwich Village. At the time she was living with us after retiring from show business. She had been a banjo player and old Grandma Ann had really been around in her time. She was a veteran of the Primrose and West Minstrels, one of the great traveling shows during the 1890s. (I also had two cousins, Etta and John Bloom, who had been featured dancers in several of the popular minstrel companies.) So, you see, Willie had a show-business tradition from way back, but this didn't mean much to me in the Goshen days.

Yet somewhere, in Goshen, and in Newark, I began to get music on my mind. And the first sound, the first musical sound, that inspired me was the cry of a newborn baby.

2

Mind and Soul Get Together

One day we've got ham and bacon,
*Next day ain't nothin' shakin'.**

Babies were always born at midnight in our house. The sound of a newborn baby is a weird, beautiful sound, and it still lingers in my head.

My education about life started when we went to Newark. We lived on the edge of the tenderloin district, known around the world as the Coast. My stepfather put us into a four-room house with an attic at 76 Academy Street, where the rent was only twelve dollars a month. We were destined to move several times in the next dozen years, as one little Smith after another got born and crowded us out and into a bigger place.

Mother told me all the facts of life when I was still very young. By the time I was fourteen I knew as much about women as I do now. I knew all about pregnancy, for instance. If it's going to be a boy, the woman carries him in the stomach, forward. If the baby is in the hips, it'll be a girl. But my mother told the other kids a 'story that babies came from Woodside, New Jersey (a suburb of Newark), where Mount Pleasant

* From " 'Tain't Nobody's Biz-ness If I Do" by Porter Grainger, published by Pickwick Music Corporation.

cemetery was located. On the nights when a new baby came, four or five of us would be sleeping in one bed in the back room. When we heard a new cry, we would get into an argument about where the new one came from. One or the other of my half brothers would come on with, "We've got a new brother coming in from Woodside." This would always bring an answer from me—"Ah, you're stupid. They don't come from the same place as the burying grounds." I then proceeded to tell them all the truth, or as much of it as I could get out, until my grandmother Ann, who was always on hand for these occasions, rushed in and put her hand over my mouth and whacked my backside.

My mother maintained as much sternness as she could. She liked to have peace and quiet around the house, and although she was very kind, she was also strict as hell. She could control us with a severe look when she wanted to. On those occasions we all knew what she meant without her saying a single word. She had expressive eyes and I learned a good deal from her about reading other people's faces. I studied her moods. You can tell a lot about a person by the way they look at you. By studying a person's face I can tell what they are thinking and if they like me or hate me. If I don't like what I see, I give them the absent treatment. Avoid a fight. My mother, who always figured I had an artistic temperament, told me to try to get along with other people, but to put a lot of distance between myself and those folks whose vibrations clashed with mine. She was afraid that when I became upset my temper would fly out of control. She was right.

Sometimes human beings remind me of animals, the way their heads are shaped, and in the expressions on their faces. My other grandmother, the one on my stepfather's side, was a good example. When she came to Newark from Paterson and wanted to move in with us, we turned her away because she reminded all of us of a hippopotamus, the way she looked and acted. She

could eat like a horse and was in the habit of putting away an
entire turkey at one sitting.

Did you ever notice the eyes of the movie actress Bette
Davis? She's an owl, as is Joan Crawford. Tyree Glenn, the
trombonist, always reminds me of a beetle. Turtles are old-
time bandleader Fess Williams and drummer Cozy Cole. In the
old days we used to call musicians by their animal nicknames.
Stephen Henderson was the Beetle; Willie Gant was the Leop-
ard; Jack Wilson was Jack the Bear; Donald Lambert answered
to the Lamb; and yours truly has always been the Lion.

It was my mother Ida who taught me and who got me started
off in the art of living. She was a very religious person in spite
of the fact that she loved to smoke her pipe, take a nip of
brandy, or sherry, cognac, beer, or whisky. Her life was
wrapped up in church activities. She played the organ and sang
solos every Sunday. During the week she would prepare the
beans for the Ladies' Guild that I had to deliver every Wednesday night.

Among my regular duties also was the reading of the Bible.
I was told to learn all about the apostles, Peter and Paul. Mother
gave me frequent lessons about the prophets, disciples, and
Moses. She also taught me about the planets and the meanings
of the stars. By the time I was five years old, I knew all about
the full moon, half moon, and the quarter moon and what to
expect whenever one of the planets is in my house. If people
learned to watch out for themselves by studying the planets,
there would be fewer wars and catastrophes rushing folks into
the ground.

As I grew older the various religious faiths began to interest
me. I made it a point to visit all the different churches. My
mother told me I could go to any church where God was in
attendance, and so I visited Catholic cathedrals, Jewish syna-
gogues, Baptist foot washings in the river, as well as our own
Presbyterian church on Plane Street. The singing, the rhythmic
singing at the Baptist services was a great inspiration. I heard

the ring shouts and I was moved by all kinds of emotional music. I would seek out places where I could hear the classics as well as the ragtime. Musical sounds were like a magnet that was constantly pulling me toward the source.

We took in washing to help ourselves out with money. My stepfather didn't make much driving that hog wagon. There were several well-to-do Jewish families who were our good customers. Some of them who could eat pork liked to give us business because we could furnish them with hog maws. John Smith could get all the maws he wanted from the plant for nothing. In those days they didn't have much use for pigs' guts around the plant and if someone didn't take them off, they were thrown away. So every morning my stepfather would bring home a bucket of hog maws and pigs' livers. We supplied our neighbors free and sold some to our best laundry customers for a low price. Of course, we fried or boiled some for our own family. Yeah, we practically lived on chitterlings and beans.

All Negro families back in the old days had their own pail, called a gut bucket, in which they used to bring home the makings for chitterlings. That's where they got the term "gut bucket" to denote a low-down style of playing music. Down in New Orleans they had a tune called "Gut Bucket Blues." But they didn't have the only gut buckets.

It was my regular custom to help my mother with the washing and ironing. I was responsible also for delivering the finished bundles and collecting twenty-five cents each for a package of a dozen pieces. Sometimes I would tote as many as five bundles for as far as twenty blocks in my bare feet. I always walked around barefooted in the summer months because my grandmother said it strengthens your legs; besides the tough Irish kid gangs didn't like "niggers with shoes on." I didn't like to walk barefooted; the pavement was always too hot or too wet, but a colored boy walked carefully in those days.

Our best customer was a prosperous Jewish family named Rothschild out on South Orange Avenue. They were in the wallpaper-hanging business. On Saturdays when I made my deliveries there, a rabbi was at Mrs. Rothschild's home to teach her children their Hebrew lessons. The chanting sounds coming out of the parlor during the lessons fascinated me from the beginning, and Mrs. Rothschild soon noticed. She permitted me to go into the study and sit and listen. It didn't take much time before I began to learn the meanings of the Hebraic words. When the rabbi saw how well I was doing, he took special pains to teach me, and it wasn't long before I was talking Hebrew as well as the Rothschild kids. It certainly did impress Mrs. Rothschild, who is still living, over ninety years of age, and whenever I go over to Newark I stop in to say hello to her.

As it turned out, I favored the Jewish religion all my life and at one time served as a Hebrew cantor in a Harlem synagogue. You could say I am Jewish partly by origin and partly by association. When I was thirteen years old, I had my bar mitzvah in a Newark synagogue. A lot of people are unable to understand my wanting to be Jewish. One said, "Lion, you stepped up to the plate with one strike against you—and now you take a second one right down the middle." They can't seem to realize I have a Jewish soul and belong in that faith.

FATHER AT THE SLAUGHTERHOUSE

If my mother hadn't told me otherwise, I would have thought that John Smith was my real father. He was always good to me and I greatly admired him. He worked for the C. M. Bailey, Pork Packers, and his job was to leave the house at midnight to drive over to the slaughterhouse and pick up a load of freshly killed pigs, then haul them to the packing house. He was due home by 4 A.M. but hardly ever made it. It was his custom to round up his drinking pals and stay out until after the day-workers had gone to their jobs. I can remember when the horses pulled him home without my father holding the reins. He was passed out in the back of the wagon or asleep in the driver's seat. My mother finally hit upon the idea of having me go along to work with him. In this way she figured he would come straight home sober. Sometimes it worked, but more often I wound up driving the horses home. I enjoyed my job, but I could only do it on Fridays or Saturdays, as my mother didn't approve of me missing school the next day to sleep. As it worked out, the nights I was able to go along were those nights that it was easiest for him to find some hell-raising companions to drink it up with.

I couldn't stand to see what I saw at the slaughterhouse. I would watch wide-eyed as the squealing pigs slid down the iron rails to the cutter where they were slashed through the middle, with the two halves falling into a tank of hot water. The kill sometimes went to as many as four hundred pigs a night. It was a sickening sight to watch.

But the cries from the pigs brought forth an emotional excitement. It was another weird but musical sound that I can still hear in my head. The squeaks, the squeals, the dipping them in the hot water, they put them on a hook, take off the head, the legs, going down an aisle—I hear it in an oboe. That's what you hear in a symphony: destruction, war, peace, beauty, all mixed.

Old man Bailey, the millionaire owner of the pork plant, was good to our family. He gave my father all the fancy clothes that his own kids had outgrown. I can still recall my first pair of blue suede shoes, given to me by one of the Bailey boys.

Our Academy Street quarters got overcrowded by 1907. We moved to a larger house at 90 Broome Street, Newark, where we lived until around 1912. The rent was a little higher on Broome Street and my mother told her husband that he was a hell of a mechanic, driving a wagon. Why didn't he get a job with a wrench and make more money? He must have agreed with her because he quit the pork-packing outfit and got a job at the Crucible Steel Works across the Passaic River in Harrison, New Jersey. My mother proved herself right when a short time later he became a foreman and did make a lot more of that green stuff.

But he still kept up with his old habits and was likely to get completely etherized on payday. It was still my job to rush over the bridge on the day he got his money to try to get it from his Irish bosses before they got him drunk—on his own pay. I became the kid who would sing the sort of "come home with me, Father, come home with me now" routine. When he was real gassed-up I was turned down flat and went home without him or the pay check.

There were other sounds I remember from those days. Like from cows—we called them moo-cows—I don't know from where, exactly, except that Newark was more like the country then. Another—a sad thing—the barking of dogs, and how they howl when a person is going to die.

When both my mother and my grandmother were around, it was hard for me to tell one from the other. They both wore long dresses with three or four petticoats underneath. When they went out shopping, it was a riot. They kept their coin purses in secret pockets sewn in one of the petticoats. It would take them ten minutes, fishing around under their skirts, to get out a dime to buy something. They looked so much alike shuffling around the house, smoking their pipes, that when I was a toddler I'd be hanging on to a long dress, following one or the other around, not knowing which was which.

Mother, who weighed less than a hundred pounds, hurried herself away from this world by working too hard. I didn't know it then, of course, but she wasn't going to get beyond seventy because she never really learned to relax. She would get up every morning at six, including Sundays, and drive herself hard all day to take care of the Smith babies. A new one arrived every two years. She made it to sixty-six, but should have gone to ninety, like Grandma Ann.

My two older brothers were named George and Jerome Bertholoff. The youngest of the two, Jerome, died when he was fifteen years old. George eventually became a police officer in Atlantic City, New Jersey, and lived until 1946. Our paths didn't cross very often in later life. His friends and connections were always on the other side of the fence from mine.

Four of John Smith's children are still alive. The oldest, Robert, tends bar on West Street in Newark. Melvin, whom I haven't seen for many years, used to live somewhere on Mulberry Street in New York. Two others, Norman and Ralph, have completely disappeared from my view. The rest of the Smiths, eleven boys and one girl in all, died between the ages of three and seven. It was my job to dress all the youngsters and see that they got to school every morning.

My home life in those youthful days was comparatively easy-going. I can remember only three whippings with a strap. Two of these were given to me by my stepfather for the same reason —getting lost on my way to church.

3

The Old Stamping Ground

In those days, Newark still had a lot of open country and it was my habit to take little detours to explore. On two of those occasions I never did arrive at church. One time I was so lost that I wound up in the police station where my folks had to come to identify me late Sunday afternoon. I really got a shellacking that time.

The only other whipping I can recall at home was given to me by my mother for something I didn't do. She walloped me real good. One of my half brothers—I can't remember which one—stole food out of the icebox. He told my mother that Willie did it. I finally got the one who did it to own up, but my mother was so shook-up when she discovered that there had been a mistake that she never whipped any of the kids again.

But that wasn't the only place I saw a strap.

Once you got to the Baxter School, you were all right until school let out. It was an all-colored, ungraded school.

The Irish and Italian kids called Baxter "The Reformatory" and they weren't far from wrong because everyone looked upon the school as a reforming place for bad kids. And if you were black, it was taken for granted that you were bad.

Gangs were often laying for us, before and after school hours, and a battle royal would take place when we heard the cry, "Here comes them niggers!" We thought nothing of calling each other wop, paisan, guinea, nigger, Irish bastard, in those days. They were real rough-and-tumble brawls. We fought each other with whatever weapons we could find in the street—sticks, stones, ball bats. But no knives. Switch blades, bicycle chains, and car-radio antennas came along later with electric refrigerators and television, and all those other improvements.

When we beat up on an Irish or Italian boy in our neighborhood, my mother and uncle would usually back me up. My mother's temper would flare up when the victim's old lady came over to put in her beef. Ida Oliver Smith would scream, "Keep your kids off the street if you don't want them to get bloody!"

My uncle Rob was my mother's brother, Robert Oliver, who also lived in Newark and drove a perfume wagon for the Odell Company. Funny, how the contents of his wagon were the direct opposite of what my stepfather hauled. They both stank —but in a different way.

To help me in the daily battling, Uncle Rob taught me to box when I was still a midget. Willie, he would say, it's a tough life for a black boy. If you can't win with your fists, you just go ahead and go after 'em with a bat. As a result of his teachings I was able to put up a good fight when it was necessary. But as I grew older, I began to stay away from fighting to protect my brittle hands. That was after I started playing the piano.

But it seems like I always managed to stay in some kind of trouble: trouble with the girls, trouble with the Irish, or trouble with other Negroes. When I was seen with an Irish girl, the colored girls would gang up on me, and vice versa. The people with whom I have had the least trouble in life have been the Jews.

Even inside the Baxter School, things weren't quite quiet. They made frequent use of rawhide straps, and when we were really bad, the principal gave us the rattan-whip treatment. He carried it up his sleeve. He was a Creole, looked like a white man, and no parents ever objected. He sort of had their consent if you were real bad.

He used to make us lie across his knee. A lot of kids resented it, but they didn't want to fight too hard because then they would be sent to an even tougher school.

The biggest mess I got into during my school days didn't take place at home or at school. It happened in Mrs. Black's fruit store when I got caught with my hand in her cash register. My intention had been to borrow a dime to pay my way into Blaney's Theater to see S. H. Dudley's traveling road show. I hadn't noticed before that every time the drawer opened a bell on the till rang. The sound caused the old lady to open the curtain to the back room and she saw me standing there, helping myself.

It surprised me when she turned me over to the police. Everybody knew that her son-in-law was the number three tough guy in Newark at that time. The whole family, they said, were cop haters and they wouldn't have a policeman in the place. But they sure didn't mind turning a ten-year-old boy over to the law.

Well, they dragged me into children's court. The judge said, "Ten dollars fine and probation." That meant weekly visits to the courthouse and I had to make a ten-cent payment on my fine and tell them how good a boy I had been during the week.

As a result of this trouble, my family transferred me to the Morton School where there was less brawling. I was enrolled in the sixth grade. My new school was a lot farther from home, but it was not classed as ungraded°—as Baxter was.

At Morton, I joined the youth cadets and wore a regular uniform that was specified by the school. Part of my troubles all along had been the way my mother goofed up my appearance. The way she dressed me. The Irish kids had always laughed because I wore one of those small, half hats that sat

---

° Denoting a school for incorrigibles.

on the top of the head like a Jewish seder cap. The girls in school would kid me about my silly skullcap so much I finally had to give up hats altogether and traveled bare-headed. Maybe it was because I was growing too fast, but it always seemed like my clothes were too small all over, especially the lengths of my sleeves and pant legs.

The cadets were a marching group and we carried wooden guns in all the parades. Those phony guns made us all mad. The boys in the high school got to carry real rifles. We fancied ourselves real sharpies, but this was all spoiled because of those wooden guns. The girls would laugh and put us on something terrible as we marched down the street.

There was one cute little brownskin girl at Morton that I set out to impress. Her name was Trixie and she had those magnetic black eyes that you couldn't stop looking into. All the boys in the school were digging her and I was trying to get a home run. Things went well until she saw me parading along with that phony artillery. She burst out laughing and got me so upset that when I talked to her I stuttered. Back in those days when I got aggravated I had a strong tendency to stutter, and when Trixie heard that, she started to mimic me. She'd come up to me and say, "My, my, my, look, look, look at him with that funny gun." She'd scream and break up laughing, while I would get raving mad and stutter all the more. It broke up a beautiful relationship.

WILLIE, ATHLETE

By the time I got to Newark High School (now Barringer High), I had learned that one of the best ways to impress the ladies was to be an athlete. So I tried all the sports—swimming, skating, track, basketball, sledding, cycling, and boxing. The old Morris Canal, now filled in, was the place where I learned to swim. But my love for swimming came to an end one day when I was fooling around in the ocean and a crab got ahold of my foot. This scared me half to death and made me forever leery of water. To this day I don't dig beaches and boats. I turned down many an invitation to appear in Europe until they perfected those flying machines that cut the traveling misery down to one day.

I played basketball regularly in high school and continued when I played with the regimental team in the Army. My only other regular activity was track. I was the only colored runner on the high school team. My brother Melvin has all my athletic equipment packed away in a trunk, and my musket, and my pack. I haven't seen him for years and when I die he'll inherit all my early possessions, I guess. Families do that. When one dies, all the next of kin make off with all his things for themselves.

My cycling career came to an end at the foot of a steep hill, where the motorcycle, an Indian, and I piled into a tree. Of all the sports, I have always been the most interested in prize-fighting. Maybe that's because I've known most of the great fighters from way back. They liked to visit the night clubs and for that reason I got to kid around with Jack Johnson, Jack Dempsey, Battling Siki, Kid Chocolate, Sam Langford (the Boston Tar Baby), Joe Gans, Bob Fitzsimmons, Harry Greb, Joe Louis, and Gene Tunney, who used to visit me when I was playing in Greenwich Village.

A couple of the Irish lads I knew at Morton were responsible for getting me interested in the ring. One of them, Patty Mc-Swiggin, later had a gym across the river in Harrison. He used to stage those battle royals where there were six guys in the ring to start and they all went after each other until there was only one man able to walk out. The rest had been carried out.

The famous Bob Fitzsimmons had a saloon on Market Street in Newark. They called that knock-kneed character "The Cornishman." He won the light-heavyweight championship when he was over forty years old. Around Fitzsimmons' bar I heard all about Stanley Ketchel, Kid McCoy, Benny Leonard, Jimmie Britt, Charlie Warner, and all the rest. Those were the guys who used to fight thirty, forty, fifty rounds with bare knuckles. Today, if they go four rounds with gloves they're gassed-out and ready for the sponge. Like some musicians.

The talk around the place was the real low-down on the fight world. White promoters would not let two big-name Negro contenders fight, because they figured they would not draw a big enough gate. The idea was always to have a white versus a Negro fighter—that was what the fans wanted to see.

We had street gangs in my youth like they have today, but we used our fists. It was sissy to fight with a knife. The gang that I belonged to had a club called The Ramblers. There were only two colored boys in the bunch. I was one and the other was a guy named Louis Moss, a sweet talker, who could take his foes apart. In later years he became known around Newark as "Big Sue" and operated a saloon in the tenderloin. Eventually I helped him out by playing the piano in his back room. He was a big man, weighing around 240 pounds and standing six feet four inches. He kept his customers in line by acting as his own bouncer. A good part of the Rambler membership was made up of Jewish boys. Two very famous Jersey men graduated from the club. They were Abner (Longie) Zwillman and Niggy Rutman. Zwillman became big boss of the Jersey branch of the syndicate and ended his career in 1959 by hanging himself in his West Orange, New Jersey, home.

Besides all the usual activities of a growing boy, I spent a good deal of time with spiritual thoughts. I used to wander all over town seeking new things to see and hear. During these wanderings I found that I could get inspiration from a vacant church or a graveyard. It was my habit to roam off by myself when these moods came over me. One of my favorite places was Mount Pleasant cemetery, out on the outskirts of the city, where everything was always peaceful. I would raid an apple orchard and fill my pockets, then sprawl out on the grass at Mount Pleasant and think about the things my mother had taught me about the stars and planets.

I also had a secret passion—music—to think about.

4

The Piano Starts Talking

When that old piano starts
talking, you'll start walking.

WILLIE THE LION SMITH

One day I was exploring in the cellar of our house on Academy
Street and found an old beat-up organ stuck away in the
corner. It had once been played by my mother but had gotten
in pretty bad shape over the years. Nearly half of the keys
were missing. In order for me to reach the keyboard I had to
stand on a box. When I started fooling around with the instrument I couldn't have been more than six years old.

My first effort was to attempt to play by ear what I'd heard
my mother play on the organ and piano at the church. Most
of the early jazz musicians learned the same way. It wasn't
like today when young musicians try to learn by listening to
phonograph recordings and copy off what they hear. We
learned a melody by ear and then tried to beautify it with our
own ideas.

After my mother noticed how interested I was in the organ
downstairs she began to teach me the melodies she knew. One
of my first tunes was the old-time favorite "Home, Sweet Home."

I soon attended every church service and would listen carefully to my mother as she played chords and sang hymns.

By the time I went to school I was able to play several tunes on the piano. The teachers selected me to play for the pupils as they marched in and out of Baxter. When one of my teachers taught me the number "Sweet and Low" it pleased my mother. We both began to think about the possibility of getting a piano for the front room. But each time it began to look as though we could accumulate enough money to get a secondhand instrument, another new mouth would show up to be fed and I would have to satisfy myself playing the old worn-out organ.

Besides the teachings of my mother and the ladies at school, I began to get help from my uncle Rob. He was a short, squatty man with a wonderful bass voice. When he wasn't busy on his perfume wagon he devoted his time to a quartet around town that he managed. Many times I would go out and hear them sing on street corners and hear their audience holler at them to "pep it up" or "rag it" while they were harmonizing away.

Uncle Rob could dance as well as sing, and back when I was only five years old he had taught me how to dance a buck and wing on one leg. In fact he taught all the Smith kids to dance. We could even do a real good old-fashioned cakewalk together.

One time I did my one-leg routine, a soft-shoe and a buck-and-wing dance, in an amateur contest at the Arcadia Theater. I won first place and a big ten dollars. This success inspired me to start haunting the theaters and dance halls around town. I remember one place in particular where they would put ordinary sand on the floor to dance on. You could really hear and feel the rhythm when the dancers shuffled around in a nice pair of patent-leather shoes. There was one guy, called Rastus, who wore wooden shoes while "sandin'"; he was really something. He was a sort of a champion and everybody stopped to watch him dance.

It got so that every time I could get a fifty-cent piece to get in I would be at one or the other ballroom or dance hall. They didn't care how old you were as long as you had the half dollar. The popular dances of the time were the Texas Tommy, schottische, two-step, and the lancers.

Although the fancy dances and dancers were of considerable interest to me, I began to pay more and more attention to the piano ticklers. It was their playing that made me want to play the ragtime tunes of the day.

During this period I had an after-school job at Hauseman's Footwear store, where my duties were to shine shoes and run errands. Old man Hauseman wanted to pay me off by letting me buy eight-dollar shoes for two dollars. It was a hard fight to get the cash instead, but he finally gave in because he admired my ability to talk Hebrew. I insisted that I had to have the money to buy an upright piano for our parlor at home. This he also liked, and agreed to pay me five dollars a week.

As it finally turned out I wasn't going to need the money. At the time Marshall & Wendell's music store was holding a contest. It was one of those guessing contests where you were supposed to estimate the number of dots in a circle printed in their newspaper advertisement. As I recall now, there were from three to four thousand dots in a space the size of a silver dollar. My arithmetic studies at school now came in handy and I set to work with a pencil and ruler to figure out the problem. It paid off. The day after sending in my number, they delivered an upright to the house.

From then on old man Hauseman, the market, and all my other employers missed me after school. I was home practicing the piano. I listened closely to my mother as she played the familiar hymns on our new piano. I'd say, "That sounds all right, but it can be beautified." Then I would sit down and rag "Sweet and Low" and make her furious. She actually would run me away from the piano when I'd play a blues or make the tunes she enjoyed playing into ragtime.

Back in those early days churchgoing Negro people would

not stand for ragtime playing; they considered it to be sinful. Part of that feeling was due to the fact that the popular songs you heard played around in the saloons had bawdy lyrics and when you played in a raggy style, folks would right away think of the bad words and all the hell-raising they heard, or had heard about, in the red-light district.

Yeah, in the front parlor, where the neighbors could hear your playing, you had to sing the proper religious words and keep that lilting tempo down!

I kept telling my mother I was tired of playing the same old melodies the same old ways. In my wanderings around town in the saloons, dance halls, and theaters, I picked up on such tunes as the "Maple Leaf Rag" by Scott Joplin, the "Cannonball Rag" by Joe Northrup, and the "Black and White Rag" by George Botsford. But in those days I didn't know the names of the rags, or who they were written by, because I had learned them by listening to other piano players. One of my favorites was the famous "Don't Hit that Lady Dressed in Green." Man, the lyrics to this song were a sex education, especially for a twelve-year-old boy.

That was the kind of song you heard in those old-fashioned saloons and cat houses back in those days. By the time I was twelve I had worked up enough courage to go right into any-place and explore. I was always able to catch a few pennies doing my buck-and-wing dances which gave me a good excuse to be on the inside. Other lively tunes I learned were such titles as "She's Got Good Booty" and "Baby, Let Your Drawers Hang Low."

Musically, I was beginning to get the mind and soul talking, and from then on it was to be music on my mind, all the time.

IN THE ALLEY AT FOURTEEN

So let's let the piano talk,
It's gut bucket, and it's low as a toad.

How low can you go? You can go low as a toad
Man, you can't go no lower.

It wasn't easy for a kid my age to get started in the tenderloin. Newark's Coast was a plenty tough section, but it was the only part of town where there was any opportunity for a young colored boy to get in as an entertainer.

Around about 1911, our family moved from Broome Street to 28 Clayton Street; a move that was again necessary on account of the growing brood of little Smiths. Clayton was a two-block-long street near the city hall and only a couple of steps away from the corner of Arlington and Augusta streets, the center of the Coast.

On my errands after school I had frequently stopped to watch a hurdy-gurdy man with an organ and a monkey. It fascinated me to watch the creature tip his little hat and then pass it around in the crowd to collect some money. Another sight that used to cause me to stop, as I walked around the Coast, was a colored lad named Bo who had been born without any arms. He made his living by giving a marble-shooting exhibition every afternoon in the entrance to an alley. He'd take a stick, draw a large circle in the dirt, and put several marbles in the center. Then, using his big toe, he would shoot them out of the ring with an agate. Bo rarely missed and was as good a shooter as any guy using thumbs. When a crowd had gathered he would pass his hat and rake in the coins.

Whenever I saw things like that I would figure out how I could make use of them for myself. Those hat passers gave me an idea. I'd do the same thing after I'd performed my various dance steps. It always brought me a good pile of coins after performing my specialty—the one-legged buck and wing.

As you walked around the Coast you could always hear the tinkling of the pianos from behind the swinging doors and the banging shutters of those houses they called buffet flats, or just plain cat houses. There was action and music at any time of day or night. That was where those "Around the Clock" blues came from. And when they opened up a new saloon they made a ceremony out of throwing away the key.

I was brave and cocky enough to walk right into the saloons and go into my dance, and then pass around my derby to collect the loot. It not only got me to wearing a hat again, but gave me an opportunity to sneak some tunes on the stomp box when the regular player wasn't looking, or was at the bar taking on a load.

It wasn't too easy to get a chance at the piano. Most of the ticklers were smart enough to stay glued to the bench—they were always afraid some guy would walk in and take their job away by outplaying them.

As I roamed around the joints in the late afternoons I began to get known and recognized. Some people called these places citadels of vice, creep joints, or the road down the primrose path; but I had learned that God gives a person power over all things that are cruel, mean, or unpleasant. You just had to mind your own business and keep your tongue between your teeth so it wouldn't waggle.

The church people used to say to my mother, "Why do you let Willie go into those saloons and play ragtime?" She was always protecting me. "He's only playing what he feels, and he isn't doing any harm. He gives me whatever money he makes. Seldom does he do anything wrong. I want him to be a man and do what he thinks is right."

I've found throughout life that people don't understand the folks in the underworld. There are as many of God's children in the saloons and cabarets as can be found in the churches. When you come right down to it, those who frequent the pleasure spots are religious souls who are singing to release their pent-up feelings. Many of the wilder spirits eventually head in the right direction and wind up at the same destination as those who spend their time criticizing them.

I came up with all kinds of sharpies, pimps, pickpockets, snow birds, gamblers, con men, and ladies of the evening. There has always been vice, from the prophets down, and there always will be.

The so-called righteous people who are evermore screaming, "Down with the saloons!" or "People should stay out of those places!" are doing more harm than good by causing rebellion in others. The do-gooders are really jealous of those who are able to let their emotions out. A man or woman, who is a searcher or a good mixer, makes for the type of person able to help others, because they are understanding. Many of the churchgoers are always tearing things down.

Take Bessie Smith, who taught others to let off steam, by teaching them to sing the blues. As much as she roared, drank, and dissipated, she was always considered to be a devout religious woman—truly one of God's children. Our great gospel singer of today, Mahalia Jackson, stood outside a New Orleans theater to listen to Bessie and derived a great deal of her inspiration from what she heard.

Bill Buss's saloon was located two blocks from downtown Newark near Arlington Street where Branford ran into Shipman Street. It was at Buss's that I held my first steady job and it was the boss's wife Blanche, a fine Creole woman, who was responsible for getting me on a regular payroll. She had noticed how popular I had become with the Thursday-afternoon crowd. Mrs. Buss liked to see her customers having their fun and noted how they gathered around the piano when I was playing. She talked her husband Bill into hiring me for every afternoon between three and five—because I was cute, she said.

On Thursday afternoons between two and six, all the kitchen

mechanics and pot wrestlers were balling it up on their afternoon off. All over the country it was customary to give the
domestic help a holiday once a week. Usually Thursday afternoons.

Those folks, who cooked for the white families, wanted their
music in the alley. They didn't dig that "Three O'Clock in the
Morning" jive. Each of the younger gals would meet her sweetback* and turn over her week's wages. I'd get some of that
money for playing tunes like "She's the Best Lover You Ever
Seen" and other fast ballads, sometimes with lewd lyrics.

When I went home for supper I'd have between three and
four dollars in my pocket. My salary was a dollar a day plus
tips. Most of the latter came in dimes and quarters. Before leaving Buss's, I was returning to work after supper to take care
of the early evening shift from seven to ten.

Blanche Buss sort of took me under her wing and saw that
I was all right as I pounded the piano there in the front across
the room from the bar. She would get raving mad when the
more boisterous customers, who had gotten lit up like Luna
Park, tried to tease me. I was still having trouble with my stut-
tering and once in a while someone would holler at me, "Hey,
da-da, dere-dere, with me-me," or some other senseless sentence
trying to mimic me. When this happened Mrs. Buss would tell
them off with a tenderloin tongue-lashing.

Many of the tush hogs† and sealskin papas‡ who had been
around the place all afternoon were still there when I got back
in the evening. The sealskin papas and the sweetbacks were always sharply dressed. The girls would greet the sealskins with,
"Hello, sweet papa do little, you don't do nuthin'." Or, if they
wanted the guy to be their sweetback, they would come on
with, "Baby, I'm your stopper!"

---

* An exclusive pimp; also her lover.
† A tough character who derived pleasure from beating up a person.
‡ A pimp who worked with all the gals, but was in love with none.

YOUNG SPORT

It wasn't long before I was sporting around. I wore my first derby, smoked cigars, and drank my whisky clear. Buss would give all the employees three checks when they came to work, good for three beers and a shot of whisky. You started off with a "Y-Z," made up of a shot of bar booze and a short-beer chaser. After that you still had two regular beers coming with your checks. But during a regular working session you were sure to have plenty more as the customers were hollering, "Give the piano player a drink, so he'll play my tune." With that kind of hospitality you soon learned to line your stomach with butter before reporting for work.

My mother, uncle, and grandmother, taught me in my early years to have a short drink as a sedative when I was tensed up. I didn't hesitate in taking their advice—it helped me to cure my stammering.

It was at Buss's that I was introduced to stick gin. This gin was kept on the bar with a stick in it that gave it a sweet taste like vermouth. They call them martinis now. It was about the strongest straight drink around in those days. Another favorite of mine was a claret punch—made up of claret, milk, eggs, brandy, and crème de menthe.

Yeah, those were swingin' times. It was easy does it on the pocketbook, too. Whisky cost us anywhere from ten to twelve cents a half pint. For eats—why you could get an entire pie for a big nickel!

When I had been in the business a little over a year I decided I wanted more money for my act. So I applied at Randolph's Cafe, a much bigger place, located in an old church building on the Coast. Randolph's was operated as a combined saloon and dance hall. During the week I played in the rathskeller on the first floor; on weekends I went upstairs to play for the dancers. When I worked the upstairs hall I usually worked with a cornetist, trombonist, or violinist. The customers had to pay an admission fee of twenty cents to get up those stairs.

The dance craze had just gotten started and there were all kinds of variations on the turkey trot and the two-step. Some of the dances were pretty wild. They called them "hug me close," "the shiver," "humpback rag," "the Grizzly Bear," and "the lovers' walk." These were just some of the frantic dances that were beginning to replace the more dignified cakewalking struts. I'll never forget an elderly English gentleman who used to pay his twenty cents just to sit and watch the dancing. Once he leaned over and said to me, "My word! That whisky certainly makes the wriggly wiggling wiggle."

While at Randolph's I got a real bad crush on a gal named Maude, whose last name was White, Jones, or something, depending on who she came in with. She was from Jersey City, New Jersey, and all the Newark pimps were trying to get her on their strings, or in their stables. I called her Little Flower because her beauty was of the delicate kind. She called me Fashion Plate because I carried a cane and wore a derby.

I was just beginning to get the inside track with Maude when I discovered she was a lesbian. It was quite a shock; I'd never run into one before. After that I left her alone and let the pimps battle over her to their heart's content.

Newark got to be known as a good piano man's town. I had several rivals there to watch out for. And then there were the pianists from out of town who wandered into places like Randolph's.

My chief rival was a fellow named Dick Huff, who could sing, dance, and play a lot of piano. He kept me on the jump, but he had one bad habit that gave me an advantage—Huff was a dope addict and would disappear for long periods of time.

Then there was Harold (Bon-Bon) Gardner, who could

play all types of piano, and was an ace showman besides. He loved cigars, like I did, and in later years married the blues singer Leona Williams. I worked with them both around New York after World War I. Back in those early days, he was the regular pianist at Conerton's Cafe on the Coast.

The visiting piano men hailed from Baltimore, New York, Philadelphia, and Washington. It was during those Newark days in my early teens, that I met two pianists who were to be lifelong friends.

It was around 1913 that I first met Charles Luckeyeth ("Luckey") Roberts§ who wandered into the Coast, passing himself off as a lemon pool player.|| They had a table downstairs at Randolph's and one day this guy showed up and began to lose game after game. When I wasn't too busy I'd watch the action at the table and noticed this character was a lousy shot and was missing set-ups. Every game was costing him a few dollars in bets. But that was just his way—

On the third day he got involved in a big money game and everything changed. He was a shark! He didn't miss nuthin'! All those local suckers thought they were going to clean him out—he turned the tables on them.

That night, while I was playing for the dancers, I noticed him standing in the doorway watching me. When I finished I went by him and said kiddingly, "Want to play some piano?" It surprised me when he answered, "Don't mind if I do."

He sat down—I couldn't believe it—the guy was a piano shark, too! He had the biggest hands I'd ever seen on a player. His long fingers enabled him to reach to a fourteenth.

This guy was too much. He wasn't the boob he made himself out to be at all. He was a short, squatty fellow, with the build of a football player. Being as strong as an ox, with a powerful right hand, he could make the piano hum like you've never heard. And spectacular—he would lift his hands off the key-

§ Born Philadelphia, Pa., on Aug. 7, 1887.
|| An expert pool player who pretends he is a novice at the game.

board with a flourish that always drew attention—a trick that Duke Ellington learned from him and still uses.

After we finished that night Luckey told me how he had started in show business when he was three years old as a child actor with one of the traveling *Uncle Tom's Cabin* show troupes, then became an acrobat on the coast-to-coast vaudeville circuits, and finally became a twenty-five-dollar-a-week piano man at the Green Dragon saloon at Nineteenth and Nordain, in Philly.

Yeah, Luckey's been one of my closest friends ever since that night long ago in Newark. During the nineteen twenties he wrote the scores for a dozen musical shows and established one of the most popular society bands of the period. He furnished the music for many of the big parties on Fifth Avenue, Park Avenue, Long Island, and Palm Beach, Florida. After he made a lot of money with his famous composition "Moonlight Cocktail," in the early forties, he opened his own saloon, Luckey's Rendezvous, up in Harlem. It was very popular for many years, but he was too generous to make a good businessman. He has never taken a drink, or smoked in his life, but when it came to helping others, he was always right there. His trouble was that when business was poor he still was dishing out too many free drinks.

I still call Luckey at his apartment, on Sugar Hill, once a week, and we rehash those old days on the Newark Coast when he first taught me how to play his original tunes—"Junk Man Rag" and "Pork and Beans." He has just finished writing a musical that he hopes to have produced on Broadway soon.

JAMES P. JOHNSON

If my memory serves me right it was the fall of 1914 that I first met James Price Johnson,¶ who was my closest friend.

¶ Born Feb. 1, 1891, New Brunswick, N.J.

He was always a sincere guy, easily hurt, and I used to sort of watch after him. He was born under the mixed-up sign of Aquarius. James P. Johnson was kind of naïve and easygoing— so naturally I nicknamed him The Brute.

James P. showed up on the Coast in the company of his wife Lillian Wright, a singer-entertainer from the South. Known as "Lillie-Mae" she had been around the business for several years. Her first husband had been Fred Tunstall, a New York City piano-playing pimp called "The Tonsil." Freddie was the kind of dandy who never took a steady job, preferring to live off his girl friends. He was a sporty dresser: green ties, high stiff collars, and a Norfolk coat with pleats that spread out when he took his seat at the piano. He was a piano player worth hearing if you could catch him when the mood was on him.

Tunstall wasn't what you'd call a good husband for Lillie, so she left him and married my boy James, a guy she could boss around; it had been the other way around for her when she was married to The Tonsil.

One of the many important things you had to be able to do when playing piano in the saloons back in those days was to accompany the singer-entertainers. Some of the larger concert saloons and cabarets had as many as ten male and female singers around the joint regularly. You had to be a fast thinker to handle them. First, it was necessary to be able to play in any key, run the chords as we called it, because the entertainers worked in them all. A singer might change into any key on the piano at any time. They themselves didn't know half the time what key they worked in. Singers like Ethel Waters, who I was to work with many times in Harlem, couldn't sing in certain keys and it was up to the pianist to play in the right key for her. When Ethel would start off in the wrong key for the song she was singing, I would quickly get her on the right track by forcing her into the right key. Some of the gals would start work at nine o'clock, singing in E-flat, but when a little draft was blowing, or they had taken on a few belts, they would be singing in G major by eleven, swearing they were still in E-flat.

Well sir, the first time Lillie Johnson came to Randolph's with Jimmy we had a time. After looking over the place Lillie decided it would be a good spot for them to work together. That's the kind of stuff you always had to be on the lookout for—somebody wanting to take your job.

Lillie figured the way to get Jimmy in on the deal was to give me a hard time. She had been taken on as an entertainer; the boss had told her he already had a piano player. So it was up to me to play for her when she sang. On that first night she announced she wanted to sing in E-flat, and then went right ahead and started out in E major. It didn't sound so good. So she started hollering for a pianist who could accompany her right—she kept motioning for young Jimmy to come over.

I started screaming right back at Lillie. "You just make up your mind what key you want to perform in," I told her, "because I've got 'em all." The boss was standing around listening and she was doing all the complainin' for him to hear. I gave it right back to her. After she ran out of excuses I said, "Come on, what song can you sing?" She said she'd like to do "That Funny Man from Dixieland" and this time we really got together and had all the customers clapping their hands right along with us.

After our first set Lillie introduced me to Jimmy and the two of us got to talking and exchanging ideas. At that time he was playing Scott Joplin's rags and some of the songs written by Victor Herbert and Rudolph Friml. He also told me about some hot numbers he'd learned while playing at a pleasure resort in the West Thirties in New York City. The funny part of these tunes was that they all had Indian lore in their titles. He said those sporting house guys and gals really loved "Red Wing," "Come with Me to My Big Teepee," and "Big Chief Battle Axe." But his favorite tune at the time was "Little Brown Jug."

Although Johnson was actually a shy, retiring type, we immediately hit it off. In later years I did a lot of his fighting for him as he never seemed to want to bother. That is, I helped him out in the brawls around the saloons. But I left him to fight for himself when he did battle with Lillie. I made myself absent when these affairs got started—as they frequently did. Back in 1914, Jimmy and I were just two young boys who played piano by ear. We couldn't read or write music, but we were to both learn very soon. As the years went by we became like twins and came up together. You'll read a lot more about The Brute in this book as we go along.

Johnson finally got a job at the Kinney Hall in the Newark tenderloin and when I left Randolph's to open at Johnson's Cafe on Plane Street, he took the Randolph job. (When I left, the place came under a new management and was renamed Lewis' Saloon.)

Until 1914, I had done all my playing right there at home in Newark, but I was destined not to stay put. Everybody went to the shore in the summertime and at the age of fifteen I made my first visit to an internationally famous pleasure spot.

5

Hot Towns Are Calling Me

My mother used to tell me I'd never reach my destination sitting in a back room. She'd say, "You go holler, holler, holler, that's the only way you'll make a dollar!"

Back in the days before the First World War it was customary for everybody to try to make it to the seashore on the New Jersey coast during the hot summer months. The top entertainers and all our working people from New York City, Newark, Philadelphia, Baltimore, and Washington would hunt jobs in Atlantic City.

Everybody wanted to go there because A.C. moved fast. There was plenty of money floating around for the smart guys to grab. You'd run into all your friends down there in July, digging the salt water and the sun.

The busiest center of activity for the piano ragtimers took place in the tenderloin section known as The Line, twenty blocks west of the boardwalk. Yeah, again you found the people of wisdom there.

Our dictys* had some fancy cabarets and cafés like Scott's, Fitzgerald's, and the combined dance hall–cabaret at Egg

* Harlem sophisticates.

Harbor, but the joints I'm talking about were centered around the corner where North Carolina Avenue crossed Baltic Avenue. As I've always said, the places where the money, fun, and excitement were found in those days could be found in the red-light districts like Newark's Coast, New York's Hell's Kitchen, Chicago's Levee, and San Francisco's Barbary Coast.

When I first started to summer in A.C., the famous places on The Line included The Boat House (a large barnlike building, once called the Belmont Dance Hall), Charlie Reynolds' Philadelphia House, Ralph (Rafe) Welloff's New World, The Pekin, The Elephant Cafe, and Kelly's Cafe on the main corner (North Carolina and Baltic). That Elephant Cafe was a crazy place as I remember—the front of the café was fixed up to look like an elephant's ass and one entered by passing under a big long tail hanging between the animal's legs.

My older brother, George Bertholoff, had become a rookie cop in A.C. and my first visit down there was to see him. He wanted me to hear Eubie Blake† play piano at Kelly's, a small all-night spot in the center of the district. They used to call the cafés "grottos" in A.C. It was quite a distance from the beach (twenty blocks), but when it rained the water flowed up the side streets and right in through Kelly's front door.

Blake, who later composed the music for the famed *Shuffle Along* show on Broadway, was a good ragtime man and could play in all the keys. Most of the songs he played at the time were the popular tunes of the day. He was a great one for performing flowery passages and told me he was influenced the most by the music of the Hungarian composer Franz Lehár.

In those days Blake spent the winter season playing in prize fighter Joe Gans's Goldfield Hotel in Baltimore. He usually worked with the singing comedian Madison Reed and a cute Creole girl named Grace Jackson. Reed was the fellow who made the ditty "It's After Hours and You Can't Come In"

† James Hubert Blake, born in Baltimore, Maryland, Feb. 7, 1883.

famous all over the world. They made a great team. Up to that time I'd never seen a singer with as large a repertoire of songs as Reed had. He had a long piece of cardboard, almost as long as the piano keyboard, on which he had listed about five hundred numbers with their keys—and he knew the lyrics to every one of them.

Blake could play any number Reed would call, and it was funny to see them both searching for a tune on that long list. Madison Reed was one of the best and he was a king in A.C. night life for many years.

There were many others I heard for the first time in A.C. that summer: Edgar Dow, another fine ragtime pianist from Baltimore, who played at The Boat House with the great Philadelphia violinist, Charlie Taylor. One night Taylor just up and left The Boat House to go and play in another dive with the Monk Sisters, also from Baltimore. The Monk Sisters, Gertie and Susie, were two of the best women piano players I ever heard. A lot of fine musicians came from around Baltimore back then.

Another old-timer, who could really make a piano talk, was a guy named Bobby Lee from Philadelphia. He stayed around A.C. for many years and ended up leading his own orchestra in the best A.C. spots.

I met the late Charlie Johnson from New York City playing in the swank Dunlop Hotel, a white establishment on the boardwalk. He was a good trial horse.‡ His big reputation was made later with a jazz band that included such all-time jazz stars as Jimmy Harrison, the trombonist, and Sidney De Paris, a trumpeter. For over a decade Johnson led the house band at Ed Smalls's Paradise Club in Harlem during the wintertime and moved to Rafe Welloff's Paradise Cafe at Egg Harbor for the summer. At Atlantic City they called Johnson's band "The He-Be-Ge-Bees."

‡ A performer who served to warm the bench until the main attraction took over.

There was still one more piano player in A.C. who impressed me a lot. He was known as Kitchen Tom. No one to my knowledge ever knew his regular name. Tom was from somewhere down South and was the first one I ever heard using what has become known as the "walking" or "boogie bass." He confined his playing appearances to one of the bigger sporting houses at the beach. They have always written that Pine Top Smith, a blues player from Alabama, brought the boogie to Chicago in 1927 and was the first boogiewoogie piano player. He may have been the first to introduce the bw to Chicago, but I heard old Kitchen Tom playing it in Atlantic City in 1914. His "Kitchen Tom Rag" was full of the figures they later called the boogiewoogie. The truth is that the familiar boogie figures can be heard in several of the old operatic scores. It wasn't anything new, even back then!

The colored piano players didn't have any personal managers or booking agents to handle them in those days. It was very hard to get one of the piano-playing jobs in A.C. during the season. About the only way to get in was to have a pull with one of the owners or to be on hand when one of the regulars didn't show up for the night's work.

I was lucky. I grabbed the regular spot at Kelly's for the summer of 1915 when Eubie tipped me off that he would not be back. He was heading for New York City to seek his fortune. I had a good deal going there at Kelly's, and later at the New World, up until the time of World War I, when everybody's habits got changed.

Kelly's had a bar in front and a back room with enough tables to take care of around seventy people. The piano was in the back and there was enough room so that I could bring in my drummer Leon White from Newark. They must have had in all about a dozen singing and dancing entertainers.

There is one important thing I mustn't forget to mention and that is about the good-looking women. It always seemed that A.C. was full of stunning brownskin gals; they were the kind of chicks you saw later in the choruses of the Tutt & Whitney *Smart Set* revues and at the Cotton Club in Harlem during the twenties. Flo Ziegfeld was a regular visitor to A.C. to look over the dancing and to dig the ladies.

It was the good-looking women waitresses that helped many of the A.C. joints get off their nut.§ That was something that couldn't happen in New York City night clubs, due to a city law that banned women from working as waitresses after eight o'clock in the evening. But in A.C. the places competed with one another to see who could get the sharpest-looking gals to draw in the customers.

Man, A.C. was a town *crammed* with good-looking legs and pretty underwear. The entertainers spent big money for their costumes; especially for the fancy garments under their dresses. It wasn't unheard of to pay around a hundred dollars for a colorful petticoat. It was the custom in those times to "show your linen," and they would reveal their red, white, and blue pants by daintily lifting their skirts as they danced. Some of the more daring gals would remove their dresses entirely so they would be sure to show their finery underneath.

It was the same with the gents. They usually slipped off their jackets so everyone could get a good look at their colorful silk shirts. The only exceptions were the pimps who were too dignified to remove their suit coats.

While at Kelly's, I often worked with Mattie Hite and Mary Stafford. Those were two of the best singers in the business.

Miss Hite had a winning way with the clientele and always got the crowd wild so that they threw a lot of coins out on the floor for her act. She had the kind of personality that made them whoop, yell, and scream for more. She was one of those tall brownskin gals, a natural showstopper, who could wreck any joint she worked in. One minute she had everybody laughing at one of her risqué jokes and then she'd turn around and sing a sweet or sad ballad that brought tears to a roomful of eyes.

§ The amount of gross revenue needed to cover expenses.

You couldn't beat Mary Stafford for pipes. Her voice was a strong, heavy soprano that really carried; if you were down a block on the next corner you could hear her!

It was sure different. The singers around today couldn't carry a suitcase compared to old-timers like Mattie and Mary. You've got to remember that in the long ago they didn't have such things as microphones—they hadn't even discovered megaphones in the era before the war.

There was always a crowd at Kelly's on Thursday nights. That was the night the madams from the houses trotted out their girls for a good time on the town—and to show them off. They all sat together around one table, behaving sedately, enjoying their relaxation. The madam—the woman in charge—would have the waitresses bring a crate of beer or a case of champagne to the table on the house—the madam's own whorehouse, of course. Anyone who dropped by the table to say hello was asked to have a taste and everyone would drink a toast to everyone else. When the lady in charge decided it was time to leave, she would call out so the crowd could hear, "Give the rest of the drinks to the entertainers and musicians!"

When I moved over to the New World Cafe, I worked a lot with Frankie (Half Pint) Jaxon, a light brown-complexioned man, who danced, sang, and wrote his own shows. He would sometimes work with his face blackened with burnt cork and a pair of white-rimmed spectacles painted on his face. His comic routines were very popular and he was one of those entertainers who couldn't stay still—always jumping up and down, and on the go. He was a great one for building up a "kitty."

At the end of each show all the various New World entertainers would do a number together as a grand finale. As the girls paraded around the floor, Jaxon would sing out, "Come on, shoot the money in, let us hear the coins drop!" The result was usually a shower of pennies, nickels, dimes, and quarters; on rare occasions we could see, but not hear, a roll of green hit the floor. It was always Christmas when Charlie (Boo-Boo) Hoff, the big-time Philadelphia hood, was in the house. He'd enjoy folding up fives, tens, and twenties and pitching them at the girls.

It was an unwritten law in all the big-time joints that all the tips given out by the customers were to go into a kitty and be divvied up equally among the musicians, singers, and waiters after the place closed for the night. Sometimes the tip money doled out was all the salary we'd get.

The vibrations in those A.C. cabarets suited me fine. The gin was fifteen cents at the bar, and for fifty cents you could get all the chitterlings, pigs' tails, fried chicken, and beef stew you could eat. For several years after World War I, the Atlantic City scene remained mellow.

But New York was always the apple of my eye—the big apple. New York City was, and still is, the place where everything happens. I started to watch it happen early.

My Grandma Ann (Oliver) moved to the old fifteenth ward at 27 Minetta Lane right off Sixth Avenue. Back around 1912 when I first started to make regular weekly visits to her place, it was located in a large Negro section.

Once I got started, it didn't take me long to get onto the trick of getting from Newark to Manhattan. In those days you had to take the old Hudson & Manhattan railway to Jersey City, where you got off and took a ferry across the Hudson to the city.

When I was still a small boy, the first big attraction for me was the horse cars running on Sixth Avenue. They used to make a turn onto Sixth close by Grandmother's place and it was my custom to sit on the curb wondering what would happen if I put a rock or a piece of iron on the track. I guess I never got around to actually doing it because the driver with the handle-bar mustache always waved at me and I considered him to be my friend.

After I'd started to play piano in the Newark saloons, I wanted to get around to the different places in New York. In those days most of the action took place in Hell's Kitchen west of Eighth Avenue from Twenty-third all the way up to San Juan Hill in the West Sixties.

At Buss's place in Newark I had met a violinist named Wilbur Hegamin. He was a shorty between four and five feet tall, older than I was, and he knew a lot about New York's tenderloin. There was an area over around Ninth and Tenth avenues where Irishman Owney (the Killer) Madden's Gopher Gang was boss. They were noted for stealing everything out of the railroad freight cars on Eleventh Avenue. These guys were also known as the "goofer gang" and they did not care for Negroes. If we strolled over into their territory they rolled ash cans off the roofs to let us know we'd better get out quick. You could always tell goofers when you saw them because they wore blue suits and blue shirts. My friend, Hegamin, tipped me off to these things.

Hegamin took me into a section where they had a lot of saloons—one on each corner. We were welcome there because we were good entertainers. This district, the old red-light area, ran from Thirty-fourth to Forty-second Street between Seventh and Eighth avenues.

That red-light district was where my pal James P. Johnson had heard the pianists play those songs with Indian themes in their titles. I remember one palace in the West Thirties run by a large woman by the name of Diamond Floss; she displayed the accepted symbol of wealth and attainment by having a diamond set in each of her front teeth.

The saloons all had "Family Entrances." Inside, each one had a long bar, sawdust on the floor, and the familiar round-top beer tables with pretzel-backed chairs. All around the place were shining brass cuspidors with a sign over them on the wall reading, DON'T SPIT AT 'EM, SPIT IN 'EM.

Against the side wall opposite the bar would be an old upright piano, sometimes flanked by a Regina music box (coin-operated nickelodeon). The walls would be covered with

pictures of naked queens and framed portraits of John L. Sullivan, Jim Corbett, Jake Kilrain, and Peter Jackson—all the big-
time prize fighters.

Everyone enjoyed the back rooms, regardless of race, color,
or creed. In some of the places there was a restriction on the
back room and that was when they had poker games, dice
shooting, and other gambling operations going on; you couldn't
get back there unless you could flash a good-sized bankroll.

The customers at the tables were served by waiters who sometimes doubled as entertainers or bouncers. They wore Eton
jackets, white aprons, and carried towels over their shoulders
with brass beer trays tucked under their arms. When someone
got too boisterous these waiters would go into action and rush
them out of there like a whirlwind.

In many saloons the pianist was a young colored fellow working with a drummer, banjoist, or harmonica player. They received hardly any salary and lived entirely on tips, which were
sometimes very high. People are inclined to be more generous
when the alcoholic spirits are on them. You saw a lot of news-
boys, colored and white, around those saloons because the
drunks would usually toss them a nickel, a dime, or a quarter for
a penny newspaper.

DRESSING UP

When I first started to visit these places with Hegamin, before
the summers in Atlantic City, I was still wearing those crazy
clothes my mother got for me. I must have looked funny with
my half hat and tight ass-beater britches.

It didn't take me long to notice that everybody in the entertainment business made it a point to dress sharp. It behooved us
to look spectacular, not only to get and hold a gal, but to make a
good impression all around. The guys that dressed to kill always

got the good jobs. There were no such things as band uniforms then; in fact, uniforms are a comparatively recent development. Entertainers worked in dress suits, tuxedos, or dark suits.

Now, I'm going to give you the correct lowdown on how we all dressed in the olden times, even though this gets ahead of my story. I didn't dress this way at first:

First, we'll take the overcoat because that was the first garment the customers would see you in—in the cold season. There were three main clothing establishments where we bought our duds. Probably the most popular tailoring store was Bromberger's on Carmine Street near Sheridan Square. The other two places were further uptown—Clemens & Ostreicher at Fortieth and Sixth, and Wilkowitz at Forty-first and Seventh.

I favored a blue melton overcoat and suit to match. You could get a melton in blue, gray, or brown, depending on your taste. My overcoat alone cost roughly 150 dollars—it could be pawned for a hundred bucks when new—and it had a full, boxlike back with a plaid lining. The shoulders were padded and the coat would stand straight up by itself. I always gave the hatcheck girl an extra dollar to take special care of my coat while I was working.

For dressing up I always wore a derby or a twenty-five-dollar Stetson hat with a soft brim. Derbies appealed to me because they were worn by the English, the rabbis, and the members of my Masonic lodge. I found that by pulling the derby down in front it gave me mental poise while in action on the piano. When I was relaxed I usually wore the derby cocked on the side. Some of the greatest wore derbies—Sir Winston Churchill, Governor Al Smith, dancer Bill Robinson, and the vaudeville personality Joe Frisco.

Some of the pianists would show up in military-type coats, coachman's coats, or in Inverness capes with skirts. You'd also see different kinds of fancy headwear—Homburgs with buttons on the side and gray Fultons.

I usually paid around a hundred dollars for my suits at Brom-

berger's. It was customary for entertainers to have at least
twenty-five suits—you couldn't wear the same suits too often. I
sometimes would go home and change my suit during our
short intermissions. You saw all kinds of suit material with fancy
tailoring. Some of the colors were oxford gray or pepper, brown
pinstripes, crocodile black and whites, and the regular blues,
browns, and grays. I preferred to have a conservative blue or
brown melton made out of the same material from which my
overcoat had been cut. The style was full or box-back cut,
square shoulders, and a padded lining. My pants were tight
with long, peg-topped fourteen-inch cuffs. I liked to have my
suit jacket single-breasted so I could show off my gold watch
fob and chain. For an added touch we had the tailor make a
pair of spats from the same material.

My shoes had to be custom-made. This was necessary after
an experience I had in Newark the first time I wore a tuxedo.
There was a special school affair and my mother rented a tux
for me. It cost one dollar and a half. There was all kinds of
trouble with the patent-leather pumps that came with the suit
(which had sleeves that were way short). I had a miserable
time that night and wound up dancing in my stocking feet because the shoes were too tight. I vowed after that never to
wear shoes again that were not comfortable from the first time
I put them on.

My favorite shoe store was French, Shriner & Urner, where
they made shoes with pointed toes or turnups, in narrow sizes.
These were short-vamp shoes designed to make your foot look
small. The cost per pair was around twelve dollars and it was
necessary to have at least fifteen pairs on hand.

One of the most important features of our attire was the shirt
—when you worked with your coat off it was a policy to have a
real fancy silk shirt. They would let you relax at the piano with
an open-shirt collar, but you had to be dressed for it.

You picked one that went with your color. I liked a soft-blue
shirt made from a plaid material. Also a candy-colored pink

silk. You'd have to pay from ten to twenty-five dollars for a presentable shirt. And you would have to own about twenty-five colored shirts to have one ready for all occasions.

Although we didn't show it like the gals did, we also all wore silk underwear.

Yes sir, the colorful ladies around those places inspired us to tiptoe on all fours to compete with their feminine poise. Many of us carried a cane to balance our stride. Like the pimps and gamblers we carried twenty-dollar gold pieces and a sizable bankroll around with us; usually the latter consisted of one C note wrapped around a pile of one-dollar bills to make us look rich.

If we had diamonds, we flashed them. Some like the late Jelly Roll Morton wore diamond fillings in their teeth. I recall one tickler—I can't remember his name—who even had a diamond set in one of his bulldog's teeth and when he sat down to play he would tie the animal to the leg of the piano. Many of us had diamond horseshoe tie pins or diamond rings—some were real and some were phony. That was the era when the sports would sometimes wear diamonds in the place of shirt buttons. You needed a pin that was pawnable. A sporting woman gave her man the money; he was supposed to have some of it to spring her if she got locked up.

Although the high style in dress gradually faded away, I've always watched my attire carefully. Today, I wear a blue serge suit with a bright-red flannel vest. My cane these days is a hand-carved walking stick with an elephant's head. I still favor the bowler and have tortoise-shell rims (brown) on my glasses. But instead of diamonds I wear under my shirt a St. Christopher's medal and a Star of David.

To get back to my first days in New York City, I had a cousin, One-Arm Gumpy, who had lost his arm in a trolley accident. He was living on the proceeds from a law suit and knew all the hot spots. He would take Hegamin and myself on tours to the live

night places and we would meet many of the fabulous characters of the day.

We'd usually start out at the Green Gates saloon (on the
corner of West Third Street and Sixth Avenue) where you
entered through swinging doors. They sold beers for three cents,
milk punches for a nickel, and whisky for ten cents a shot.
There was an old piano in the back on which I could play. I
didn't get any salary; the best you could do in those places at
the time, if you did get paid, was ten dollars a week. But I
managed to make enough in tips, sometimes from eight to ten
dollars, to make it possible for us to have a night on the town.
The old passing-the-hat routine did it. The big-time ticklers
walked into these places and played for kicks because they
made their real money hustling the gals for whom they pimped.

My repertoire then included all the rags I had managed to
learn by ear. Such tunes as Ben Harney's "Cakewalk in the
Sky," Irving Berlin's "Alexander's Ragtime Band," "Bon-Bon
Buddy" from the show *Chocolate Drop,* and the traditional
"When I Walk I Walk with Billy." These were the big-time hit
songs of the day, great pop tunes. But the thing that helped
with the tips the most was my dance.

There were some celebrated fellows hanging around the
Green Gates, but you never knew much about who they were
before you saw them, or, sometimes, where they went afterwards. Guys like Kitchen Tom in A.C. never revealed their real
names. One regular who comes to mind was a little colored
fellow named The Lamplighter. He only weighed 110 pounds
and had tuberculosis, but he was what you'd call a real toughie,
as well as a noted ladies' man and gambler. He killed an Irish
cop in 1912 in self-defense and was destined to be the cause
of a race riot fourteen years later.

Another colorful character was a lad known as Crackerjack.
Like Luckey Roberts, he was a lemon pool player, and a pretty
slick article. They said he had once been a successful jockey
in Cuba. He was always going someplace to get his hair

straightened. A lot of our sports were heavily pomaded on the head, but Cracker was just too much. He was the first guy I ever knew who used Kink-No-More, which we called "Conk," a hair preparation invented by a barber on 153rd Street named William Hart.

Conk worked but the big trouble with it was it would make the user become bald in time because it ate up the roots of the hair. But in those days we didn't know that. Hart made millions. It was used all over the country and the musicians in New York were using it a lot. They'd go to Hart's and get their hair washed, trimmed, and straightened. Crackerjack used to look like he was wearing a wig all the time with his hair plastered down with Conk.

There were some crazy gals around the Gates as well as wild men. One was a gal known as Detroit Red, who looked Japanese. She was a dancer and made fame for herself by doing "the ups."‖ It was a sight to see when some man called out, "Come here, Red, and grab a dollar with your third leg."

But as much as these characters fascinated me they didn't knock me out as did those piano men I began to hear there in that hot town.

‖ A common practice in the old days, where a girl would pick money off of a table without using her hands.

6

Big Ears in New York City

Whenever I went to New York from 1913 on, I made it a point to get around to hear all the piano pounders I could find. Some of the guys I saw have never been heard of or written up by the jazz writers.

Most of these ragtimers were regulars around the big town, but there were also pianists from Memphis, St. Louis, Atlanta, Charleston, Baltimore, and even New Orleans, who would drop into town for a short stay. Many of the transients had gotten run out of their home towns because their stable of women had been caught pulling a fast one and the local cops were after them. Many of these got as far as Newark or Jersey City, where the railroads coming up from the South ended in those days. When they crossed on the ferry to New York they wouldn't stay long because the local players resented the intrusion on their territory.

Wherever they were from, the old-time piano men tried to develop their own individual style of playing. Because, you see, if one player had a way of performing that made him stand out from the others it would make him a big hit with the ladies and that was the one thing we were all looking for all the time. You had to be real sharp in the way you dressed, the manner in which you approached the piano, and in the originality of your ideas; that is, if you wanted to compete for the ladies. A piano player who put on a good show was said to have a sharp "attitude" and would draw the queens to stand alongside his piano. Today we call it showmanship, but back then it was called "attitude."

Jelly Roll Morton, the blues player from New Orleans, used to shine that way. He first came through New York around 1911, pimpin' for a stable of women. The east coast pianists were more impressed by his attitude than they were by his playing of the rags, stomps, and blues.

When Morton entered a place he would come in smiling so everyone would get a glance at his diamond-studded tooth. As he arrived at the piano, he would take off his coat with a fancy flourish and lay it on top of the piano with the expensive lining turned outward for all to see. Then he would carefully wipe off the piano bench or stool with a large silk handkerchief. Out of the corner of his eye he would look to see whether or not he was getting the proper attention. If so, he would sit down, and like all the pianists of the day, hit his signature chord. You had to have a special chord with which you started off all your performances. It served the same purpose as the theme songs later —it announced your presence.

One of the first so-called jazz joints we had in the early days was a café on Thirty-seventh Street near Seventh Avenue, run by William Banks. Remember, there were very few Negroes in Harlem then and the big colored section was still downtown on the West Side. In 1917 Kid Banks moved his famous café uptown to 23 West 133rd Street between Lenox and Fifth avenues.

When I first started going to Banks's, the entertainment was furnished by the Shelton Family made up of Pa Shelton on bass violin and his two daughters on regular fiddles. Hegamin, a violinist himself, always wanted to catch the Sheltons. I was more interested in Banks's piano man, Willie (Egg Head) Sewell, an old-time ragtimer from Baltimore, who made the piano hop, skip, and jump. He really did have a head shaped like an egg and was well along in years. As I recall he played with a strong rhythm and a lot of syncopated vamps on tunes like "Wait Till the Sun Shines Nellie," "That Barbershop Chord," and "Take Me Back to New York Town." I don't know whatever became of old man Sewell after he left Bill Banks's Cafe.

There was a place called the Douglass Club over on Twenty-eighth Street run by Edmond Johnson, an ex-pugilist, who owned his own night club for many years until he became a doorman. The Douglass was located one flight up over a stable. The piano man was a character known as Jumbo, and like Sewell, he was an old-time ragtimer. I haven't heard anything about him through all the years. Those pianists would sort of disappear, like old soldiers.

One of the best ragtimers around was One-Leg Willie Joseph. You could catch him at a joint run by Mule Johnson and a man named Davis.* Willie would walk in, park his crutch on the piano, and then proceed to take charge.

Willie Joseph originally came from New England—he was born in either Boston, Massachusetts, or Hartford, Connecticut —and was supposed to have been educated at the Boston Conservatory. Eventually he took Eubie Blake's job at the Goldfield Hotel in Baltimore when Eubie moved to New York.

Joseph made quite a name for himself among the popular ragtime stars of the day. He once won a big-time ragtime contest at the Madison Square Garden. His ragging of "The Stars and Stripes Forever" beat out the phony Mike Bernard, the Jewish ragtime kid, who copied the great Negro ragtime originator Ben Harney's style. Bernard, who made his on "Dardanella," got more money out of ragtime than did all the colored stars put together.

You see, before World War I, the profession of playing ragtime piano in saloons was very active and growing all the time.

* At 108 West Thirty-second Street.

Many famous stars of music and entertainment started their careers in that way. Jimmy Durante started playing ragtime at Diamond Tony's on Coney Island. Later he played Carey Walsh's saloon, also on Coney Island, where Eddie Cantor was a singing waiter. Then the great composer Irving Berlin was at one time a singing waiter at Nigger Mike's in Chinatown. Pianist-bandleader Vincent Lopez, famous for his version of "Nola," (his left hand's like the bear, nowhere) started as a pianist on the honky-tonk circuit. He played at Frank Clayton's saloon in Brooklyn and later at the Atlantic House on Coney.

I did not get to hear the above guys when they first started out—they were either before my time or worked in saloons where Negroes were not found—but they would show up in the saloons where we played. Now you know where a lot of them got their ragtime styles.

To get back to One-Leg Willie; after moving from Thirty-second Street up to Barron's Little Savoy Club on Thirty-fifth Street near Eighth Avenue, I heard him many times. That was around 1915 when Barron D. Wilkins was operating downtown. He later became one of the most celebrated cabaret owners in Harlem. His place in the tenderloin was one of the most popular dives of them all.

Yeah, Joseph was one of the best of the old-time ragtime players. He had original ideas and never played the same number the same way twice; the melody would stay the same, but he would always vary the harmony. He was fast, real fast, and his fingers and brain seemed to be working together like a flash of lightning.†

It was at Walter Herbert's joint on Thirty-seventh Street that I heard the famous Jack the Bear, whose real name was John Wilson. He hailed from either Pennsylvania or Ohio and was a well-known dope addict who played piano when he felt like it; his chief callings were those of a sporting man and a gambler.

† Another regular at the Little Savoy was John Europe, the piano-playing brother of the great bandleader James Reese Europe.

Wilson's most famous rendition was a tune called "The Dream," which had actually been written by old man Jess Pickett, another piano-playing gambler who died around 1920. This number was also known as "The Bull Diker's Dream";‡ it was a tune dedicated to lesbians.

Although Pickett may have originally composed "The Dream," it sort of became the Bear's tune by the way he played it. It had a tango bass and Wilson would start playing it at a fast tempo and then take it into slow drag style where it got mean and dirty. It was one of those "put out the lights and call the law" things and went over big just before dawn.

The area around the West Twenties and Thirties really jumped back in those times. You could hear plenty of fine piano in the houses on Twenty-seventh Street, and in Mrs. Brown's Nickelette, a small movie-vaudeville theater at Thirty-seventh and Eighth. It was there that the great Florence Mills started her career. During her early days Miss Mills was in an act known as the Mills Sisters: made up of Florence, Maude, and Olivia (a non-sister) Mills.

In those days the famous Negro music-publishing firm of Gotham & Attucks had their offices on Thirty-seventh Street, right off Broadway. All the fine Negro writers and performers of that period could be seen hanging around that corner—Bert Williams, Jim Europe, Tim Brymn, Cecil Mack, Will Marion Cook, and Gussie Davis, among others.

That was the way it was around New York when I was a boy and I would come over and get right into the middle of it all as often as I could possibly get away from my busy activities in Newark.

‡ Also called "The Bowdiger's Dream," "Ladies' Dream," and "Digah's Dream." Fats Waller recorded the number on organ under the title "Digah's Stomp." (Reference: Blesh & Janis *They All Played Ragtime* published by Alfred A. Knopf.)

7

I Went to the Gypsy

Don't cheat it—
if you can't beat it.

Willie the Lion Smith

My uncle Rob, the Oliver who drove the perfume wagon, once took me to Vauxhall, an amusement park near Irvington, New Jersey. We were strutting up the midway when all of a sudden a gypsy grabbed my arm. "I'd like to read your fortune, boy," she said. I must have been fourteen years old at the time.

I've never forgotten what the gypsy told me that day. Every one of her predictions came to pass, one after the other.

First, she said I would marry a white woman, but I wouldn't stay with her very long.

Then she said I was slated to take a trip over the seas with an army. She added that I should enlist on my own or my chances of getting back home alive would not be good.

Finally, she finished her predictions by saying I was in for all kinds of trouble until I made fifty years of age! It didn't take long for her prophecies to start. When I reached nineteen, I married a white piano player and stayed with her a year. We've never gotten unsheiked,* and when I die she'll get a third of my estate. When World War I came along, I remembered the gypsy's words—man, I didn't wait to be drafted! I hurried to join the U. S. Army before President Wilson even got around to declaring we were at war with Germany. I was sent over in the first shipment of troops and, as the lady said I would, got back in one piece. Then, in 1918, while still overseas, the planet Mars entered my house and stayed for thirty years, casting its shadow.

Here's how the first prophecy came true. Johnson's Cafe in Newark was one of the best spots in town. It had the reputation of being a real dicty, cabaretlike place with tables of good food. You weren't anything in show business around Newark unless you played Johnson's or the Hotel Navarro. I played both, but my first job away from the Coast was at Johnson's.

I met many of the greats in show business at Johnson's, where the famous Empire City Four had originated. (They were booked there after one of the owners heard them singing on street corners around town.) Another Newark-born entertainer, guitarist Nick Lucas, "The Troubadour," worked his first jobs at Johnson's. Tess Gardella (Aunt Jemima) played there regularly, and singer-entertainer Bee Palmer, Joe (Wanna-buy-a-Duck?) Penner, and Blanche Merrill, the singing pianist.

My first work there was at night and the many traveling shows I saw at the Newark theaters made me want to learn all I could about big-time show business. I caught Tutt & Whitney's *Smart Set* revues—with the best-looking women I think I've ever seen—J. Leubrie Hill's *Darktown Follies,* the S. H. Dudley dramatic presentations, and the late, great Bert Williams in *Load of Kole.* These were the best shows of prewar times.

Other wonderful vaudeville acts of those days come to mind.

* Harlem expression meaning divorced.

Dudley White, the first comedian to talk to a mule on the stage; Ada Overton Walker, the champion cakewalker, who had been married to George (Bon-Bon Buddy) Walker, Bert Williams' partner, and many, many others whose names escape me now. There was always much doing in Newark's four big-time vaudeville houses—Proctor's, B. F. Keith's, the Orpheum, and Blaney's ten-cent gallery theater.

Dramatic productions got my attention too, especially tear-jerkers. *The Way of the Transgressor,* and *Willie Live, The Boy Behind the Gun.* That had a big war scene; everybody got killed off. I was sure to remember that one soon.

How did I get to see all this? Admission was ten cents.

I wanted to learn to read and write music. It was a good break when I made the acquaintance of a fellow named Arthur Eck, who played the piano in a vaudeville act. Every time Eck would play Proctor's or the Loew's State in New York City, I would look him up after the show. At that time I was in my early teens and I could play ragtime. He was quite a reader. So he said if you teach me some of those licks you play, I'll teach you something about music. And this is the God's truth, I'm telling you. We exchanged lessons. Everybody who has a musical gift should learn his reading—that's the easiest part. The really hard part is still to learn to play creatively.

Most of the men who played in those vaudeville orchestras were good arrangers. There were twelve pieces in the pit and for acts that didn't have their own orchestrations, they worked out music. You could get music arranged for an act for about a dollar or a dollar and fifty. (Now you pay five hundred to one thousand dollars for a "lead sheet.") They were good men. If the drummer didn't catch a switching hip, he lost his job. They had to be fast.

BLANCHE

While I was at Johnson's, around 1916, a ragtime pianist and singer from Poughkeepsie, New York, joined the show. This was Blanche Merrill. She had been married to an entertainer named Norman Watters, in 1912. Watters, whose stepfather's name was Merrill, was a singer and dancer who had paired up with Blanche. Her maiden name was Howard. The act went over well, they got married, and then Watters was rushed away with tuberculosis in 1915.

Blanche was a popular entertainer at that time. It so happened that we were both Sagittarians and shared similar ideas. That is to say we both had the typical Sagittarian temper tantrums. Although those born under the sign of Sagittarius get mad easily, they are also able to get along with each other unusually well. I've always had a vicious temper, but I know it, and have been able to master it.

We had a lot of laughs together there at Johnson's. Like the Green Gates in New York, Johnson's drew interesting characters. There were the Irish gambling bosses, the two brothers, Squawk and Squire Riley. Blanche and I were great favorites of the Rileys. Then, you didn't know what was going on unless you'd met Dutch Frank, a white man and a bare-knuckle fighter, known to be one of the sharpest card sharks of his day. Or, Bend Them Bootsie, a colored cat who made the dice talk. And Georgie Forbes, who had things fixed so that he never lost at three-card monte (a technique which became known as "the Old Army game" or "Which pod is the pea under?"). I also remember the boys at the bar pointing out the Saratoga Kid to me. He was one of the best-known confidence men of all time. But no one ever knew any of the men's real names— they didn't want you to. They were all Deadeye Dicks.

Blanche and I decided to get married. It was one of those overnight ideas people sometimes get. We moved into an apartment and tried to set up a normal housekeeping routine.

My mother had warned me about getting married. She told me to find a girl either ten years older or one ten years younger than myself. Never one your own age, she'd say. I guess she was right because Blanche and I were about the same age and it didn't take long for the battles to start.

Those were days when you could shave and wash with champagne. Blanche and I got our share. With the drinking, the fights began to become unbearable. She had a wild mind, always wanted to travel, liked nothing planned. She loved night life. I was just in it because everybody else was in it. In those days a woman could go out at nine o'clock at night and stay out until 9 A.M.

We had a friend, an entertainer named Mamie Kelly from Newark, who went down to Panama City to open a cabaret. She wanted Blanche and me to come down and work for her. Blanche wanted to go, but I wanted to stay close to New York. (Mamie Kelly's place eventually became famous and she later opened another night club in New Orleans.) We fought.

And there were more fights.

Shortly before I went into the Army, the gypsy's prophecy came true. We separated and I went back to live with my folks on Clayton Street, while Blanche headed for Panama City and Mamie Kelly's. I don't believe in divorces. Divorce is not right. If you can't get along, separate, and don't slanderize. The almighty has the timetable set for us, anyhow.

Blanche Merrill is still around and we talk to each other over the telephone frequently. She lives in midtown New York on a pension and still takes in piano pupils. For many years she has coached other performers in partnership with Jack Stanley, a dance instructor who once worked for the *Ziegfeld Follies*.

Through the years, there has been some confusion because there were two Blanche Merrills in show business. The other

Blanche is older than my friend, a woman who once wrote special material (songs) for Eva Tanguay, a headliner in vaudeville. That Blanche Merrill is a member of the American Society of Composers, Authors, and Publishers. When in later years I became a member of ASCAP it would startle me to see that familiar name on the membership lists—until I learned to remember that she was an entirely different person.

Blanche and I never got back together after she went to Panama. Over the years we've gone our separate ways. There never seemed to be any reason to go through the formalities of a divorce. Anyhow, the Lord takes care of everything and you do unto others as you would have them do unto you.

MOVING UPTOWN

During the years before World War I, colored folks moved uptown. Harlem itself did not become heavily populated until during the war when a great many Negroes from the South came up to work in the plants. But the section called San Juan Hill, or The Jungles, located west of Broadway from Fifty-ninth up to Sixty-fourth, was growing steadily. West Fifty-third Street started to become *the* meeting place of entertainers and musicians. Partly this was due to the location of the famed Negro hotel, run by Jim Marshall, at 127-29 West Fifty-third. Across the street was the Clef Club, formed in 1912 by Jim Europe, to give us a headquarters—a sort of booking agency for jobs, especially those where some leader of white society wanted colored entertainment for a party. The Clef Clubbers were mostly legitimate men who read the popular music of the day and played in the large banjo orchestras around the metropolitan area. They didn't get much chance to pretty the music up on their own. It was at the Clef that I met Irving (Kid Sneeze) Williams—a legit pianist who loved to sneak off and rag it by ear—bandleader Happy Rhone, and other celebrated personalities of the period.

Down Fifty-third from the Marshall and Clef Club, toward The Jungles, was Georgie Lee's cabaret. It was at Lee's that I again ran into James P. Johnson, who was living close by in The Jungles. The third member of what was to become the Big Three was also living in that area at the time—bouncing baby Fats Waller, whose family had moved up from Waverly Place— but I hadn't met him yet.

Another one of the youngsters who was coming along about this time was William D. Gant. He hung around with James P. and myself at Lee's. A short time later Gant became one of the first pianists to work at Bill Banks's new uptown café on 133rd Street. Willie's home was in Hell's Kitchen, where he lived in a building (at Forty-first Street and Eighth Avenue) that also housed Alberta Simmons, New York's best woman jazz pianist; Raymond (Lippy) Boyette, a piano-playing whiz who later sort of managed the Big Three; and Russell Brooks, a good friend of the Waller family. Brooks was the first one to haul Fats around to the saloons while the kid was still in short pants.

We, all of us younger cats, used to follow around guys like Thad (Snowball) Wilkerson, who played by ear in one key— B natural; Jack the Bear; and Richard (Abba Labba) McLean, a sporting-house piano player who had once worked in a vaudeville act with my good friend Luckey Roberts.

Old Abba Labba wasn't easy to hear because he rarely took a regular job. He would just walk into a place and play for thirty minutes before walking out again. We—that is, James P., Willie Gant, Corky Williams (I can't recall whatever became of him), and the Lion—sure dug that cat. He used tenths in his bass and could swing like mad, just like an old-time Baptist preacher shouting at his congregation. James P. thought so much of Abba that he had a tendency to pick up on his style.

My favorite during those happy days was Bob Hawkins, one

of the first to play at Barron's† (Barron D. Wilkins), after he moved uptown to 134th Street and Seventh Avenue, sometime in 1916. Barron's became one of the main headquarters for the piano men in Harlem and it was there that Luckey Roberts eventually became the house man. But before that, Hawkins was the main guy and he was really something. One of his big numbers was a ditty named "Don't You Dare to Strike Me Again!" The customers, especially the girls, would gather around his piano and urge him to get loose or to step on it. He later got a twelve-piece band together that rocked Barron's and was one of the first cabaret jazz bands.

Back in those days there were several large halls that had some good music. Up at 100th and Third Avenue was an Irish Society hall known as McFarland's. I was reminded of that joint many years later in the 1950s when I played weekends at Central Plaza on lower Second Avenue. McFarland's was a place where people found it impossible to control their emotions and they really let themselves go. The cops were frequently called in to stop a riot. Like Central Plaza, the 100th Street hall was open two nights a week and was a center for dancing the Texas Tommy and other jazz dances.

The manager at McFarland's was a man named Harry Souser from Jersey City, who also played good piano and was a passing reader and writer of music. They usually had a four- or five-piece band—a piano, drums, violin, and flute or clarinet—to play the early part of the evening. One of the groups they often featured was the New Amsterdam Orchestra under the direction of Miss Hallie Anderson, a dancing teacher. The climax of an evening at McFarland's came after 2 A.M. when the orchestra had gone home. At that time Souser, who was quite a juicehead, would wheel a piano out into the center of the floor and start playing rags. We younger guys would line up to take our turns at the box after Souser got tired, etherized, or as we

† Roy Campanella's liquor store occupies the premises today.

used to say too "sousered" to play. It was long after daylight before we got home on those occasions.

There was another place uptown called Sontag's, a sort of roadhouse, located at 110th Street and Lenox Avenue, where the pianist was John Europe. Close by Sontag's was old Dan Williams's cabaret at 111th and St. Nicholas Avenue. Williams also used piano players in a small sporting house he ran in the Chelsea district on Twenty-seventh Street between Eighth and Ninth avenues.

Then there was a place called The Campus, 104th Street and Columbus Avenue, where my old pal from Atlantic City—Eubie Blake—worked when he first came to New York City from Baltimore. By this time he had left Madison Reed and was teamed up with a big handsome guy, a ballad singer, known as Broadway Jones, who had a voice like Caruso's. I used to pester Blake to let me sit in on piano just for the privilege of accompanying Jones.

By this time Eubie Blake was becoming known as a composer, and we all liked a rag he had written called "Chevy Chase." I think some of his earlier tunes were better than the ones that he became famous for in later years. Everybody should remember his better-known songs like, "I'm Just Wild About Harry" and "Memories of You."

The place where the real action was in those days was right in the heart of The Jungles. One wild place was called Drake's Dancing Class (on Sixty-second Street) because they couldn't get a license to operate unless they taught dancing. We called it The Jungles Casino and it was really a beat-up, small dance hall; it was in a cellar where the rain used to flow down the walls. It was so damp down there that they used to try to keep the piano dry by placing lit candles around it. The furnace, coal, and ashes were located right in the same room with the old upright. There were plenty of dancers but no teachers down there. It was some "ratskeller."

Many of the customers came off the boats that docked in

the West Sixties. The piers in that area served the ship lines
that ran between the southern ports, like Savannah and
Charleston to New York and Boston, via the Ward Steamship
Line. These people came from around the Carolina and Georgia
sea islands. They were called Gullahs and Geechies.‡ These
folks worked and played hard; they were able to dance all
night after spending the day throwing boxes around as long-
shoremen.

Quite a group of us made that Casino because those Geechies
really went for our style of playing. Besides James P. and myself, the regulars included Abba Labba, Luckey Roberts, Freddie Singleton, and Stephen (The Beetle) Henderson. Our soft,
slow, four-o'clock-in-the-morning music got to those folks from
the South. They danced cakewalks and cotillions; by this time
we had learned to play the natural twelve-bar blues that
evolved from the spirituals. We all knew W. C. Handy's "St.
Louis Blues," "Memphis Blues," "Beale Street Blues," and "Yellow Dog Blues."

The Gullahs would start out early in the evening dancing
two-steps, waltzes, schottisches; but as the night wore on and
the liquor began to work, they would start improvising their
own steps and that was when they wanted us to get-in-the-
alley, real lowdown. Those big Charleston, South Carolina,
bruisers would grab a girl from the bar and stomp-it-down as
the piano player swung into the gut-bucketiest music he could.

It was from the improvised dance steps that the Charleston
dance originated. All the older folks remember it became a
rage during the 1920s and all it really amounted to was a variation of a cotillion step brought to the North by the Geechies.
There were many variations danced at the Casino and this
usually caused the piano player to make up his own musical
variation to fit the dancing. One of James P. Johnson's variations was later published as a number called "The Charleston,"

‡ Geechies come from the Ogeechie River country in Georgia.

and was used in the show *Runnin' Wild* on Broadway in 1923. Yes sir, The Brute's "Charleston" became a dance craze by the mid-twenties and is still being revived.

Of course there were other joints in The Jungles. These included Jim Allan's on Sixty-first Street and Tenth Avenue, another cellar protected by an iron-plated door; here they had an extra feature of big-time gambling in the rear. As I recall now, their regular pianist was Bob Gordon. He had a number called "Oh, You Drummer!" which featured a lot of breaks for a drummer.

Some of the other piano players we ran into during those days were Fats Harris, who had his own rag in D called "The Fats Harris Rag"; old Fat Dan Cary, who could play up a storm; Kid Griffin (appearing uptown at the dicty Connor's Cafe on 135th Street), who hailed from Trenton, New Jersey, and was a 250-pound dandy with wide-leg pants and number-four shoes; Charles Cooke and Floyd Keppard, both from Jersey City; Leroy Tibbs, Joe Breen, Pat Toy, and Louis Emore, all originally from up in Boston; and the Washington, D.C., bunch, including Louis Brown, Louis Thomas, Doc Perry, who were followed later by Duke Ellington, Cliff Jackson, and Claude Hopkins.

This story wouldn't be complete if I didn't mention one of the most fabulous piano men of them all—Walter (One-Leg Shadow) Gould. He came from Philadelphia and he must have been over a hundred years old when he died in Albany, New York, in 1959. The Shadow was one of the first to start sprucing up the quadrilles and schottisches that were popular around the time of the Civil War. He never bothered to learn to read music and this gave him trouble in later years when he was called upon to accompany singers. When he was working at Edmond's Cellar (at 132nd Street and Fifth Avenue, around 1919), Edmond Johnson had to fire him because he couldn't learn some of the popular tunes of the day that were sung by Ethel Waters. When he died, One-Leg Shadow was making a good living writing policy numbers (running a "bank" for the illegal numbers racket) in Albany.

Speaking of Albany, I remember another piano man who came from up around there, by the name of Nigger Nelson. He was a good man but would only work in white cabarets and didn't get much of a chance to play the real blues. Another man like him was Bud Howard from Detroit, Michigan. He also died about two years ago.

There were some good piano men who came in from the West. I remember one guy in particular from Toledo, Ohio, but his name escapes me now. I do recall he had a pint of whisky for breakfast every morning and featured such tunes as "Walking the Dog," "All That I Had Is Gone," and "When the Cold Cold Wind Blows." My friend, Roy Bargy, who used to be Paul Whiteman's featured pianist, told me he learned a good deal from that Ohio guy.

Both James P. and I liked a guy named Mike Jackson, who came from either Louisville, Kentucky, or St. Louis, Missouri. He was featured at Barron's Exclusive Club for a spell and always did a number called "Chinese Blues" (in D minor). During this rendition he would imitate Chinese dialogue and use a muffled bass drum to get an oriental effect. The lyrics to his vocal choruses would compare the mutual troubles of a Negro and a Chinaman. It was both sad and funny; a listener never knew whether to laugh or cry.

A noteworthy thing to mention is that in those days we always had to have a couple of classical selections in our repertoires. I worked up my own arrangement of the "Polonaise Militaire" and a special ragtime version of a chorus or two of *"Miserere"* from *Il Trovatore.*

We were inspired to always include classics by such pianists as Fred K. Bryant of Brooklyn, known as "The Harmony King," and Sam Gordon of Trenton, who had been trained in Germany. Both of these men were great technicians: classically trained Bryant had very small hands and was the inventor of what we called "the backward tenth," and Gordon had the fastest right hand I've ever seen. Sam Gordon's New York spot was the Elk's Cafe on Lenox Avenue between 137th and 138th streets.

Another good man, with a classical repertoire, was New Jersey-born Donald Lambert, who died in May of 1962. Don was about seven years younger than I was and came from the town of Princeton. His most famous classical rendition was Beethoven's "Moonlight Sonata," which he featured for many years at Wallace's cocktail lounge in Orange, New Jersey.

I must not forget to mention the man who was probably the most inspirational in getting both James P. and myself to include as many concert pieces as we could. He was Ernest Green, a classical pianist and teacher, who would come into Barron's and play such numbers as the *William Tell* "Overture" and the *White Canary* "Overture" for us.

Here I've tried to give a picture of New York as a piano man's town before World War I. After the war and during the 1920s, the Harlem striders really began to get under way. We'll go into that after a time out to squabble with the Boches.§

§ World War I expression for Germans.

8

A Lion in Forty-nine Days

*A weak cat never made a fighting tiger,
and a fighting tiger never licked a fighting lion.*

WILLIE THE LION SMITH

That fortune-telling lady wasn't kidding when she said I would be going on a long, long trip with an army.

There were all kinds of rumors after World War I started in Europe on that August day in 1914. I remember when the S.S. *Lusitania* was sunk by German torpedoes; everybody was saying the President (Wilson) had ordered three million army uniforms complete with boots. What the gypsy had told me started to worry my mind, as the news from Europe kept getting worse and worse.

One night when I was out with the boys we happened to go to a saloon in Harrison, New Jersey, and ran into three or four soldiers there in their uniforms. My friends and I started to talk and to have a few with them. They were from the 15th Infantry Regiment, the only colored troops around New York City at that time, and they were all for us signing up with their fighting bunch. (It was the 15th that later took Jim Europe's Hell Fighters Band to war with them.)

Those soldiers were convincing talkers. Before the night was out, my friends and I had made a pact to meet at the enlistment headquarters in downtown Newark the next morning. This was around November 1916, and we were all old enough to get in—I was going on twenty.

There was a lot of excitement at our house on Clayton Street the next day when I announced I was going to join the Army. A lot of colored folks at that time thought the war in Europe was a white man's battle and they all hoped our country would stay out of it. They would say that we should let those ofays* across the ocean shoot each other down.

My mother was inclined to be of that frame of mind and, like all mothers do during time of war, tried to talk me out of my plans. But not my stepfather, John Smith—he was all for it. He said, "Good boy, Willie, you go over there and show 'em." The fact was, he was on one of his benders and followed me all the way to the trolley line offering me good-by drinks from his jug.

But, wouldn't you know it? When I got to the recruiting office I was the only brave lad of the night before that showed up. The other cats had stayed home to nurse their hangovers. But remembering what the palm reader had said a couple of years before—as well as beginning to feel the gulps from John Smith's bottle that had killed *my* hangover—I barged right into the office and announced, "I'm here. And I want to join the 15th Regiment at Camp Upton on Long Island." They didn't argue. The man in charge smiled and signed me up on the spot. The next thing I knew I was in Camp Dix, New Jersey.

There, they were organizing a new Negro regiment for the field artillery. When I asked why I hadn't been sent to Camp Upton, the head man said, "Oh, we thought you would rather be in a cannon-shooting army than in a marching society."

Everybody knows who is boss in the Army and it sure isn't the soldier boy. So I traded in my red garnet English suit with

* Pig Latin for foes, or whites.

the tight pants and my cloth-covered, patent-leather shoes for a khaki outfit complete with puttees.

That winter we did setting-up exercises at dawn while stripped to the waist in the icy wind and snow. As time went on our chances for getting over to see some of the fighting kept getting better and better. After it was announced that our President declared the United States was at war with Germany in April of 1917, we got a lot of instruction on how to fire a four-inch artillery piece.

OFF TO FRANCE

We must have been damn good at our work; they sure didn't lose any time rushing us toward France. Our regiment was proud of itself when it was given us straight—we were scheduled to cross over with the First American Expeditionary Forces in the first convoy to go in July. It made us feel real important because the jive was the United States had to get a million men into France right away or lose the war.

Our regiment was moved secretly, in unlighted trains, from the camp to the docks at Hoboken, New Jersey. We were marched aboard a boat in the middle of the night, nine thousand of us were piled on top of a cargo of wheat. It wasn't very long until some of our bravery began to abandon ship. Word got around that we were on the one boat that had been a German passenger vessel. We found out the next day we were on an impounded German liner, renamed the *President Grant*. Every German submarine located off the coast was on the lookout for just that ship.

They should have placed us in the middle of the fifty-ship convoy with those U-boats out gunning for us—instead we were right on the outer edge of the formation. Three hours after leaving New York harbor, sneaking out at that, a U-boat got a bead on us. They fired a shot that caught us right across the bow. It sure looked like we were designated to sink!

That was when the bravery of our regiment began to not look so good. We were all getting scared. Our officers had told us right before we left the dock that if anything happened we would leave the ship in sections like in a fire drill. If anyone got panicky or tried to get off he would get shot.

When I heard the torpedo scrape our ship, I was standing guard on the No. 4 deck and had to rush to find my section. By the time I found my group and was ready to march off in single file, they turned our tub around, and announced we would stay on board. We then limped back to Hoboken all alone like a sitting duck.

That's how I finally made it to Camp Upton. We were then sent out to Long Island where we pitched our pup tents and relaxed for two days. The repairs on the ship were made on the double-quick. Soon we were back on deck. Then our tub raced out of the harbor to try to catch up with the convoy.

Our all-colored unit—officially, the 92nd Division, 153rd Negro Brigade, 350th Field Artillery, Battery A—landed at Brest, France, eighteen days after leaving Hoboken. They issued us steel helmets, gas masks, and puttees, or wrap-around leggings.

As soon as we landed we ran into more grief—heavy rains had the ground five feet deep in mud. We had to march in this stuff carrying a seventy-five-pound pack and a heavy helmet that made our heads bow. It was a rough period on the way from the coast to the front up beyond Paris, I'm telling you. Although we rode in wagons part of the time, there was a long distance we had to pile through mud and mire. There were some, in spite of the good condition we were in from the months of training at Dix, who just couldn't take it and dropped in their tracks. We'd give them brandy and help them drag their packs. Some of the meekest, who got tired the easiest, turned out to be real soldiers later on.

Yes sir, as we struggled along, one thing after another came along to tear at our nerves. As I said, some of us were tough guys, so young we didn't know what nerves meant, but there were others who as soon as we found out we were on our way to the death spell (that's what we called the front lines) began to chicken out on us. There were a lot of scared men in that man's army, especially after we got within range of the sounds from the big guns. The guys in charge kept a lot of cats from cutting out by saying that there was from ten to twenty years on the rockpile waiting if we went AWOL.

This boy decided there was no use to cheat 'em if you couldn't beat 'em. Better to join the gang and fight than to just sit back and think about it. The top brass was right when they told us we might as well make up our minds to die fighting because we would die faster if we hung back scared.

The boss of our battery of two hundred men was Colonel Prosser of North Carolina. He was the kind of man who wanted his men to have a look that was mean and ferocious—if you couldn't look him right in the eye he didn't want you in his outfit. He always had a fast answer to complainers and goldbrickers. If you said to him you were sick, he'd growl and reply, "Die and prove it!"

One of our biggest problems on our march in the mud through France was sickness. It was said we lost more men through illnesses like pneumonia than we did later from battle casualties on the firing line. They gave you aspirin for all possible pains and diseases. They gave it to me for a bad tooth and to my buddy when he got a letter from home telling him his wife had run off with a slacker.

There was one thing about Colonel Prosser—he loved music. We had Tim Brymn's brass band in our division. They got to be known all over Europe as the Seventy Black Devils of the U. S. 350th Field Artillery. Their nickname came from the Senegalese soldiers in the French Army, who fought next to us at the front. These colored folk from West Africa were known far and wide as the French Blue Devils and they were savage cats; if they saw a man get his head blown off, they thought it was funny and laughed. . . .

I had the honor of being the drum major for the Black Devils' band when we were marching. But when we were resting someplace I would play the piano, if one could be found, and some of the horns from the band would join me in a sort of early jam session. There happened to be three fine cornetists in the group, who later played with me in America. Two of them were from the cornet-playing Smith family. Their names were Luke and Russell, and back in the States they had a younger brother, the famed Little Joe Smith, who was too young to go to war. (Russell became famous later in Fletcher Henderson's orchestra, as did Joe, but Luke took to bad hooch and rushed himself off before he could make a name for himself.) The third cornetist was a fellow, Addington Major, who was destined to play in my band when we made a historic blues record with Mamie Smith in 1920.

As we marched in the mud toward Paris and the front lines, we had our good times as well as our bad. Sometimes we rode in freight trains, wagons, or just walked. We never made more than ten miles in a day. We marched so hard on some days that we were cross-eyed at night. In spite of being tired we still looked around for a good time at night wherever we stopped. The Army put plenty of saltpeter in our food to keep nature down, but you still saw lines waiting to get into a house where there would be seven or eight French tarts waiting for us. It became well known after the war that we left a lot of babies behind when we returned home.

The French are a very affectionate people. They move you. They kept our canteens full of cognac, which helped a lot; the water was full of poison. I became very fond of the French girls with the red cheeks and the bicycles. One of our big problems was sneaking away from our camp at night and getting back on time in the morning. That was where those bikes came in handy—they would meet us with their bikes. In the dawn there

was always a weird parade of soldiers wheeling toward camp
with chicks on the handle bars.

But things began to change as we got nearer and nearer to
the front. It was disturbing to see the hospital trains returning
from the front loaded with the soldiers, badly wounded. We had
to spend the nights in abandoned trenches rather than in soft
beds in a farmhouse. Those trenches were full of gray, white,
and black rats. Man, we were beginning to see whatever fun
there was in war was over for us. To battle the rats, we'd pour
crude oil into those trenches and then set fire to it. Then we'd
have to get what sleep we could in those stinking, burnt-out
holes in the ground.

One of our largest worries had to do with the poison gas they
used in that war. We had been carefully told all about it and
given a good deal of instruction in how to use our gas masks.
I remember there were several different kinds of gas—mustard
gas, chlorine gas, and a cloud gas they shot into the air from
cannons. You'd cough your lungs out if you happened to inhale
any of those gases and German Fritzie had plenty of it to shoot
into the air.

Thinking back now, it was the cloud gas that worried us the
most, because the wind could carry that stuff anywhere over a
long distance. The hell of it was you couldn't see it coming because it looked like any other cloud. As we neared the firing
line we walked with our gas masks always around our necks;
we had to be ready to put them on at the slightest suspicion
that the air was gassed. We had been taught how to get the
masks into the proper place on our heads in eight seconds but
I could play that tune fast, too—my record was four-and-a-half
seconds!

After the war many of our boys returned home with gas sickness—and it lasted the rest of their lives. People today should
think about that in relation to the fallout dust from the atomic
explosions. Just like that terrible gas, it can make you sick for
the rest of your life.

By the time we got up near the front lines the German soldiers were only about ten miles from Paris and their Big Bertha cannons were bombarding the city from seventy-five miles away. Those shells were landing right on the outskirts of town. I recall they hit, but didn't knock down a statue outside a little church in the Paris suburbs. It wobbled but didn't fall. It was a statue of Joan of Arc.

Some of the soldiers would cry like babies when they were sent up to the firing line. The noise up there, or anywhere near to it, was something terrible, I'm telling you. Some of the boys lost their hearing for life just from the racket. I put cotton in my ears, but even that didn't do too much good. The din up there made us punch-drunk.

If you busted out or refused to go across to the action, you got "deranked," as well as court-martialed. And you didn't even have to be right at the line; those damned Huns were lobbing shells high over the trenches to blow up the reserves on their way up. It was hell on earth.

There were some real fighters up there, including the Blue Devils, and a French brigade made up of women who had shaved off all their hair so they could enlist for fighting.

The guys who had the most dangerous job of all were the ones who got assigned as snipers, and to string telephone lines out beyond the trenches. When they asked for volunteers to fire the French 75s I didn't think much about it—I was real glad I didn't have to go out in the open like those snipers—I stepped forward when they made the call. There were damn few others who wanted to take any chance.

First, they gathered us together to show us the mechanism of the big cannons. Of the few who volunteered not many of us were destined to get back in one piece. I believe the stars and planets were with me all through that fracas. We had been trained on obsolete Civil War cannons. They were four-inch pieces and our training had not been too long. Our men were up against the crack German mathematicians, who had been

at it with the latest shooting equipment for over four years.
Yeah, now that we were in Europe we learned we were far behind in gunning matters.

The French captain in charge of the volunteers told us,
"Well, I think it will only take you fellows a month to learn
the mechanisms and then we'll shoot you up to the front."
There was some talk of sending us to school at Fontainebleau,†
but before doing so they checked to see just what we did know.
They were surprised to see how well we'd been taught.

I'm telling you the truth: I learned that mechanism in six
hours and they sent me right on up to that smoking front line
where everything was breaking loose. They tabbed me as an
A-1 gunner right off the bat.

I shot those 75s at the Fritzies for forty-nine days without a
break or any relief. Word got back about the several hits I had
to my credit and a colonel came up and said, "Smith, you're a
Lion with that gun." Before long everyone was calling me "Willie the Lion," a name that has stuck with me ever since.

Things sure moved fast on that firing line. Our guns had a
nine-mile radius and we kept the Boches behind that arc. If
they began to come forward to throw gas at us, which was
usually the case when things got quiet, we would "box-barrage"
them with our 9.2, plus a special gas. When those Huns got
cornered in one of those box barrages, where the gas came at
them from all sides, you could hear them sizzling like fish frying. Wow, they couldn't escape; we had the gas shells dropping
on all sides of them. The bad part of it was that sometimes some
of our own men would get accidentally in the way. Like General Sherman once said, war has always been a hell of a mess.

When they decided I had been up there in the thick of the
action long enough they proceeded to retire me. They gave me
an award, too; I was made a sergeant with leadership over
twenty-four other men who had been up there with me. We

† French Army Artillery school.

were all given passes and sent to a place called Aix-les-Bains, a beautiful health resort up in the mountains. It was the place where they sent soldiers to relax after they had been in action. I had a wonderful time there, meeting lovely people, and playing a lot of piano for the French natives, who all seem to love music. It only lasted for three short weeks.

Only a few days after we returned from the rest camp the Armistice was signed (November 11, 1918). The news came while I was stationed at a suburb of Paris waiting to go on a seventy-mile march. When the news seeped through that the war was over, we threw our hats in the air and whooped it up. We all began to hop with joy because we thought we'd soon be on our trip back to the good old United States.

Now came the time that I'd wished I'd hung onto the name Bertholoff. Because it took a whole year for them to get around to the Smiths. Yeah, they demobilized us by the alphabet. It was to be a real misery.

You lost all your spirit after the fighting and excitement was over. The Smiths were left behind to do the police work and to clean up the battlefields. The fast action I'd had with the gunnery crew was replaced by dull, shovel leaning in a labor battalion. The kind of tired you got from that dirty pickup work was harder on me than the battle fatigue.

While digging around the battlefields with a spade I had a lot of time to think. Those Germans might have won that war if they had timed their actions with what the moon, stars, and planets had to tell them. Yes sir, if that Kaiser had been hip to his astrology he might have got home first. Goodness knows, the Allies weren't paying much attention to the stars, either.

The best thing that comes from a war is that it causes medical science to advance. If it hadn't been for the World Wars no one today would live to get over fifty years old. The horrible things that happen to men in war stimulates the medical investigations, and results in discoveries that prolong life. During peacetime the buggers‡ like to sit relaxed and count their dollars. Their answer for everything is, "Give the man an aspirin." But when they're forced to devise ways to repair the badly damaged human body they come up with something useful. Look at the drugs that came out of the last war that are a great benefit to man.

My big day, leaving for New York, finally arrived late in 1919. But our trials weren't over yet as we were to have plenty of excitement on our return trip.

The only ship they had to take us home in was an old beat-up Japanese fruit boat, the *Muri,* recently taken out of the merchant shipping service. It was docked at Brest. Our unit was given a chance to vote on whether or not we wanted to take a flyer on getting across the Atlantic in such a decrepit tub. The only other thing we could do was to wait, Lord knows how much longer, until they had another ship available. We were so anxious to get back we would have taken a rowboat.

One of the crew members informed us the Atlantic was still full of mines. Packed like sardines, like before, we were told that in case of disaster we were to get off the boat—in alphabetical order.

The Lion figured that the planet Mars had entered his house sure enough as we drifted across the sea in that glorified raft. The spirits were right—but late. One day out of New York the stern began to come apart in a violent storm. The guys around where things were happening sent out word the propeller had broken and we were about to sink. Well, maybe we had been hardened by our battle experiences because everybody somehow managed to keep his head. Twelve guys crawled down to the prop and got it fixed well enough so that we made Hoboken still afloat. As it turned out we got back a lot quicker than it had taken us to get there the two years before. We made it in seven days, a week of worrying. There was a great deal of

‡ Medical doctors.

whooping and hollering as we walked down that gangplank.

Yeah man, you have to learn how to handle mental tension if you want to stay here for a while. I've seen the Number I war and the Number II war, and I don't want to be here for Number III, because there'll be no finish for anyone when that one strikes.

The things we went through in 1917–18–19, nobody could live through them today. Medicines, automobiles, and doctors prolong our lives, but wars, planes, and buses take lives away. As the Bible says, man will wreck himself.

It was only a matter of a few days after we got back that we were mustered out in New York City. On my discharge papers they wrote: *Sergeant Smith went through the war with the 92nd Division and his conduct was excellent in battle showing nerve, faith, and intuition.*

The Lion took his nerve and faith where his intuition told him to and immediately went back to the saloon wars, pounding the piano.

Harlem Stride Piano

BY GEORGE HOEFER

The histories of jazz speak of a unique phase of the music's development: Harlem Stride Piano. This serves to name a particular style of improvisation and variation. As with the word jazz itself, any strict definition has a tendency to compound confusion. In a chapter on Ragtime from his book, The Story of Jazz,[1] Marshall Stearns points out that the ancestry of the piano music played in New York City during the late teens and early twenties was ". . . long obscured by labels such as 'house-party,' 'rent-party,' 'parlor-social,' or, simply, 'Harlem' piano style." Actually, as Stearns states, this music was ". . . a big step, involving a new and deeper fusion of European harmony and African rhythms."

Most of the stride-playing performers were composers as well as pianists. In their younger days, most of these men considered themselves to be ragtime musicians. The outstanding members of the "school," as Willie the Lion tells us, were such men as Richard (Abba Labba) McLean, Charles (Luckey) Roberts,

---

[1] This reference and other numbered references appear in notes in the back of the book.

James Price Johnson, Stephen (the Beetle) Henderson, Raymond (Lippy) Boyette, Thomas (Fats) Waller, and, of course, Willie himself. The period between 1900 and 1917 was the heyday of ragtime, another term used by some of the men and some writers to denote almost any form of expression not considered to be serious music.

Present-day musicologists have probed ragtime thoroughly. As a style, its lifetime was largely over by the end of the 1920s. True ragtime was essentially piano music and, as Guy Waterman[2] has written, it was "a composed, not an improvised or arranged, music." This points up the essential difference between the classical ragtime of Missourian Scott Joplin (composer of the "Maple Leaf Rag") and the "ragtime" piano played on the eastern seaboard. The latter was jazz piano, and it involved much individual improvisation.

Eastern jazz piano can be said to have been derived from two major influences. Probably the strongest of the two was the rhythmic music of the Negro church, stemming from the old ring shouts, and the African dances that were once central features of Negro social life and as important a part of a church service as the sermon.[3] As the Lion tells us, "Shouts are stride piano—when James P., Fats, and I would get a romp-down shout going, that was playing rocky, just like the Baptist people sing. You don't just play a chord to that—you got to move it and the piano."

The pulsing African rhythmic factor was coupled with European influences. The latter were drawn from folk music, quadrilles, schottisches, and other dance steps. Here again the Lion has told us of the impressions made by the Gullah dancers in The Jungles. These dancers literally challenge the New York pianists to improvise music to accompany their own improvised dance variations of cotillion steps brought from the South. These took the form of stomps, slow drags, and other steps.

Also, ranging up and down the Atlantic seaboard were itinerant piano men from the Deep South, who were blues players.

The blues, with both religious and secular origins, started out as a vocal expression. The human voice was the principal instrument as blues singing developed. The banjo, guitar, and then the piano took up the blues, not as voices in themselves, but as stringed and percussive instruments accompanying the voice. This was followed by an improvising piano style based upon the use of the "blue notes"—the flatted third and seventh notes. The slow drag, defined by Blesh and Janis as "a rocking music of medium tempo," derived its techniques from the blues piano style, both in its "blue" harmonies and in its dragging rhythms. From the lower Mississippi River area there came a slow blues style, to be called later boogiewoogie often speeded up and characterized by a persistent bass rhythm (of eight to the bar) executed by the left hand, while the right improvised and repeated a series of riffs which are often in opposition to the powerful rhythm produced by the left hand. It is interesting to note that the Lion recalls hearing this style as long ago as 1914 in his reference to "Kitchen Tom."

Sometimes Willie tends to be unspecific when he uses ragtime, gut bucket, lowdown, or in the alley, as equivalent terms. The historian and reviewer must be more specific. Willie is not always specific and his memory is as generously flexible as the man himself, but there are fascinating details, and always new ones, in every one of his descriptions of the past.

The late James P. Johnson[4] has left a descriptive account of how the "ticklers" would exchange ideas, steal from each other, and concoct their own individual tricks: "I did double glissandos straight and backhand, glissandos in sixths and double tremolos. These would run other ticklers out of the place at cutting sessions. I was playing a lot of piano then, traveling around and listening to every good player I could. I'd steal their breaks and style and practice them until I had them letter perfect."

There was some reason, then, for the assorted styles to become assimilated and to an extent interchangeable.

New York pianists tried to get an orchestralike effect with their instruments. They assimilated some of the harmonies, chords, and techniques of the European concert pianists. In any consideration of the development of this music in Willie's town, it must be remembered that the New York striders were, unlike the jazz and ragtime pianists from other parts of the country, steadily in the aura of big-city sophistication and closer to the rhythms of Broadway.

Attempts have been made to give firm technical definitions of stride piano. John Wilson (jazz critic of the New York Times)[5] has written, "The stride effect is produced by the left hand hitting a single note on the first and third beats and a chord of three or four notes on the second and fourth beats." James P. said, authoritatively, "The difference between stride and traditional piano ragtime was in the structure and the precise bass played in a rag style by the left hand, while the characteristic strides were performed by the right hand." Obviously, definitions can lead to confusion about the source of the "stride" effect.

Whitney Balliett of The New Yorker *recently offered a useful definition when he wrote,[6] "Stride piano is characterized chiefly by an oompah left hand (a two-beat seesaw, whose ends are a powerful mid-keyboard chord and a weaker single note played an octave or a tenth below) and by an arabesque of right-hand chords and arpeggios, fashioned in counter rhythms."*

The eastern branch of ragtime can be heard in almost pure compositional form in Luckey Roberts. It is said that the last of the great ones to retain the stride bass were Waller and Art Tatum; Count Basie and Thelonious Monk are later developments of the stride school.

The Lion comes closer to the spirit, certainly of his own style, when he says: "Stride piano means playing with both hands performing in perfect unison—like walking in balance." Per-

haps that is what Duke Ellington meant when he once said, "When you came into the Capitol Palace [in 1923] you were either in step with the Lion, literally, or you had to stop and get into it."

9

Low It, and Take Charge

Down it, and get from 'round it,
Low it, and you can't owe it,
I'm a poet, and I know it.

WILLIE THE LION SMITH

You can't talk about the old days in Harlem unless you talk about Leroy Wilkins' club at 135th Street and Fifth Avenue. That was the place where all the dictys from the Negro show world, the prize fighters, and the sports stopped in for an evening's entertainment.

Leroy's was the oldest cabaret in Harlem and was internationally known. For over ten years it was *the* place to go in uptown New York. Wilkins opened it up around 1910 in the basement of an old brownstone building. Harlem club owners located their places in cellars for several good reasons. There were fewer complaints from people living close by regarding the noise and later, during the prohibition era, it was discovered that the Irish cops patrolling the neighborhood were afraid to venture down the dark stairways for fear they wouldn't get back up in one piece.

That doesn't mean there was always brawling and hell-raising like they had in the saloons down in Hell's Kitchen. It was just the opposite because the guys who ran the places were Negroes and they kept order. That is up until 1920 when things changed and the hoodlums, who furnished the booze, came up and took over. The early Harlem club owners were both sharp and tough. Men like Edmond (Mule) Johnson and the ex-heavyweight champion, Jack Johnson, ruled with a one-two punch.

Leroy was the older brother of Barron Wilkins, and he wouldn't stand for any bad actor's acting up and everybody knew it. In those days the owners, whether they were fighters or gamblers, knew how to use both their dukes and a knife. They would station themselves right by the front door where they could see everybody coming down the stairs. Yeah, they knew the troublemakers and the bad eggs knew them. If two guys got into a brawl over a woman they were hustled right up the stairs to the sidewalk to do their fighting. Probably a third guy, who had been behaving himself, would wind up with the woman.

Leroy Wilkins was a nonsmoking, nondrinking man weighing in at 250 pounds and as slippery as an eel. He always appeared to be very honest and strict about everything—a stickler for high-toned manners and good conduct. He wouldn't allow the customers to throw coins on the floor for the entertainers, nor would he let any of the girls do the ups. He refused to let the gals remove their dresses so they could show their pretty underwear like they did in Atlantic City.

He was the first Harlem cabaret man to insist on the proper clothes for the floor managers, the waiters, and the musicians. On weekends *everybody* had to wear tuxedos, including the customers. The traditional dress-up night in Harlem was Sunday and on that occasion Wilkins always wanted the music to be high class—operatic and semiclassical pieces preferred.

Bob Hawkins had the band in there, twelve pieces. He was famous, very fast, a good reader, good improviser, and the style that you hear—well, I'd say the bass that you hear myself and

Jimmy and Fats play, that's the way Hawkins played. He had
a terrific left hand, I mean beautiful. He had a style of swinging
and James P. was quick to—you don't call it a thief, but James
was quick to play counterpoint. You see something, you dress it
up quick. Well, that's what Bob Hawkins had, a keen style of
playing and everybody who heard him would love him because
he really played the piano. But in those days, white people
hadn't gotten to coming around.

I had spent quite a bit of time in Leroy's before the war listening to my favorite old-time ragtimers like Bob (The Hawk)
Hawkins, who alternated between Barron's and Leroy's. One
thing good I noticed about playing the piano in Leroy's was you
didn't have to play against the noise from a long bar—he only
had a service bar in a small anteroom and all the customers
were served at tables. There was no cover charge and the price
of the drinks was the same as at any ordinary saloon or bar of
the day. You could have a pleasant evening for as little as a
dollar fifty per person.

One day in late 1919 I was strolling up 135th Street, at that
time the main drag in Harlem (125th Street was then in a
white neighborhood), and ran into Barron Wilkins who hailed
me.

"Hi there, Sergeant Smith. My brother Leroy is looking for
you. He says he needs a good piano man to take charge."

I decided to play it sharp. "The name is the Lion and you
tell Leroy to phone for an appointment if he wants to audition
me."

Since getting out of the Army I had been doing a little gambling, drinking, and piano playing in the various bars just like
I'd been doing before the big mess in Europe had started. After
meeting Barron an old saying of my mother's came back to me,
"It is far better for the soul to have a crust of bread and plenty
of sleep than to have a turkey and a hundred dollars in your
pocket." I decided it might be a good idea to settle down some-

where for a while. The vibrations at Leroy's had always seemed good to me.

I was living at the time at Lottie Joplin's boardinghouse. That was where all the big-time theatrical people stayed and everything was free and easy. Mrs. Joplin was the widow of the great ragtime composer, Scott Joplin, who had died back in 1917. She only wanted musicians and theater people for tenants. The place was a regular boardinghouse but sometimes operated like an after-hours joint. She had the entire house at 163 West 131st Street and it was a common occurrence to step in at six in the morning and see guys like Eubie Blake, Jimmy Johnson, and the Lion sitting around talking or playing the piano in the parlor. We used to play Scott's *Maple Leaf Rag* in A-flat for Mrs. Joplin. Before she died she took me down in the cellar and showed me Scott's cellar full of manuscripts—modern things and even some classical pieces he had written.

The Lion decided to have himself a big dinner at the Libya* and then go over and talk to Leroy. The Libya was Harlem's high-class restaurant of the day; it was the dictyest of the dicty. They served tea between four and five in the afternoon and featured dinner dancing until one A.M. The music was furnished by a string orchestra made up of members of the Clef Club. They were hidden in a grove of potted palms and were not allowed to rag it or to beautify the melody using their own ideas—they had to read those fly spots closely and truly. We used to kid them about having to read their tails off.

During supper they served the Lion a muskmelon filled with ice cream doused in champagne. These vibrations were *too* tony for a guy who had just gotten out of the trenches. Leroy's was gonna look good to this piano man.

* 139th Street near Seventh Avenue.

LEROY'S

When I walked in and announced to Leroy, "The Lion is here," he glared as per usual and replied, "You know where the piano is at; go ahead and take charge."

Back in those days "takin' charge" meant the pianist had duties and responsibilities. He played solo piano, accompanied the singers, directed whatever band was on hand, and watched the kitty to be sure no one cheated on tips. That cigar-box kitty was very important at Leroy's, since the boss didn't allow any coins to be thrown around. Everybody's tips, including those given to the musicians, singers, waiters, and bartenders, had to go into the box to be divvied up at closing time. The piano man was *it!* The man in charge.

He had to be an all-round showman and it helped if he could both dance and sing. It was like being the host at the party, you were expected to greet everyone who entered to establish favorable feelings. I used to chat with the patrons at nearby tables in order to get their immediate moods. When I'd run into a noisy, rude one, I'd end the set abruptly, and holler "Man, go get lost!"

The bosses expected you to stay rooted to your stool from nine at night to dawn. Man, if you got up to go to the men's room those guys would scream. Leroy would come up wailing, "What are you trying to do, put me out of business?" And in those days you worked seven nights a week.

Furthermore, you'd rather piss in your pants than leave the piano when a rival was in the house. That was the best way to lose your gig.

Another thing that was different in those days was that you couldn't eat or drink in the joint on an entertainer's discount, yet you were expected to drink all the booze brought to your piano at a customer's expense. To the Harlem cabaret owners, to all night-club bosses, the money was on a one-way chute—everything coming in, nothing going out.

And that wasn't all. In addition to all this takin'-charge service to the establishment, the tickler was required to build up for himself a big following. It got so that whether or not a place had any business was decided by who the piano man was—and there was no advertising done to help. It was your job to draw in the customers. All the owner had to do was count the money.

For all this, they paid you off in uppercuts. That was a saying we got up in those days; it meant you were allowed to keep your tips, but you got no salary. Sometimes they would give us a small weekly amount—like twenty dollars. That was known as a left hook.

When I started at Leroy's he acted as though he was doing me a big favor by letting me sit at the piano. After I'd been at the club for a couple of weeks I noticed the place was packed. It was time for me to have a little talk with Mr. Leroy. So one night I took time out and sent for an order of southern-fried chicken, the specialty of the house, served with hot biscuits. Instead of the chicken I got Leroy hollering, "What the hell you think you're doin' now, Lion? Ain't you got any food at home? You tryin' to take advantage?"

I looked calmly around the crowded room. "I want a small left hook, man, or else I'm movin' on." It was common practice for a piano player to keep on the go because you weren't considered too good if you stayed at the same place too long a time. It signified you were not in hot demand.

Well, my little move was a success. I wound up with a salary of eighteen dollars a week plus tips—and I was taking home around a hundred a week from the kitty. Old man Wilkins could see which side of the bread had the butter.

At Leroy's they didn't pretend to give out with a fancy show or revue. The show actually consisted of the pianist, occasionally accompanied by several instrumentalists, six or seven sopranos, and a bunch of dancing waiters who also sang.

Our sopranos could sing any kind of music in the book or requested by customers. These gals, like the piano players, worked all the cabarets in Harlem and Atlantic City at one time or another. I recall at Leroy's we had Josephine Stevens, Mattie Hite, and Lucy Thomas, including a cute little Creole girl from New Orleans named Mabel Bertrand—she later married Jelly Roll Morton. All these girls sang at the tables as well as doing their turn on the floor.

On the nights when I had help to keep the music rocking, we had fun. The helpers were usually a drummer, a banjoist, or a violinist. Once or twice we had a tuba player. Most frequently it was just a drummer and we sure had some good ones around New York at that time. Such guys as Carl (Battle Axe) Kenny, George Hines, Harry Green, George Barber, Freddie (Rastus) Crump, Charles (Buddie) Gilmore (the regular drum ace with Jim Europe's Hell Fighters), and a lame guy known as "Traps" (I think his real name was Arthur McIntyre). Traps could make a fly dance with his ratchets. He and Gilmore drummed most of the time in a show band. He was knock-kneed, and like all those people with crazy legs, he was as strong as a bull. Every time one of the girls moved her eye old Traps would hit a lick. The chicks would tell him, "Just brush me lightly, politely, slightly, and get soft—give me that real low gravy." Man, the women sure did love his drumming. When the gals ran out of songs, Traps and I would take over and make up lyrics for them. And talk about blues, we really had 'em, choruses after choruses. It was like Ethel Waters once said over the radio, "I don't care what you talk about. You can talk all about the modern musics, but when it comes down to feeling the music and interpreting it, that we can do. We have the gift to send the message—the blues— Yeah!"

When the word got passed around at Charlie Thorpe's bar on 135th Street that the Lion was making his stand at Leroy's, a lot of the Harlem show people began to make the club a regular stop. At that time there was more real talent in Harlem than in all the rest of the country put together. Nightly we had folks like Bill (Bojangles) Robinson, Bert Williams, Florence Mills, Ethel Waters and her sidekick Ethel Williams, the team of Greenlee & Dayton (dancers), Mantan Morland (comedian), Clarence (Dancin') Dotson, Marie Lucas (a trombonist-pianist), Moss & Fry (comedians), and Miller & Lyles (also a comic team).

We also got the sporting and fight crowd; the gang that hung out at Barron's on 134th and Seventh, they always came to Brother Leroy's to catch the show. In this group you'd see such famous people as Jack Johnson, Sam Langford, and Harry Greb, the fighter with the glass eye. Not many people ever knew about Greb's false eye.

The gals from the *Smart Set* shows would drop in when they were in town—and could they ever dance? They cut the girls who came along ten years later in *The Cotton Club Parades* to ribbons. The sharp dancin' cats were still doing the "Texas Tommy," where they would hop-skip three times and then throw a doll over their shoulders. Then they would hop-skip three more times and squat on their knees as they skated right on down the floor. It was somethin'.

On the nights when Ethel Waters stopped by, Leroy's old house would rock. The audience would holler for her to do her "Shim-Me-Sha-Wabble" number. She was thin in those days, with a beautiful body, and when she sang and danced it was a quivering-shoulder, can-shaking event. They called her Sweet Mama Stringbean at that time and she was working at the hincty† Edmond's Cellar, only a couple of blocks from our joint.

Florence Mills was a frequent visitor with her husband, the dancer U.S. (Slow Kid) Thompson. At the time (1919–20), Miss Mills was a member of a group called the Tennessee Ten.

† The opposite of "dicty"—a low-life dive.

A year later she was destined to rise from a chorus girl to a featured star in the musical *Shuffle Along*.

I hadn't seen Florence since the days she and her sister had an act at the old Nickelette downtown. While I was away she had worked in another act with a couple of friends of mine. The act, called the Panama Trio, had included Ada (Brick Top) Smith and Cora Green. Brick Top went on to become famous with her Paris night club in the Rue Pigalle and Cora Green was an inspiration to the great blues singer Bessie Smith.

Florence Mills became a girl who was loved by all mankind. Her early death at twenty-six years of age in 1927 was one of the hardest blows ever given to Negro show business. She was at the peak of her career and creative powers when she overworked herself into an early grave.

Sometimes Florence's sister Maude would drop in and we would have a ball. She was not blessed with the same kind of talent as Florence but she was what we called a "one-legged" dancer and our favorite nickname for her was the Mule. Yeah, Maude the Mule. She danced like some of the piano players today play—the one-fingered ones or the one-handed pounders, as we used to term them.

Playing for Maude as she did a dance turn, I'd be hollering at her, "Dance with the *other* leg! Dance with the other one!"

"I ain't got time to teach the other leg!" she'd shout back.

My comeback always was, "That's right, you can't make a race horse out of a mule."

But we sure had some two-legged dancing when Bojangles Robinson showed up. The floor would shake so much it would make the piano rock when Bill's two feet were tapping out the riffs. It was no mule walk with him.

When Robinson came into a cabaret, he made sure everyone in the joint knew he was there. It was just the opposite with Bert Williams, the star of the *Ziegfeld Follies*. He would slip into Leroy's and quietly take a back table. At first no one would know he was there, but he was so popular it was not long before someone would notice him and then his table would fill up with friends. Williams was another one who overworked. He was only forty-six when he died in March 1922.

As word got around town that a lot of show-business celeb- rities could be seen at Leroy's, we began to get some white- folks trade from downtown. Leroy didn't particularly like this because he thought the mixing of the races was tindery. There were three groups of ofays allowed in—personal friends of Leroy's, big names in the show world, and anyone brought to the place by an ex-pug cab driver known as Mississippi or just plain 'Sippi.

'Sippi, who had once been an entertainer as well as a fighter, was the only Negro then driving an old-fashioned horse-and- buggy hack around Central Park. It was 'Sippi's colorful big plug hat that inspired bandleader Ted Lewis to feature a high hat in his act.

'Sippi's custom was to collect a group of VIPs downtown and take them on his own personally conducted tour of the Harlem night spots. He favored Leroy's, Edmond's Cellar, and the tony J. W. Connor's café at 71 West 135th Street. He would collect a fat fee from each party he took uptown. It was his way to be very careful of his charges and he would come down the stairs to see that they were given the best pos- sible table. Then he would retire to a back table where he could keep an eye on the proceedings. From the sidelines he made sure they got good service and when they were ready to go he watched to see that their tabs were not padded. On rare occa- sions he would step out on the floor and go into his old-time song-and-dance act.

Everybody uptown was fond of old 'Sippi. Even when he didn't have any clients he would drive up to see what was going on. Many a dawn I spent with 'Sippi in his hack sauntering through the park, sharing a quart.

Another character we saw a lot of at Leroy's was a dancer whose real name was Russell Brown. He hailed from Charleston,

South Carolina, and he was always dancing somewhere for tips; either in the saloons and cabarets, or on the street corners. His dance was a Geechie step like those I had seen in The Jungles. He took a special liking to the way the Lion played the piano for him and so I let him get in the show and share our tips.

Brown, a small sickly fellow destined to die from TB, was given a nickname by the people in Harlem. When they met him on the street they would holler at him, "Hey, Charleston—do your Geechie dance!" Some folks say that is how the dance known as the Charleston got its name.

I'm a tough man for facts and I say the Geechie dance had been around New York for many years before Brown showed up. The kids from the Jenkins Orphanage Band of Charleston used to do Geechie steps when they were in New York on their yearly tour.

The Reverend Jenkins had this kid band that he had been taking on tours since 1911 in order to raise cash for the institution. They had a kind of circus brass band that marched up and down the streets of Harlem. They'd play concerts on street corners and then pass the hat. They sometimes had as many as twenty pieces and none of the kids were over fifteen years of age. Such jazz men as the drumming Wright brothers; the Aiken brothers—Gus on trumpet and Buddy on trombone; trombonist Jake Frazier; the Benford brothers—Tommy on drums and Bill on bass; and Geechie Fields, all came out of that Jenkins school.

It was always the Lion's custom to keep on the move and spend time working at as many places as I could to get a different slant on things. There was a period of over two years, not all in one stretch, that I was the regular piano man at Leroy's.

To get a short rest from Leroy's, I would sometimes go back to Newark and put in a few weeks at Jimmy Conerton's on Academy Street, Pierson's Hall, or in the dining rooms at the Hotel Navarro or the Robert Treat Hotel.

Several of the times I left to go up 135th Street and help out gambler Jerry Preston, who had just started an upstairs joint called The Orient. I was the first pianist to work for him and talked him into hiring three girl singers to make his place into a regular cabaret. It started him off in the business. I worked again for him years later when he ran Pod's & Jerry's. He was a congenial boss and we always got along. My only complaint was that he hired the damnedest waiters and bartenders—they were a band of crooks. He paid them good salaries but was always firing them for being snooty to the customers. Being a first-rate gambler he had very good connections.

Whenever I would cut out from Leroy's, it was my custom to leave the piano in the custody of a trial horse. In this way I felt I could get my job back when it came time to return. My favorite trial horse was a pool shark named Charles Summers, who had been a pianist at Leroy's before I went in there to take charge. He was a fair tickler, he could only play in three keys, but he made so much playing pool that his piano playing was just for kicks.

But, there came one time when I really goofed and almost lost the job. That was when I left the stool in charge of a sixteen-year-old fat boy, whose name I didn't even know at the time. He used to hang around wherever there was a piano on 135th Street. I was told they let him play the box at the Crescent dime movie down the street when the regular man was off. (This was long before the time this kid was bugging Maisie Mullins, the pianist-organist at the Lincoln Theater, to let him play the ten-thousand-dollar Wurlitzer pipe organ.)

Yeah, man, I'll never forget how good old Fats, when he was still a stripling, would walk into Leroy's eating one of those caramel-covered apples on a stick. He was never without one.

IN COMES FILTHY

James P. Johnson brought him down one Sunday afternoon. We were all dressed in full-dress suits and tuxedos and in comes this guy with a greasy suit on, walks down to the bandstand, and says, "Hello there, Lion, what do you say?" He made me furious. I turned around to Jimmy and said, "Get that guy down, because he looks filthy." "Get them pants pressed," I said. "There's no excuse for it." From that day on I called him Filthy.

So he sat down until I got finished and when I got finished he was insistent, very persistent. He insisted he wanted to play Jimmy's "Carolina Shout" and when I got through he sat down and played the "Shout" and made Jimmy like it and me like it. From then on it was Thomas Fats Waller. He sat down also and heard me play a couple of strains of something, and then he improvised and the next time I turned around he had a tune called "Squeeze Me."

The Lion was only gone for a few days and when I got back Filthy had built up quite a following for himself. You could tell by the ovation he got when he walked in casual-like. I gave him a listen and made my famous prediction: I said to James P. Johnson, who was in the house again that night, "Watch out, Jimmy, he's got it. He's a piano-playing cub!"

10

Those Crazy Blues

Now I got the Cra-zy Blues,
Since my baby went away,
I ain't got no time to lose,
I must find him today,
Now the doctor's gonna do all that he can
But what you're gonna need is an undertaker man,
I ain't had nothin' but bad news,
Now I got the Cra-zy Blues. *

While the Lion was still appearing nightly at Leroy's an event took place that was destined to change the entire music business. I'm talkin' about the first blues record made by a colored artist. The record was Mamie Smith singing "Crazy Blues" and the Lion was at the piano as leader of the accompanying band.

The music that is known today as the true blues originated wherever there were Negroes. This would mean that most of the blues songs came from the southern section of the United States because that's where most of the colored people lived in the early days.

My close friend, the late William C. Handy, who came from Alabama, was the greatest blues composer we have ever pro-

* From "Crazy Blues" by Perry Bradford; published by Pickwick Music Corp.

duced. He wrote beautiful songs from the various blues strains in field hollers and church shouts he had heard as a young lad in the South. There is nothing new under the sun and he heard the same Negro music that every other band instrumentalist, singer, banjoist, or piano player heard early in this century; it was just that Handy had more talent for putting what he overheard into an original composition.

Another fast man was the late Ferdinand (Jelly Roll) Morton from New Orleans, who as a ragtime piano player evolved a lot of original blues, stomps, and shouts. Jelly and my man Handy got into a big argument as to which one originated the blues, but nothing could be decided either way because the blues songs were around long before either of them showed up.

Jelly was a good talker, had lots of tunes, and lived long enough so that the tunes belonged to him. But the Lion favors Handy; nobody ever wrote a greater tune than the "St. Louis Blues."

Down through the years there have been thousands of blues players and blues writers. Every piano player or singer from the Deep South had his own "original" blues. Many of these blues tunes sound alike, and are alike, using identical notes and ideas. You've got to remember that most of these players could not read or write music.

The average Negro family did not allow the blues, or even the raggedy music, played in their homes. The earthy blues were considered to be sinful songs. Many of the New York City colored folks, including quite a few of the musicians, did not go for the blues music. Among those who disliked this form of entertainment the most were the Negroes who had recently come up from the South to seek a better life. They wanted to forget all about the things for which the southern Negro was noted. They also hated the way their people were portrayed in the theater.

Those were the days when the colored folks wanted to be as white as possible with straight hair. There were preparations to help get both of those characteristics. Not only the hair straight-ener put out by Dr. Hart; you could also buy a bleach for those who wanted a light complexion. It was a laugh. At the same time this was going on, the white people were knocking them-selves out to be suntanned and have curly hair. Guys like Al Jolson and Eddie Cantor used blackface routines and in doing so they made it necessary for poor Bert Williams, a light-brown-skinned man, to put on blackface for his act in the *Follies*. He always resented that, but he never said anything in public. He was a proud man and you couldn't buy him for a song. Williams had that same kind of class that Duke Ellington possesses.

That was the way things stacked up when the first blues rec-ord was made in 1920. I am going to tell you exactly how it all came about; there have been a lot of inaccurate stories printed about that "Crazy Blues" record.

One night at Leroy's one of my oldest and dearest friends in show business came in and asked if I would help him out. The man was William Smith. He was known as Sweet Singing Smitty. He was working as the headwaiter over at Preston's Orient and like our floor manager, Bob Smith, he had been a member of J. Leubrie Hill's musical stock company in years gone by. His was a fine tenor voice.

MAMIE SMITH

Some years before, Smitty had married one of the popcorn goodies from the chorus of the *Smart Set* company. The one that Smitty got was a raven-haired, dark-brown beauty by the name of Mamie Smith. She was originally from Cincinnati, Ohio, and when she got to New York with Smitty she became one of the most popular singer-entertainers in town.

By the time I'm telling you about now, Mamie and Smitty had

become separated, but my friend still had big eyes for her. The trouble had come about when Mamie, while singing at the Digg's Cafe, got a mad passion for Digg's porter—a tall, handsome guy, named Ocey Wilson.

Also involved with Mamie at the time was pianist-composer Perry Bradford, who was trying to be her manager. He was always pestering her to feature his songs.

Well, Smitty figured he had thought of a way to get back with Mamie, so he came to see me about it. He approached me with this proposition: "Look here, Lion, as an old friend I want you to do me a favor. My Mamie has got an audition to sing a couple of songs for a guy down at the General Phonograph Corporation on West Forty-fifth Street, where they make those Okeh records. She needs a good piano player. I know she likes you because I've seen her over here listening. Would you go over to Digg's place and maybe look over her songs? I'd sure like it if maybe you went down to the studio with her and played for her audition."

You see he figured it would make a good impression on Mamie if a friend of her husband's looked after her. She'd listen to anything that had to do with her career. At that time I had not yet had an opportunity to hear Mamie sing.

So one night between sets at Leroy's I took a trip over to Digg's Cafe and gave Mamie a listen. She was O.K. When I talked to her she told me she had two Perry Bradford blues songs she wanted to record. It seemed that Ocey Wilson was also making like Mamie's manager. He didn't dig Bradford's trying to move in and so he was all for me taking her down to the Okeh office to play the accompaniment.

As I remember it now, Mamie and I went down to an old-fashioned studio and performed some selections for Ralph Peer, the guy in charge at Okeh, and he told us to get a band together. The band I organized for the deal included Addington Major on cornet; Ward (Dope) Andrews, an uncle of the famous trumpeter Charlie Shavers, on trombone; Ernest (Sticky)

Elliott, a Clef Club musician I taught how to jazz it on clarinet (he wanted to learn to sing in Jewish—I also tutored him on that); and to round out the group we had violinist Leroy Parker. In those days they couldn't record drums and bass fiddle, so we didn't bother to use them. We decided to call the unit The Jazz Hounds and it became a famous name for the bands working for Mamie Smith.

The day, in August 1920, we went to make the sides there was only Mamie, Ralph Peer, myself, and the band in the studio. I can't recall that Bradford was anywhere in sight. We waxed two tunes "Crazy Blues" and "It's Right Here for You" (If You Don't Get It, 'Tain't No Fault o' Mine). The former was a Bradford composition.

I taught the bandsmen their parts from the piano sheet music given to me by Miss Smith. All stood, except the Lion, in front of a large megaphone-like horn and Mamie really let loose with her fine contralto voice. As I recall, we got twenty-five dollars apiece for the two sides, and we had to wait two months to get our money. In those days it didn't matter how long it took you to get the sides down satisfactorily—the money was always the same, regardless of the time, and no royalty deals. Major, Elliott, and Parker are still alive and will bear me out on the details of the first blues date. Andrews, a man who loved his booze, died a few years later from tuberculosis.

The side that took off like a prairie fire was "Crazy Blues." It was released in November 1920. In no time at all it was selling like hot cakes in Harlem. The tune was just an ordinary old blues strain that had been used in other songs. Mamie said she had first used it in a show called *Maid of Harlem* at the Lincoln Theater under the title of "Harlem Blues." James P. Johnson once claimed he used the same strain in his "Mama's and Papa's Blues," which he had composed back in 1916. Other pianists remembered that part of the melody came from an old bawdy song played in the sporting houses, "Baby, Get that Towel Wet."

The success of "Crazy Blues" put Mamie Smith on the map and she was in demand for appearances all over the country. She wanted, or her manager Bradford wanted, to take The Jazz Hounds on a tour of the Theater Owner's Booking Association (T.O.B.A.) circuit, playing theaters in Georgia, Alabama, and all through the Deep South. This chain of theaters had a nickname, "Tough on Black Artists," among show folks, and the people who worked it were "Uncle Toms"—if they weren't, they were expected to act like they were.

It has always been the Lion's policy to stay away from climates that don't fit my clothes—in those areas the vibrations are *always* bad. I turned the T.O.B.A. tour down flat and stayed at Leroy's.

The Jazz Hounds were revamped with Perry Bradford on piano and they went South with the great Johnny Dunn on cornet. Dunn was from Memphis, Tennessee. Mamie had a hard time keeping her musicians because she was a pretty bossy gal. Dunn was soon replaced by Bubber Miley, who was in Duke Ellington's first jazz band in 1924. While on tour in Missouri, Mamie discovered a young tenor saxophonist practically in short pants—that was Coleman Hawkins and the first band he ever played in was The Jazz Hounds. So you see, that little band I picked up for that one recording date was destined to become a famous group in the history of jazz.

It wasn't long before Mamie was rolling in the green. She appeared in Atlantic City sporting an ostrich-plume cape that was supposed to have cost her three thousand dollars; Bradford was also getting rich and showed up in Harlem with a fancy racoon coat. Mamie kept on recording during the early twenties and, in all, made about one hundred sides with her Jazz Hounds on Okeh. The company was new in 1920 and it was the success of that "Crazy Blues" that really put them in business.

There are some other things that are not too well known about Mamie Smith. For one, she was a very high-class entertainer, as well as being one of the best-looking women in the business, and the truth of the matter is she really didn't care too much for the blues. Yet it was Mamie Smith who was actually responsible for the big business that was to come about from recording the blues. After "Crazy Blues" became a big hit, every record company and every colored singer got on the old bandwagon. They began to turn out blues records by the ton.

Mamie Smith and Miss Lucille Hegamin were ladies and were both higher-class singers than many of the other female performers of that day. All the other blues-singing Smiths—Trixie, Bessie, Clara, and Laura—were rougher characters. Those other Smiths, no relation to each other, sang what you might call the real blues and were much more earthy in their private lives. But, it was Mamie who broke the ice, and made it possible for all those others to make records.

There have been some things written about Mamie Smith that give the people the wrong impression of what she was really like. They say she was always chasing after her men with a gun. I recall she did get into a jam once when she had a pistol on 135th Street, but it was the usual jealousy thing involving that bum Ocey Wilson. She never did go back to Smitty and kept up her frantic affair with Wilson for many years.

Bad luck overtook Mamie when the record business began falling apart. Bradford had long since broken off their manager-artist arrangement and Wilson was spending all her money. When she was on top she had invested some of her profits in apartment houses—she was reported to have owned one in New York and one in Chicago. Somehow or other Wilson managed to get the properties away from her and squander the proceeds. Then she got sick with arthritis. Wilson refused to pay any attention to her. She died penniless in an Eighth Avenue rooming house in 1946.

It is the same old story. Artists, especially colored entertainers, get pushed around like cattle. No one can make so much money that it can't be taken away from them.

Pre-Prohibition Harlem

BY GEORGE HOEFER

Harlem, originally a small Dutch village in the wilderness far from the heart of New York became first a city suburb, then a residential area more thoroughly citified, and eventually the world's largest and most densely populated Negro community. It is located within the upper reaches of Manhattan island directly above Central Park. Today, there are over seven hundred thousand people concentrated within its area.

The assimilation (but not integration) of Negroes into New York's population goes back to the days of New Amsterdam. There were Negro freemen on the island before the Revolutionary War. Through the years, as the city's boundaries crawled uptown, Negroes lived in clustered groups in many different neighborhoods. In the waning years of the last century, more than half were living in the dingy red-brick blocks south of Washington Square. That section, known as "South Fifth Avenue" or "the black and tan" neighborhood, ran from West Third Street down to Houston Street.

A northward trek started slowly around 1900 as the Italians and Irish began to close in on the old Negro district from the east and west sides, respectively. They took over by force of numbers and the Negroes migrated further uptown to San Juan Hill (west and north of Columbus Circle in the lower Sixties); to Third Avenue and East Eighty-eighth Street in the German section of Yorktown; and into Harlem itself.

It has been written[1] that the surge into Harlem began around 1901 because of a deflated real-estate bubble. Stanford White, the great architect of Madison Square Garden, had designed a row of elegant houses on 139th Street, between Seventh and Eighth avenues, surrounded by tree-shaded streets with rows of handsome brownstones kept up by well-to-do German families. The fine apartments built by White remained untenanted. The transportation facilities from the active center of the city were inadequate. A Negro real-estate agent, Philip Payton, persuaded the new landlords to accept colored residents. The first families to move in were from wealthy and middle-class groups, people who had been unhappy on San Juan Hill. The environs of the Hill were considered to be the northern fringe of the notorious tenderloin district known as Hell's Kitchen. The area —now the site of the Lincoln Center for the Performing Arts— was called The Jungles. The move to the countrylike atmosphere of Lenox Avenue with its rows of trees was a relief for many quiet and sedate Negroes.

Before World War I, much of the Negro population in New York had either been born there or had been in the city long enough to become reasonably acclimated. As Willie suggests, many were trying to forget the traditions of the South and emulated the whites in their ways of life. As Negro clarinetist Garvin Bushell told writer Nat Hentoff,[2] "When I first came to New York I drove a truck and you couldn't deliver a package to a Negro's front door. You had to go down to the cellar door. And Negroes dressed to go to work; they changed into work clothes when they got there. You were not allowed to play the blues or boogiewoogie in the average Negro middle-class home. That music supposedly suggested a low element. And the big bands with the violins, flutes, banjos, and piccolos didn't play them either."

Some of the early music emanating from Harlem was designed for the entertainment of white society. During the first decade of the twentieth century, Negro singers, dancers, and instrumentalists attracted favorable attention at dinners, receptions, and dances held at the old Waldorf-Astoria. James Reese Europe founded the Clef Club in 1910 as an agency to represent colored talent and to sponsor the formation of a large concert orchestra.

It was not long until Clef Club members were playing in string ensembles and orchestras that appeared regularly at the famous restaurants of the day, Delmonico's, Sherry's, Shanley's, Martin's, Rector's, and Churchill's. These groups were also in demand for parties and receptions held in the Fifth Avenue mansions of the rich whites.

The Clef Club orchestra followed their inaugural 1910 concert at Manhattan Casino (now the Rockland Palace) at 155th Street and Eighth Avenue, with an evening of "Negro" music at Carnegie Hall in 1914.

Large Negro orchestras of that day were not jazz bands by any stretch of the imagination. They were composed of twenty to fifty musicians, and in one large band of the period there were twenty men playing bandolins, a combination banjo-violin that was plucked. Charters and Kunstadt in their Jazz—A History of the New York Scene,[3] list the instrumentation of the Clef Club orchestra for their Carnegie Hall concert: "Eleven banjos, eight violins, one saxophone, one tuba, thirteen cellos, two clarinets, two baritone horns, eight trombones, seven cornets, one tympano, five traps, two string basses, and thirty pianists taking turns playing ten pianos on the stage."

But the Negro bands—led by Will Marion Cook, Allie Ross, William F. Patrick, Happy Rhone—did not confine themselves to playing for white audiences alone. They were also on hand when young girls were introduced to colored society at Har-

*lem's debutante cotillions held in the Manhattan Casino or in
the New Star Casino (at 107th Street and Lexington Avenue).*

*When the dance craze struck New York before World War I,
the dancing teams of Irene and Vernon Castle, Maurice and
Florence Walton, and others enlisted the help of Jim Europe
and Luckey Roberts to play accompaniments as they taught
the world to dance. Ford Dabney was regularly leading an
orchestra for the Ziegfeld shows on the New Amsterdam
Theater Roof. Other Negro bands played in the prewar cabarets downtown, Reisenweber's and in Ted Healy's Golden
Glades.*

*As Willie has said, the jazz playing of the day was largely
confined to performances in small, downstairs cabarets. He has
mentioned the rather high ethical standards of Leroy Wilkins'
establishment, a few details of the specific code of morals, and
how on Sunday nights they were required to feature semiclassical and operatic selections.*

*When the First World War came along, many changes were
made in the size and structure of the Harlem community. These
began when an influx of Negroes came up from the South and
from the West Indies to work in factories and shipyards. Agents
were sent South to recruit whole trainloads of people who were
thrown into unskilled work against the Irish and Italians, who
were beginning to demand higher wages. Shortly after the war,
thousands more came up to escape the unrest and individual
trouble in some Southern cities.*

*To accommodate all the people crowding into the area, land-
lords converted the old brownstones into rooming establishments by partitioning the large rooms into cubicles—just big
enough in some cases to hold a bed, a dresser, and a chair. In
this way they managed to obtain five times as much rental in-
come as they had been getting and they set a noxious tradition.
The rent schedules in Harlem have been, and still are, notorious.*

*Ethel Waters has written[4] about the Harlem she saw in 1918
when she first arrived in New York. "In those days Harlem*

was anything but an exclusively Negro section. The black belt ran only from 130th to about 140th Street, between Fifth and Seventh avenues. The fashionable thoroughfare at that time was Seventh Avenue."

The main street of Harlem today, 125th Street, was a white boulevard in 1918. Miss Waters recalls, "We weren't welcome on 125th. Colored people could buy seats only in the peanut gallery in B. F. Keith's Alhambra Theater, and none at all in the other white show houses." The aforementioned segregation did not apply to the Alhambra's stage, however. The acts playing the theater included Bill (Bojangles) Robinson, Moss and Fry, and Dancin' Dotson, alternating with such famous white acts as Sophie Tucker (doing a blackface comedy bit), Belle Baker, Blossom Seeley, Eva Tanguay, and Trixie Friganza. Close to the theater (on 125th between Seventh and Eighth) was a downstairs cabaret called the Alamo, where the featured attraction was Jimmy (Schnozzola) Durante's New Orleans Jazz Band.

In 1919 when Willie Smith dug in at Leroy's he was on the then main drag of Harlem—135th Street. It was there that the night life centered. One of George Gershwin's first compositions was an obscure opera entitled simply 135th Street, based on impressions of the vitality of the life flowing up and down that street.

The Crescent, the first colored theater in Harlem, opened there in 1909. Many of the famous names in Negro show business were first presented to New York audiences from the stage of this small theater (it had less than two hundred seats) that later became a ten-cent movie house. The Lincoln Theater, seating around a thousand, opened in 1915 on 135th—only a few doors from the Crescent and took over the presentation of Negro stage acts.

The history of the larger and older Lafayette Theater, 132nd Street and Seventh Avenue, was stormy. The details are given by Charters and Kunstadt:[3] "The Lafayette had a turbulent past. It opened with a variety bill of white acts and a policy of segregated seating, white downstairs and colored in the balcony. Within a few months the owners were being sued by patrons who had been discriminated against; the entire community was aroused against the managers and business had dropped off to almost nothing. The courts ordered them to discontinue the seating arrangements, and the audience insisted on Negro musicians and Negro performers. In May 1913, a Negro orchestra led by William Tyler was hired to play in the pit, and the Lafayette's business took an upward turn."

By 1919, the growing number of Harlem cabarets, sprouting up like dandelions in the spring, had begun to use four-, five-, and six-piece jazz bands. This music was different in sound and spirit from that presented by the large overstringed bands. The new bands were installed in the cabarets for dancing and after each singer-entertainer had performed the band would play a dance number.

These jazz bands, featuring improvised blues, were to help usher in a new era in Harlem—the Harlem the world heard about during the prohibition days.

11

A Taste of the Road

*. . . you try out everything from the sublime
to the ridiculous; every corner, hole, dump,
saloon, back room, on up to the top houses;
you even go out on the road, where your
clothes don't fit.*

WILLIE THE LION SMITH

The Lion took charge at Sontag's for a short, limited engagement after leaving Leroy's. While there the famous Clarence (Dancin') Dotson caught my act and made me a proposition. He wanted a good pianist to help him break in a new vaudeville act.

In those days they tried your act out at Proctor's Fifth Avenue Theater before booking you for a regular tour. It was a tough deal, friend, because those guys—booking agents for B. F. Keith, Poli, the Orpheum chain, and the Pantages circuit from out west—would sit and read newspapers on you while you auditioned. You never knew *what* they were thinking! Yes, sir, I don't care how fast your act was, they'd be reading their newspaper. Sometimes they even went to sleep and didn't wake up until the show was over.

Well, I was no more anxious to go out on the road than I'd

been when Mamie Smith wanted me to lead The Jazz Hounds. You travel in a band, you wear old suits some other guy has worn, your clothes don't fit. But, I liked Dotson, he was a real sport, and I knew I could learn a lot about show business from him. Dotson was the kind of man who would drink whisky all day, every day, but no one ever knew it. He went on for years like that. It was as recent as 1958 before things caught up with him. He broke his hip performing on the stage of a Boston theater and died shortly afterwards while suing the theater for damages.

There was one important fact that I learned from my experience working with Dancin' Dotson. And that was the meaning of the No. 1 and No. 2 spots in vaudeville talk. When you are the piano player accompanying a singer or dancer and they put you in No. 1, it means you are seated, with your back to the audience, way over by the curtain on the left side of the stage. That's no good. The good pianists always got the No. 2 spot, where the piano is located downstage, and the audience can not only see you, but they can hear you better.

While we were breaking in the act at Proctor's tryout house, two old friends of mine from Newark dropped by—the crooner and guitarist Nick Lucas and his wife. They immediately tipped me off to get myself into the No. 2 spot. I was squabbling with Dotson about it when Will Mastin came by and offered me a better job, which at that time didn't look like it would take me out of town. So I told Dotson I had to leave to become a member of Mastin's *Holiday in Dixieland* show that was scheduled to go into Reisenweber's café near Columbus Circle.

Will Mastin, a fine dancer and entertainer, is still going strong. He is the leader of a trio that has become famous because one of its members is Sammy Davis, Jr. The third member of the Will Mastin Trio is Davis' father Sammy Senior. In the days I'm talking about—1922—Sammy Senior was a dancer with the *Holiday in Dixieland* troupe.[*]

[*] A year or so later, after I'd cut out from the show, he married Elvira Alpino, also a dancer in the chorus, and Sammy Davis, Jr., the famed star of screen,

Will and his wife Vergie put together *Holiday in Dixieland* with a cast of thirteen colored artists. The musical director was a young cornet-playing pal of mine named Algeria (June) Clark from Philadelphia.

Man, we had trumpet players all over the place with that show. Besides Clark on horn we had cute, light-skinned Valaida Snow, who danced on one end of the chorus line and every now and then would step out of the line and stop the show playing her trumpet. Everybody in the act had eyes for Valaida. June Clark went overboard for her; Bunny Allen, our tenor vocalist, spent most of his spare time chasing after her, and he carried a gun; and finally even Will Mastin showed interest. When Vergie showed up one night in a hotel lobby and Valaida cut out through the first-floor window, the Lion decided it was time to leave the show before something worse took place—it was in Detroit.

As if Clark and Miss Snow were not enough horn players, we also had in the chorus Dolly Jones, who could blow a mean trumpet. (She later married a saxophone player by the name of Hutchinson and became a featured horn soloist with Lil Armstrong's band.)

Yes sir, in those days you had to be a Jack-of-all-trades. Our clarinetist, George McClennon, could spin like a top on his stomach, or on his backside, while playing his instrument. The trombone man, Sammy Vanhurst, and the drummer Tommy (I can't recall his last name) were both crack dancers. The Lion wore a derby and mugged with a cigar clenched between his teeth; a routine for which he was to become internationally known.

Vergie and Will Mastin both sang and danced in the act, when they weren't fighting or trying to keep the wolves away from Valaida and Dolly. They had help from Dolly Jones's

television, and records, was born in 1925. Of course, today, Sammy Senior has long been divorced from Junior's mother and has remarried; Vergie and Will Mastin have also split up; but Will Mastin and Sammy Davis are still together in that trio.

mother, who was also a dancer in the chorus. And there was still another popular chick in the show—Mabel Bertrand, the Creole from New Orleans, who had worked with me at Leroy's. When she later married Jelly Roll Morton, he wrote a tune for her entitled "Fussy Mabel" and dedicated it to her temperamental ways. Yeah, that *Holiday in Dixieland* outfit was a liberal education, especially after we got out on the road.

The show was originally organized to be featured in a New York cabaret. There were two large cabarets near Columbus Circle that were managing to stay open in spite of the Prohibition law. One was Healy's Golden Glades in a large building situated on the corner of Broadway and Sixty-sixth Street. It was a café for whites near the old Jungles neighborhood. In that same building was where they had the first ice shows in Manhattan and in still another part of the structure was the ballroom known as Busoni's Balconnades where the Original Memphis Five played for the dancing.

The other hot spot was John Reisenweber's layout located in an old building still standing at Fifty-eighth Street and Eighth Avenue. It was there that the famed Original Dixieland Jazz Band from New Orleans appeared in 1917.

The Lion once pointed out this building to a jazz-record collector; you can still see the faded lettering "—EISENW——" on the south side of the old three-story building. The young jazz fan stood staring at the place as though he'd just seen Jelly Roll Morton's ghost.

At Reisenweber's, *Holiday in Dixieland* was first presented. The place had two large rooms for entertainment. On the third floor was the Paradise Roof Garden, cooled by natural breezes, but on the second landing they had the "400" room, and that was where they advertised that the cooling was done by "typhoons." Whatever it was they had blowing there gave all the entertainers a fit. Our entire company came down with bad colds working there in that room one flight up from the street.

We opened in April 1922 and everything seemed to be going along pretty good, except for our health, when bam-bam-bam came the (Prohibition) agents and padlocked the place up for good.

I thought that would be the end of it. Then Mastin announced we were going out of town to tour the Orpheum vaudeville time. That was when I wanted to quit but June Clark talked me out of it. He said we were headed for Chicago and that was one town I ought to see. I fell for it because Clark and I had been such good friends. He often dropped into Leroy's with his cornet to pay his respects and we had some real tear-it-down sessions together. I remember one night he came in with banjoist Buddy Christian, a New Orleans musician who had come to New York around 1915, and the three of us got into a session that lasted until almost noon the following day. Clark could take as many as sixteen consecutive choruses on his cornet without tiring.

Well, we started out doing two shows a day on a split-week basis. We'd play the first three days of the week in a town the size of Akron, Ohio, and the last four days in a town close by, like Youngstown. Sometimes we did so bad in the first part of the week that they canceled us out in the town where we were supposed to finish out the week. That road tour was part of the Lion's show-business education. It was part of that first thirty years of bad luck the gypsy had told me about back in Jersey.

Will Mastin knew the ways of the business and he wised me up on a lot of the points. He showed me how important it was to be able to talk, sing, dance, in addition to playing the piano. In some of those theaters we had to contend with pianos that had broken keys; that was when you had to learn to mug. Mastin would say that when you don't get the attention you should, you had to demand it. He put into action the same things that the famous lone wolf of the dancers—Clarence (Dancin') Dotson—had told me when we worked together. Dotson would say, "I like to work by myself because then when you are on the stage it belongs to you. Take it, and don't let anyone wave you off." You've got to know enough to get right down to the microphone, in the spotlight, as soon as your name is mentioned. And so, with Mastin showing me the tricks of the show world, and brother Clark wising me up on all the sharpies you run across on the road, my short detour into vaudeville was worth the experience.

UPS AND DOWNS

Besides learning to run, jump, fight, hop, skip, sing, talk, and dance, you learned to be a good mixer and to socialize with the other performers backstage during the midnight suppers and other activities we used to have going. But I think the most important thing was learning how to get on and off a stage, and how to handle your hands when you were in the spotlight. Those are the things the young folks going into show business today just don't know how to do. The kids today never had the chance to go through those rough spots that we did. After they make that one hit record, they are through because they don't know how to act on a stage or in front of a television camera. And the musicians today let the stage hands push them around.

Another thing you've got to learn about involves the fact that there are always women following the troupe around who have just got to have a musician friend. Sometimes they are hometown girls and other times they are members of your company.

Our show was playing on the white vaudeville time. There were usually from six to eight acts on the bill with us. When we got into the Middle West an act joined the bill made up of a couple of gals who played ukuleles, cracked jokes, and performed a singing turn. Margie Ogden and Venza Noblett, both French-Canadians, became pals with the Lion. Venza Noblett, a red-haired doll with green eyes, took a real shine to me. She took it upon herself to "save me" and bought me silk shirts to get me in a good humor.

There is always a lot of emotion in show business as all the actors, actresses, and musicians are highly inflammable people. Talk about your small-town gossips and how next-door neighbors can get involved emotionally with each other—man, show folks are ten times worse. We fight about the billing, our position on the bill, and about each other's wives and girl friends.

Bad tempers flare up easily while you're traveling with the same folks every day. I remember we were once on the same bill with Gus Van and Joe Schenck, a popular act, made up of singing, dancing and piano playing. These two guys wouldn't speak to each other off the stage. Yeah, they worked together two to four times every day, and managed to stay mad at each other. But when Joe Schenck passed away, Gus Van couldn't bring himself to hire a new partner and continued to go on as a single for many years.

Then you take the vaude team of Clayton, Jackson, and Durante—they were always splitting up because of jealousy, but never failed to go back together. It was because Jimmy Durante, who had a big thing about their long association, was always faithful to his partners. It got so he didn't need the other two, but even today he usually gets Eddie Jackson in on the television shows on which he performs.

Sometimes all you'd hear backstage was gossip coming out of the dressing-room doors. Some gal would be screaming, "—that bitch is no better-looking than I am—how does she get her act next to closing?" The next-to-last turn was usually reserved for the biggest star on the bill and was considered to be the climax of the show. The last act was the killer because the crowd was filing out of the theater. They frequently gave this position to the acrobats. A man had to watch himself to stay out of all that jive going on. You had to learn to tend to your own business. It was the same thing as the problem of accepting drinks from the saloon-owner's wife when you worked the pianos in the bars. To keep straight with the boss, you refused those drinks.

Our act opened with the entire company playing and singing the title tune, "Holiday in Dixieland." This was followed by Vergie Mastin stepping down center front to sing "Can't You Hear Me Callin' Caroline?" June Clark was supposed to also go down front and accompany her on cornet. He was always late and that was where the term "scratch time" came from. If an act didn't show up by the time it was supposed to go on, it would get scratched by the theater owner. The act we had could always go on as long as Vergie was there, but she used to get raving mad when June wasn't on hand. Clark would sometimes get plenty flustered as he rushed on stage. One time he came on playing "Three O'Clock in the Morning," our closing number, while the band and Vergie were performing "Caroline." Old June would be closing the show before it opened. He also had several short speaking lines and I always had to prompt him from where I sat at the piano. The band opened and closed the show from the stage, but between the first and last numbers we performed from the orchestra pit.

We were a sharp-looking outfit in the tuxedos the Mastins gave us to wear. They were so old that we had to coax them to fold up when we put them in the trunk to move on to the next stop. If we didn't keep our eyes on them they would just up and walk away.

It was customary in vaudeville for the home office to employ spies to keep tabs on the various acts and their conduct. These stoolies or "spotters," were usually a regular act on the bill and no one was supposed to know they were reporting back to the office in New York. These spies would not only check on the behavior of an act, but they would also send back information pertaining to how good business had been and what acts were getting the most applause.

We began to worry about the reports being sent back. The big blow-up came at about the time we were finishing up the swing through the Orpheum Theaters and getting ready to go west on the Pantages time. The show was scheduled to go all the way to Spokane, Washington.

The first date for the Pantages circuit was at the Rialto Theater at State and Van Buren streets on the edge of Chicago's Loop district. It was a one-week stand and toward the end of the engagement one of the ladies carved a notch out of one of the big men. The next week, when we were at the Koppin Theater in Detroit, we got word we were canceled out of the western tour on account of the knife incident.

There was an act billed as the Noodles Fagan Family, a comedy turn, at the time our musical revue was canceled. The Fagan family was made up of Noodles, his wife, and his daughter; we were pretty sure it was one of them that turned us in.

It didn't seem to bother Mastin. He assured us we would be rockin' on easy street and livin' in peaceful alley, as he was lining up a long list of split weeks through Michigan, Illinois, Ohio, and up into Canada. It looked more to me like we were stranded. I was getting tired of the five shows a day, six or seven when it rained. In Chicago, at the Rialto (we called the place "The Workhouse") we'd been doing two extra shows on the days it rained—to bring more people in from the street.

So like I said, when Valaida went out of that hotel window in Detroit, I decided to take a good look at Chicago's South Side. My friend Venza Noblett had said I'd do well pounding a piano in one of the back rooms in the Windy City.

It felt good to be working as a single again. A noisy band is always hemming a man in. Every group manages to have one horn who wants to blow his sound over the piano.

12

Chicago, Chicago, That Swingin' Town

Chicago's all right to visit
But please don't hang around
You'll find the smooth chicks and high slicks
and—Boy, all those mellow fellows,
But when your bankroll is gone,
You're just another chump that's dropped in town. *

A piano man had it made like a hair-cutting man or an undertaker back in those good old days. No matter where you went, there was work waiting for you. Many of the other entertainers, like the singers and dancers, did not have it so good; nor did the drummers, fiddlers, or horn men. These folks were helpers and a good pianist didn't always need assistance.

Chicago's rough-and-tumblin' South Side reminded me of The Jungles in New York. Things were wide open. Mayor Big Bill Thompson's cops were on the take and managed to look the other way whenever something was happening, regarding that

* From "Chicago Blues" by Lonnie Johnson; published by Leeds Music Corporation.

Prohibition law. My friend, Venza Noblett, had been right when she told me I'd make out fine in the windy town.

My first Chicago stop was at the Columbia Hotel, where anyone in show business could get a room for a buck and a half a night (one dollar, if you were pressed for funds). It was located at the top of "The Stroll," which was the promenade down State Street from Thirty-first to Thirty-fifth. And we did stroll.

All the right cafés and theaters were located right around that part of town in 1923. They tell me that today it is all gone, with every one of the old buildings torn down and replaced by brand-new brick places.† They are hurrying away the buildings faster than the people in both New York and Chicago.

Right next door to the hotel was the famous Grand Theater (3110 South State), a stopping-off place for all the colored acts from Harlem. Who was playing there when I arrived but my old pal Ethel Waters with her Jazz Masters band in the "Bom-Bay" show. It was just like old home week on that corner with Fletcher (Smack) Henderson, who was Ethel's accompanist and the leader of the band; trumpeter Gus Aiken; Gus's brother Buddy and Lorenzo Brashear on trombones; clarinetist Garvin Bushell; and drummer boy Raymond Green. They were all out plugging Ethel's blues for the Black Swan record people, a Harlem firm owned by Harry Pace. Miss Waters had started making her blues records right after our "Crazy Blues."

The Aiken brothers and Bushell cut out from Miss Waters' band when she decided to close the Grand and head for the Deep South. They stayed in Chicago an extra week before heading back for New York and we made the night spots, listening to all the pianists, singing entertainers, and the hot bands. The bands proved to be the real treat because we hadn't heard groups in the East that could play the blues and stomps like these guys in the Middle West. A lot of them had played in

† This area is now the site of the Illinois Institute of Technology.

those carnival and circus bands that used to barnstorm through the southern states. Man, if those circus bands were a brass-player's graveyard (as they were called), the Chicago cabarets were a brass-player's paradise.

The horn men around Chicago had cutting contests too, like piano men had in Harlem. They were great out there for brass teams. These included Ol' Bad Eye Oliver, the King of New Orleans cornetists, and his young pal Louis Armstrong; Freddie (King) Keppard, another New Orleans man; and Bobby (White Shirt) Williams, from Louisville, Kentucky. The Schiller at that time was the favorite after-hours joint and early in the morning was when the wild carving would take place. I heard both these brass teams take off after each other there in the Schiller.

LOUIS, PROTÉGÉ

That was the period when Joe (King) Oliver had a band at the Lincoln Gardens. The place had once been named the Royal Gardens and was called that when Clarence Williams introduced his "Royal Garden Blues" in 1919. After they were through playing the shows at the Gardens, Oliver and his protégé, Satchelmouth Armstrong, would come over to the Schiller. Oliver would refuse to let Louis get off on his own sometimes. Louis at that time was beginning to outblow his boss and so Oliver would try to keep them both working on those famous cornet duets so Armstrong couldn't outshine him. This got me mad. I'd slip Louis a five-dollar bill and tell him to go out and solo by himself. "Let that boy play something," I'd say. When Louis really got warm he could blow them all out of the room. That's how he came to tangle with Bobby Williams.

Williams and Fred Keppard played together in the band known as the John H. Wickliffe Jazz Kings. Wickliffe, a drum-

mer, had come from Kentucky, like Williams, and in the band
Williams usually played the first trumpet parts and let Keppard
play the hot-jazz solos. They played duets together, but didn't
take the same kind of breaks that Oliver and Armstrong were
famous for playing. Keppard was one of the most powerful
cornet players of all time, but he didn't have the technical
ability of Oliver, Armstrong, or Williams.

Williams, as I recall, didn't play as loudly as the New Orleans
boys, but he had the most beautiful phrasing I've ever heard.
He was a good reader. And he had a tone that came to my mind
in later years whenever I heard Joe Smith with his sweet and
mellow horn.

He had been in Chicago and Milwaukee with Wickliffe since
about 1915, Williams told me, and when he was in the 803rd
Regiment band during World War I, with pianist Ed Bailey,
the latter wrote the famous "Bugle Blues." Williams featured it
and set everybody back on their haunches when he did the
number in the parade down Michigan Avenue after the war
was over.

One night at the Schiller, the two horn rivals, Bobby and
Louis, tangled in a long blowing contest. Armstrong hit a peak
when he took around forty choruses on "The Sheik of Araby."
Williams followed, holding his cornet in one hand, and fingering
the valves with the same hand, and almost blew Satchmo out
into the street with a tricky version of "Bugle Blues." The thing
that seemed to get the listeners was Bobby's sweet tone and the
way he made chords—something like Sidney Bechet later handled the soprano saxophone.

Williams had a weak heart, although he seemed to be able
to keep going all night long. It was just probably a question of
time before he would have blown himself away, but he didn't
get that chance. Late in 1923, Williams' wife poisoned him with
some bad booze she had gotten her hands on for the purpose.

There has been very little written about him, but a lot of
musicians will tell you that if Williams had lived he would

have been one of the great trumpet wizards of all time. This is not meant to say I would take anything away from Louis Armstrong. He deserves every dime he gets. He works like a horse, knows how to pace himself, and knows his chord construction.

One night Trevie Woods and Teddy Horne (Lena's father) took us to Schillers' to hear a piano player who went by the name of Peachtree. As far as I know no one ever knew him by any other name. He was from somewhere in Georgia and was playing the blues style that later became the boogiewoogie. He had the best rolling bass I've ever heard, even better than old Kitchen Tom's.

Well, when I heard ol' Peachtree beating the board, I got inspired to find a spot for myself. That Georgia blues man with his phony diamond stickpin and his fancy ring with the stone that wasn't real either got the Lion on a blues kick.

I soon took charge at a place called the Fiume Cafe, a place near Thirty-fifth and State. It was my headquarters for eight or nine months in Chicago. My job was to play a twenty-minute dance set with the band and then do a half-hour solo turn.

From some of the stuff that's in the jazz history books you'd think we didn't play anything but "Royal Garden Blues" or "King Porter Stomp," but we played the popular tunes of the day like "Aggravatin' Papa," "The Sheik," "Mama Loves Papa," and "Barney Google." We played what the customers asked to hear and in those days everyone had a wind-up phonograph at home.

One of the tunes I performed frequently was "Love Will Find a Way" (so they always say), a hit song from the Noble Sissle-Eubie Blake score for *Shuffle Along*, the great colored revue that had opened in New York in 1921. The requests for this tune came from the cast of the show, *Honeymoon Lane*, then playing in the Loop. They would come down to the Fiume nightly and stand around the piano, singing the song like a choir. The star of the show, Eddie Dowling, and I got to be good friends. Somehow it seems, looking back on it now, that there was a lot more mixing of the races in Chicago at that time than there was in Harlem. I sure found the "toddlin' town" to be real friendly.

You got a chance to get around to all the spots; they were close together then. You'd start out in the afternoon by making your first stop at a barber shop near the hotel. They would give you a relaxing shave and it was the policy of the shop to give each customer a half pint of gin to sip on. It got you off to a nice start. And then you went on, down The Stroll, toward Thirty-fifth Street. You'd pass the Vendome Theater, across the street from the Grand, and it was the movie palace of the South Side. Erskine Tate directed a semisymphonic orchestra there that later featured Louis as soloist. The Vendome's mammoth pipe organ was taken over a few years later by Fats. And down near the corner of Thirty-fifth and State was the New Monogram Theater, the official Chicago house for the T.O.B.A. circuit. There was the States Theater, with Joe Jordan's Pekin Orchestra in the pit. Jordan, who composed "That Teasin' Rag," had produced shows at the famous Pekin Theater up the street at Twenty-seventh and State, but he left there because they changed the place into a night club, the Pekin Inn, where things went full blast all night. Later they turned that place into a police station.

Most of the theaters had matinees and there was always someone in town from Harlem with one of the shows. There was the Lincoln, the Owl, the Indiana, the Avenue, and the Peerless. The big-time cabarets were around the corner at Thirty-fifth and State: the Elite No. 2, the Deluxe Gardens, Bill Bottom's Dreamland Cafe. Going east on Thirty-fifth, you passed the Entertainer's Cafe, the LaFerencia, the Paradise Gardens, and finally the famous Sunset Cafe at Calumet. A little off the beaten stroll were the Lincoln Gardens, where they advertised King Oliver's Jazz Syncopators, and the Radio Inn.

And in those times they went all night and up into the day. The last event was the Radio Inn where Tommy Ladnier played his cornet for the Breakfast Dances. That was the time and that was the place where a lot of jazz history was made.

It was at the Elite that I first met Bricktop (Ada) Smith, a singer with a magnetic personality and red hair, a girl who would give you the shirt off her back. At that time, Bricktop had a good word—she had to leave New York to make it. It was so much at our heels here, she would say, people forget that you live on the main street here in Harlem. But she knew exactly which way she wanted to go and was known in all the places on the South Side. A few months after I saw her there, she returned to Harlem and was responsible for getting Duke his first job in New York at Barron's.

It was my custom, while getting around, to challenge the piano players. They didn't have the competition out there that we had in the East. One of several good piano men as I remember was Glover Compton, who worked as a duo with his wife Nettie, at the Paradise Gardens. He was from Louisville, a hard man to take. He had a lot of technique.

And one night I walked into the white-tiled Elite No. 2 and ran into a smart-alecky kid manning the keyboard. Bricktop thought she would have some fun with me and sicced this piano-playing kid from Pittsburgh on me that night. I told him and Ada that I would take him with one hand. As I have pointed out, a pianist in that era had to have at least a hundred songs to make any kind of impression. Well sir, I sat down and started to beat a few out. The kid listened and then disappeared before I was through. His name was Earl Hines and they told me he didn't know but three or four songs then. He just got too scared to stay and count on the couple of tunes he knew. But he won so much fame out there a few years later that they called him the Fatha. He turned into a fine one after he acquired some experience.

The Elite was one of my favorite places because they used a lot of singing entertainers in there, like the places around Harlem. I'd run into Alberta Hunter, Mary Straine, Mary Stafford, Mattie Hite, and Josephine Stevens. Miss Stevens had one fine effect—she was a coloratura who was able to hold a note while the rhythm strode along and when she wanted to pick up the rhythm again she did so without breaking the note.

There was another entertainer out there who made a good impression on me. He was a large Creole man, Ollie Powers. He was a drummer as well as a great baritone vocalist and for a while led his own group at the Paradise with Glover Compton on piano, Jimmie Noone from New Orleans on clarinet, and Freddie Keppard. They were known as Ollie Powers' Syncopators.

They had the bands and the good horn men out in Chicago, while we had the piano men and the best drummers. The only thing wrong with the western and southern jazz musicians was that they could not read. Maybe it was like Henry (Red) Allen, a New Orleans trumpeter, once told me: "In New Orleans, if you read music, you're considered a sissy."

The one thing those instrumentalists could do was to play the blues so that you could dance on a dime. The right blues tempo means a half step and a slow drag. And the blues a musician plays depends a great deal on the mood he is in at the time. A man's blues come from the hard work in the cotton fields or wherever, and from his religion. You could say the blues are really a sacred thing with the Negro by now and are represented in his hymns. They sing and play what their heart tells them to express. If one is in trouble, sad and downhearted, he can really express the blues. That's where the spiritual thing comes in—it reverts back to the Almighty God and the spiritual power He sends through the mind and body.

Toward the end of 1923 it was getting to be time for me to look back to New York. I would find big changes. In the old days, uptown or downtown, they would often chase you away from the piano when you played the low-down blues. The time was coming that if you couldn't play the blues and get in stride, you couldn't find work.

Harlem During the Twenties

BY GEORGE HOEFER

The world conflict, Willie's "mess," of 1914–18, indirectly brought an end to Harlem's relatively quiet and compact middle-class neighborhoods of New York-born Negroes. As the population expanded, the limits of Harlem expanded with it and the area became a teeming metropolis in itself where urbane New Yorkers were intermixed with others whose backgrounds were Birmingham, Memphis, St. Louis, New Orleans, and the exotic culture of the West Indies. As a young Duke Ellington saw it in 1923, "Here is the world's greatest atmosphere," he said. "It's like the Arabian Nights."

Eventually Harlem was to extend from 110th Street (at the top of Central Park) up to 155th Street; but the area from 110th to 116th contains Spanish and Italian Harlem. Negro Harlem is bounded by 116th Street on the south, Morningside and St. Nicholas avenues on the west, 155th Street and the Harlem River on the north, and the East River on the east. The main thoroughfare of the district became 125th Street.[1]

There, during the twenties, over 300,000 people lived in

housing designed for 60,000. The overcrowded and overpriced tenements took in more people in some city blocks than could be found in the Negro sections of average-sized southern cities.

The national prosperity of the twenties brought more clearly defined class distinctions to the area. Although a high percentage of the new inhabitants had never seen, much less earned, the amounts of money they got in Manhattan, they were still earning less than the average wages on a national scale. But up in the northwestern corner of the district, Sugar Hill had its handsome apartment houses for the affluent doctors, lawyers, and businessmen, including some who were getting into the millionaire category.

On 139th Street, called "Striver's Row," many up-and-coming hopefuls lived in the Stanford White-designed brownstones. These included people who were prospering in the entertainment industry, figures like bandleader Fletcher Henderson and prize fighter Harry Wills. They were very much a part of the Harlem middle class that also included small businessmen and certain professional people.

Below Sugar Hill toward the east was "The Valley," a section also called "The Black Ghetto," where vast hordes of the working class, as well as the "sporting" element, were crowded into a tenement section that under other circumstances would have been classified as a low-rent district, but which was, in Harlem, anything but. . . .

Although the people who lived in Harlem were in some ways less sensitive about themselves during the twenties, than they were to become in later years, there were already signs of a strong Negro pride in Harlem as an entity. There was a form of organized rebellion against the Negro image created in the South and constantly given a showcase by both white and colored show business. Harlemites raised considerable fuss in 1921 when a Senator Williams of Mississippi got a bill through the United States Senate to erect a monument to "The Faithful

Colored Mammies of the South." Although the legislation finally passed, it was vetoed by President Harding.[2]

Business establishments, with notable exceptions, were starting to be owned and operated by Negroes. The first large Negro-owned department store opened in November 1922. In 1921, Harry Pace and composer W. C. Handy started, as Willie records, the first all-Negro recording company, Black Swan Records. At first they operated out of a small office in Pace's home on Seventh Avenue between 134th and 135th streets. Their advertisements included a motto: "all other colored records are by artists only passing for colored." This firm, which thrived at first, lasted three years, and grossed $110,000 during its first year. Partners Pace and Handy were not shrewd entrepreneurs over the long haul, perhaps, but they did ride the blues wave triggered by the Mamie Smith-Willie Smith "Crazy Blues" record of 1920. In spite of their motto, they made use of white performers under disguised names.

As Willie has said, Harlem was a talent center. It was the home and favored stomping ground of the greatest acts in colored show business. During the twenties, people from the world of entertainment, people from all over the country, would go "uptown" to see the latest techniques in music, dancing, and comedy.

Early in the decade, the unprecedented success of the musical Shuffle Along, starring Florence Mills on Broadway (actually, the 63rd Street Theater—uptown from the heart of the traditional theater district), inaugurated a long list of Negro revues: The Plantation Revue, Liza, Strut Miss Lizzie, Runnin' Wild, Blackbirds of 1926, 1928, and 1930, Keep Shufflin', Hot Chocolates, How Come?, Brown Buddies, Africana, Rhapsody in Black, The Chocolate Dandies, and others.[3] The most successful of these sprang from tab shows (shortened versions of full-scale revues) originally presented at the Lafayette Theater, or from floor shows produced at Connie's Inn, uptown on Seventh Avenue.

The Broadway shows became progressively more sophisticated as years passed. By 1930, the professional Southernism was rapidly disappearing. And no longer did the billboards show us the pickaninny with the August ham.* The performances of such entertainers as Bill (Bojangles) Robinson, Ethel Waters, Snake-Hips Tucker, Hamtree Harrington, were able to stand on their merits. The music from these shows was recorded by performers of all kinds and a substantial percentage of Tin Pan Alley output originated from the scores of top Negro revues.

While Negro composers and performers unveiled their talents on Broadway, colored audiences at the Lafayette were seeing humorous take-offs by their own stars of such white dramatic shows as White Cargo and Lulu Belle.

As the tempo of the twenties increased, a new and lucrative fact of show-business life took hold uptown—the exotic Harlem night life. The original impetus for the trek uptown was Prohibition, which had become the law of the land, so to speak, on January 16, 1920. By the mid-1920s, police estimated that Prohibition had distilled at least eleven "white trade" night clubs in Harlem.

These included the world famous Cotton Club, whose opening nights became as important as a first night in Broadway theaters, particularly because of the Cotton Club Parades.[4] Floor shows changed twice a year and Connie's Inn, the Saratoga Club, and Small's Paradise flourished.

Liquor could be purchased at all the spas if the customer had the price, which was high. It could also be obtained at one hundred lower-rank Harlem cabarets, perhaps five out of seven cigar stores and luncheonettes, and at numerous "buffet flats" sprinkled around in the apartment houses.

At first, the Negroes themselves were in complete control of the places they ran, but as time went on, the illicit liquor

* Harlemese for watermelon.

suppliers began to see the profits in proprietorship as well as supply. They took over some of the better-known places by furnishing capital to make them more attractive to the increasing clientele from downtown. It was said that Owen (Owney) Madden and George (Big Frenchy) DeMange, took over the ownership of the Cotton Club, but as in other spots where Madden and his colleagues took over, they usually left the former owners installed as managers and "fronts" for the operation.

Madden was rarely seen at the Cotton Club. His energies were devoted to operating the Phoenix Cereal Beverage Company on West Twenty-sixth Street. There, "Madden's No. 1" beer was made and distributed to many of the bars in New York.

Most of the Harlem clubs, whether owned by white gangsters or not, were managed by Negroes. Some of the more powerful figures during the era were Barron Wilkins, who finally, it was said, crossed the boys from downtown and was wiped out (their agent was Yellow Charleston, a man said to use dope and a knife with equal appetite); Edwin A. Smalls, a former elevator boy from South Carolina who, on October 22, 1925, moved his site of operations from the Sugar Cane Club on Fifth Avenue to 2294 Seventh Avenue and renamed it the Paradise, which was billed as "The Hottest Place in Town"; Jerry (West Indian) Preston, who opened up Pod's & Jerry's on 133rd Street; Mel Frazier, in charge at The Nest; Johnny Carey; and many others who as gamblers, floor managers, or sporting gentlemen were well known on the Harlem scene during the twenties.†

Liquor was not the only draw. Some went uptown to see Florence Mills, "the little black mosquito," a magnetic personality who was a potent ambassadress for Harlem's entertainment. The music was becoming more and more impressive. Cotton Club productions had scores written first by the team of Jimmy McHugh and Dorothy Fields, and later by Harold

† Others: Pop Steele, Pop Lewis, Bub Hewlett, Des Verney, Gershwin Meyers, and the Lion's friend Rudolph Brown of the Capitol Palace.

Arlen and Ted Koehler. These were white composers, of course, and the Cotton Club was actually an "ofay" night club uptown. (It later moved downtown.) The entire show became designed for white trade and, in 1927 when Duke Ellington's band opened, it was for the entertainment of a white audience made up of Park Avenue society and celebrities in all categories. Harlem citizens were not admitted. According to Carl Van Vechten there were doormen he described as "brutes" to enforce the rule. Apparently, big names in Negro show business were admitted because they worked there from time to time. Yet there is some evidence that the revered W. C. Handy was refused admission one night, even though they were using some of his music in the show.

A year after Smalls Paradise opened in its new location on Seventh Avenue the proprietor took an ad in Variety, *May 1926, announcing:*

> *Word-of-mouth plugging has made Smalls an all-season playground. To see the "high hats" mingle with the native stepper is nothing unusual. Where formerly the dance floor was either all white, or all black, the races mix and the atmosphere permits for no class distinction.*

A popular feature at Smalls was watching the waiters dance the Charleston late at night, while carrying fully loaded trays.

The publication of Van Vechten's novel, Nigger Heaven, *in the mid-twenties, which described some of the more exotic activities taking place uptown, stimulated a rush of white trade to the best-known cabarets. Sensitive to Van Vechten's revelations, the club owners and producers of the floor shows tried to give the sensation-seeking clientele what they were looking for; the shake dancing with its grinds was stepped up and the more primitive, junglelike aspects of the entertainment were highlighted. To get the story over to the downtown public, Harlem night-club owners hired Lee Posner, a publicity man, who helped to build up fame for the Cotton Club and other black and tan establishments.*

This was all conducive to the establishment of a staged night life that was to thrive from about 1927 to 1933. Harlem, like any other community, didn't mind the large sums of money that appeared to be pouring into local coffers, but the truth was that most of the prosperity went back downtown to the controlling hoodlums.

Van Vechten's Harlem did exist, but it was not open to the public in general. Only a small percentage of the visitors saw Basement Brownie's after-hour spa, Helen Valentine's sex circuses on 140th Street, the floor shows featuring the "drag parades" of homosexuals, the marijuana parlors illuminated by blue lights, the small joints where white jazz musicians sat in with six-piece jump bands to jam, or the neighborly house-rent parties and parlor socials. A special sort of guide or a friend was needed to make these places available to an ofay.

Few, if any, tourists journeyed to the Lafayette to hear Bessie Smith shout the blues or to the Savoy Ballroom to listen to Chick Webb's Chicks. These people could hear Ethel Waters, the ebony Nora Bayes, sing at the Palace and dance to Fletcher Henderson's band at the Roseland during the so-called fabulous decade.

Most of the whites who saw nontourist Harlem were in show business as singers, dancers, and musicians. People like Mae West, Ann Pennington from George White's Scandals, *and bandleader Phil Harris picked up helpful techniques to use in their work. Many white musicians interested in jazz rhythms regularly made an appearance in after-hour places and small clubs to absorb as much of the music as possible. Many of these spots were unknown and hard to find, but jazz men found their way through the underground.*

During the winter of 1925–26, the Galewski (Gale) Brothers built the block-long Savoy and labeled it THE WORLD'S MOST BEAUTIFUL BALLROOM. *The enterprise, managed by young*

Harlem real-estate agent Charlie Buchanan, was an immediate hit. It offered the section for the first time a place where there was room enough for everybody to dance. Buchanan's outstanding feature during the Savoy's early days were the famous competitions between bands. Sometimes it was city versus city. On a Sunday night, May 15, 1927, for example, it was war between New York City and Chicago. The Middle West was represented by King Oliver's band and the Fess Williams Royal Flush Orchestra; New York offered Fletcher Henderson from Roseland and the Savoy's house band, under the leadership of drummer Chick Webb. The record battle in terms of numbers took place in 1929 when six separate jazz bands had at each other, brass and beat.

The Savoy's wider fame came during the Depression Years when it became the center of acrobatic dancing. Then known as "The Home of Happy Feet" it was the spawning grounds for the Lindy Hop, the Susie Q, and Truckin'. Somehow these dances drew wider attention to Harlem than had the Charleston and Black Bottom of the earlier ten-year period. As the Lion has mentioned, the Charleston came from the South Carolina area, while the Black Bottom, featured in George White's Scandals, originated, says Perry Bradford, in the "Dark Town" section of Atlanta, Georgia.

A daytime focal point for show-business celebrities and the sporting crowd was the corner of 131st Street and Seventh Avenue. There the "Tree of Hope" was located. Gamblers and entertainers on their way to work touched the tree for luck. It grew in the middle of the uptown lane of Seventh Avenue in front of the downstairs entrance of Connie and George Immerman's Connie's Inn. Fats Waller, it has been reported, composed "Ain't Misbehavin'" one afternoon in Connie's Inn during a rehearsal of Hot Chocolates. His lyric writer, Andreamentana (Andy) Razafinkerifo (Razaf), has said it took Waller all of forty-five minutes to come up with the melody. Waller's col-

laborator, Razaf, was the nephew of Ranavalona III, the African Queen of Madagascar.

During the early twenties, composer William Grant Still conducted the orchestra in the pit for the Lafayette's tab shows. The Schiffman family, now owners of the Apollo Theater on 125th Street, ran the old Lafayette for many years after taking over from the Coleman Brothers. They featured special Sunday-night shows regularly attended by all of Harlem's dictys in dress-up finery. Those few with big names in the entertainment world might then go on to the Sunday Celebrity Night at the Cotton Club.

Then the custom of breakfast dances on Sunday mornings (from 7 A.M. to 11 A.M.) began in Harlem. At Smalls, the Lenox Club, and other all-night places, these early-morning shows featured ad-lib entertainment and music, sometimes from the biggest names in the business. Frequently the club announced beforehand the names of the guests expected to be on hand and, if not, the customers hoped they could stay awake anyhow because surprise guests usually showed up to perform.

Harlem's night life held up unusually well through the stockmarket crash of 1929 and during the early years of the great Depression.

When 3.2 beer appeared in 1933 there was a definite slackening up of the travel uptown. The beer didn't bring an abrupt end to the gay Harlem night life but it did help bring on a decline. The Depression, easy-to-obtain liquor, and the end of the vogue for Negro shows on Broadway lessened Harlem's attraction to downtown celebrities and it had been these people who had brought along the "big butter-and-egg men." The larger clubs were forced to close. The Cotton Club moved to Broadway and Forty-eighth Street, only to fail after two years.

The only redeeming feature of the end of the entertainment Golden Age uptown was that many of the big-name entertainers and jazz bands had developed their showmanship to the extent they were sought after by white theaters and ballrooms all over the country; this was especially true for musicians connected with the bands of Duke Ellington, Cab Calloway, Jimmy Lunceford—they were ripe for the era of swing music.

13

Reduce It to a Low Gravy

Some people used to call them speakeasies,
But I call them sneakeasies,
You sneaked in and spoke soft,
When the door bell rang you got a thrill,
'Cause when it rang three times the cops were on the kill.

WILLIE THE LION SMITH

When the Lion got back to Harlem in late 1923, things were romping and stomping. There were a lot of new spots and they were all beginning to use five-piece jazz bands.

Mamie Smith now had a fast band with Bubber Miley playing cornet at the Garden of Joy, an open-air cabaret with canvas sides. It was located atop a big rock on Seventh Avenue between 138th and 139th streets. (They cleared the rock away in the mid-twenties when they built the Abyssinian Baptist Church, where Adam Clayton Powell is now the preacher.)

The New York pianists would hang out at this roadhouse-like place, nicknamed "The Rock," on summer afternoons. The breezes coming off of the Harlem River made the spot nice and cool. Japanese lanterns were strung around for decoration and at night when they were all lit up it gave the dive a real exciting look, like an amusement park. You climbed a couple of flights of stairs to enter from the side. Everything was fine until it rained; the place was wide open to the sky overhead.

The Lion performed with George McClennon on clarinet at the Garden of Joy for several months. We played nightly and did matinees on Thursdays, Saturdays, and Sundays, as was the custom in those days. In Harlem there was always a matinee going at times when a lot of folks weren't working, like the kitchen mechanics' days I mentioned in Newark and Atlantic City, when all the working women and pot hustlers had their afternoon off.

THE CAPITOL PALACE

It was about this time that I got another good deal. I took charge for a long spell at a large and fancy place called the Capitol Palace on Lenox Avenue between 139th and 140th streets. The Capitol was another one of those clubs located in a basement. A Chinese restaurant was on one side of the main entrance and a greasy-spoon lunch counter was on the other. Upstairs, there was a twenty-four-hour-around-the-clock pool hall.

The smoothly waxed dance floor would hold about forty couples, but on a Saturday night they would try to squeeze a thousand people into the room. The bandstand was way back at the end of the large room.

One reason they were always packed was because the Lion was fronting a good jazz band and because they always served good food. The house specialized in fried chicken, steaks, and sandwiches. There was a fifty-cent cover charge at the tables, but considering the entertainment and food it was well worth the price.

Then, of course, you could get your booze. It was kept in pitchers under the bar. That made it easy to dump if the

Prohibition boys dropped in for a visit. They sometimes came in for a drink instead. Just like everyone else, they dug that special potion they used to serve uptown called "Top and Bottom." It was made of a mixture of gin with wine, had a pink color, tasted like perfume, and sold for thirty-five cents a pint. Man, it would send *anybody* sailing.

The boss at the Capitol was a large Negro from Detroit named Johnny Powell. He came up to me one night and said, "Look'a here, Lion, I been open eight months and business ain't nuthin' to brag about. Maybe that fiddle, piano, and drums outfit I got there isn't hot enough. Maybe I need me a *loud* jazz band. You interested in talking business?"

I looked around the place and noted that I was reacting favorably to the vibrations. It was larger and more modern than Leroy's had been and seemed to be attracting a fun-loving crowd. That liquor law was making good sports out of a lot of quietlike folks. This looked like a good spot for about five pieces —without the violin. You could tell the customers would rather do the bellywobble than dance the waltz. Yeah, these red-hot chicks wanted to dance it up with their cold-weather papas. The Lion could tell!

The band I got together had some good men in it. It was real brotherly. We had the Aiken Brothers—cornetist Gus and trombonist Buddy; the Benford Brothers—Tommy on drums and Bill on bass; and Buddy Christian on banjo. When Tommy Benford left I got another drummer, who came from a famous set of brothers—the Wright Brothers. The one I hired was Black Steve. His brother, Herbert, also a drummer, had been the fellow who stabbed Lieut. Jim Europe to death during the concert played by the Hellfighters in Boston, back in 1919. All of these guys, except banjoist Christian, had at one time played with the Jenkins Orphanage Band I talked about back aways in this book.

That was some band! We had frequent changes in personnel, as did all the bands back in those days, and we had a lot of

sitting in. The Capitol Palace became quite the place to hear
the jazz men with all the latest tricks. We had guys like
trombonist Dope Andrews, who had been in my outfit on the
"Crazy Blues" recording date, and the team of cornetist June
Clark and trombonist Jimmy Harrison, coming down almost
every night. Clark and Harrison were working a duo deal like
the King Oliver-Louis Armstrong combination had done in
Chicago, except Harrison made his trombone sound like Armstrong's cornet.

There has been a lot of argument about who was the first
brass man to use a bathroom rubber plunger for a mute. I
remember that a trumpeter leader named John Smith, who had
a large society orchestra made up of Clef Club members, was
using a rubber mute way back around the time of the First
World War. Sometimes he would use an ordinary drinking glass
to mute the bell of his horn.

The two most creative guys in the early days with mutes
were cornetist Bubber Miley and trombonist Charlie Irvis. They
both used to stop in at the Capitol to blow. Miley was ahead
of Johnny Dunn, who the Lion recalls as a guy with a big mouth
talking about himself too much. He was also a flash in the pan
compared to Miley. It was the team of Miley and trombonist
Irvis that later developed Ellington's "jungle style," when Duke
had a band at the Kentucky Club near Times Square.

Irvis carried a regular gut bucket around for a mute and
when I'd tell him to play soft he'd come on real low down with
that bucket on the end of his slide trombone. We would get
some sessions under way there at the Capitol. The bandstand
had room for eleven men, and many a night the platform was
loaded until you couldn't get another musician up on it.

At that time my boss, Johnny Powell, was riding high with
the boys downtown—he was to later get sent back to Detroit
by the mob because he withheld some of the funds rolling in
as the place kept getting more popular. Powell's assistant and
floor manager was a Harlem sharpie named Rudolph Brown,

who knew exactly how to keep the customers in line and the police happy.

There was very little trouble at the Capitol, in spite of the fact we had some of the toughest Harlem characters coming down every night. The joint was a hangout for the West Indian gambler Dashy Grant, a lad who had big eyes for our star singer—Lizzie Miles from down around New Orleans.

We also had plenty of visits from Yellow Charleston, a dope fiend specializing in happy dust,* who later took care of Barron Wilkins, with a knife, for the syndicate. Then we had three of the biggest gamblers around—Big Blue Ranier, Bub Hewlett, and Des Verney. These boys all had lots of money and loved to sing, fight, dance, and make love. They believed in the old expression, "If you are man enough to satisfy your gal, you are man enough to fight." The notorious knife wielder, Chippie Mamie, saturated in gin, would quietly sit in a back corner when she came to see us. Yes sir, the Capitol Palace was their playground and their fight arena, but Powell and Brown always made sure their customers did their fighting upstairs on the sidewalk or back in the alley. Powell's riot squad of six bouncers were not afraid of the worst men in Harlem and could handle them all.

The only time I ever saw Rudy Brown fussed was the night a fighter named Battling Siki showed up with his lion cub.

There was always a close relationship between the prize fight world and show business. Lightweight champion Joe Gans, the owner of the Goldfield Hotel in Baltimore (where Eubie Blake started his piano career), was once married to the gal who later married bandleader Ford Dabney, one of the most prominent New York orchestra leaders before World War I. The first saxophone player in New York, Nappy Lee, was married to fighter Harry Wills's daughter. And Siki, the Senegalese fighter, had eyes for our Lizzie Miles.

Siki was famous all over New York. He wore a long black

* Cocaine.

overcoat with a stovepipe hat and a monocle, and was always a great one for animals. You would see him strutting down Seventh Avenue, then a fashionable street uptown, with a monkey riding on his shoulder and a lion cub on a chain leash following along behind him.

Well, about the time I was a regular at the Capitol, Siki had just returned from France, where he had a suburban estate outside Paris, after whipping Georges Carpentier. He came over here to challenge the winner of the Firpo-Dempsey heavyweight title match. He was also looking to fight Harry (Black Panther) Wills, the only man Dempsey was said to be afraid of going into the ring with. As it turned out the Senegalese bruiser didn't get a chance to clash with either Dempsey or Wills.

One night after Siki had taken on a cargo of gin, he got in a playful mood and came down the stairs into the Capitol with his pet. He let the lion's leash loose and hollered, "Sic 'em." Rudy Brown, who was always stationed at the entrance to determine who came in and who stayed out, didn't get much of a chance to bar the onrush of the lion. In passing Brown, the beast lunged at the floor manager's pants leg and couldn't, or wouldn't let go. Brown screamed, "Get this damn monster off of me!" and Siki tried to talk the animal into letting go, but instead the baby lion was pulling Brown around and around in a circle.

Lizzie Miles, who had been singing "Please Don't Tickle Me Babe,".rushed over to Siki and spoke to him in French. I don't know what she said but he got the cub and quieted it down. This didn't seem to satisfy floor manager Brown, who turned and said something to the Battler—it would have had to have been in English—that infuriated him. The next thing I knew Brown was on the floor from Siki's powerful one-two punch.

When the floor manager got himself back upright and brushed off, things began to quiet down. Lizzie Miles joined Siki at his table and the lion hopped up into her lap and went sound asleep. Then, and only then, did the bouncers and customers come out from the dark corners of the room to return to their tables.

It wasn't long after the above incident that Siki sicced his lion cub once too often. He wandered over to Tenth Avenue one night and set his pet after a big tough Irishman. The next morning they found Siki lying dead in the gutter. The cub never did show up again.

There were so many entertainers, musicians, and customers taking turns at the Capitol it became necessary to keep a close watch on the kitty. As had always been the custom, the gal singers, waiters, and bartenders were supposed to put their tips in the box to be split equally at closing time. To be sure everything was on the up and up, the Lion had the management place a large mirror on the piano so he could keep his eye on everybody. They still use that idea today in some stores. Everybody has noticed those mirrors mounted on the ceiling and bent in such a way a watcher can see you if you stick something in your pocket.

Some of the girls had developed a neat trick of palming quarters or other coins off the tables by using the sweaty, sticky palms of their hands. They would lean all their weight on the coin as they placed the hand over the coin; the loot would stick to their hand until they got a chance to stick it in their gowns somewhere. They also developed sleight-of-hand methods with a handkerchief.

Besides the mirror, I used waiters whom I could trust to help me keep tabs on things. I'd slip the guy a little taste† to keep his eyes open and let me know when he caught somebody cheating on the tipping system. There was one waiter named Whistling Seith at the Capitol who could whistle like nobody's business and was famous all over Harlem. He would carry his tray loaded with drinks while whistling a fine blues. Seith was

† A small gift, either in cash or a drink.

noted for getting into the acts at the Lincoln Theater from his seat up in the balcony. If he whistled along with the singing and dancing of an attraction it was considered a sort of Good Housekeeping Seal of Approval. When the balcony crowd wanted some low-down blues they would call out, "Put us in the alley!" Then, if the whistler joined in, the act knew they had it made and would become a favorite there at the Lincoln.

But you couldn't always trust the waiters and bartenders any more than you could the entertainers. That is how they came to design a waiter's uniform with a tight collar and no pockets. This helped to stop thieving waiters who would just as soon pocket a five-dollar bill given them for the piano player to perform a particular tune.

The bartenders had to be watched closely. Still, it was always a good idea to stay on the good side of them, whether you were a customer or an employee of the place, because if you didn't they could lay a Mickey Finn or a Bronx cocktail on you. If a piano man got one of those bombs he would probably end up fired because they made it necessary to make frequent trips to the men's room and the cabaret bosses just wouldn't go for that at all.

That's the story of the night club—everybody watching everybody else. This even extends to the partners owning a joint. There'll be one cash register in a spot with three guys standing around it watching.

During the dry years, the waiters and barkeeps had an added responsibility—watching for raiding parties. If the cops or Feds came down the stairs everybody on the staff knew the signals. One of the warnings that was often used when a waiter or bartender spotted trouble was to dash a glass to the floor, breaking it with a crashing noise. When that crash was heard the men behind the bar grabbed the pitchers of booze and started pouring them down the drain. Some of the places had a bell-ringing system and when the law arrived there was buzzing all over the place. Others flickered the lights and sometimes the piano player would give the signal by playing a certain tune. All the tip-offs were signals to destroy the evidence so they couldn't pin a charge on the boss that would close up the operation and put us all out of work.

All in all, a raid in one of the big-time places was a rarity. The bosses gave out a goodly sum of gold as protection. In fact, you could see a Prohibition agent or cop almost any night in the Capitol partaking of a big juicy steak and a glass of red-eye hooch on the house. People were on the level in those days—everybody gave value for value.

ENTER, DUKE ELLINGTON

It was at the Capitol Palace that the Lion first met Edward Kennedy (Duke) Ellington, then a young piano man from Washington, D.C. He was with a band under the leadership of banjoist Elmer Snowden. It wasn't until Bricktop Smith went to Barron Wilkins and talked them into a job at his place that they got on the eating list.

When the Duke came to New York the band had Elmer Snowden on the guitar, Alton (Sonny) Greer on drums, and Otto Hardwick on saxophone—there were six of them in all. At that time I was pretty well liked around Harlem and I was doing all right for myself. I had my usual twenty-dollar gold piece on, my stickpin, diamond ring, and about a hundred one-dollar bills covered with a ten on the top. Big deal, they call it now.

At that time Duke and his pals weren't doing so well. They used to come into the Capitol and sit down and listen to me and my band rip. When Duke came in, I used to set him down to play. He was always a good-looking, well-mannered fellow; one of those guys you see him, you like him right away; warm, good-natured. I took a liking to him and he took a liking to me. I introduced him, and all the girls took a liking to him, too.

I often said to Duke, "You might as well hang around and wait for me till I get off." In those days there were a lot of Jewish-owned restaurants on Seventh Avenue. I knew them all and that's where the first hog maws and chitterlings were introduced and came to be widely known. The colored people used to make them and cook them with fried chicken, but the Jewish people who could eat them went them one better. They took them and made them so they were cool in the morning, and they took all that grease off them and the people went for them like hot cakes. So I introduced Duke and his band to chitterlings on Seventh Avenue. I used to share half of what I had with Duke and the boys every morning.

Things were so tough that they had about decided to go back to Washington. But I said, "Why go back to Washington when I'm doing all right? Let's stick it out. You've gone this far." I was a guy who was handling a few bucks then and was always willing to split it down with them. We'd stand on street corners and I'd give them lectures each morning. I'd lecture them on the ladies. There was no way for them to miss. To buck them up, I showed them that I always had a couple of hundred skins in my pocket. "I've been riding calves ever since they had a calf," I said. So he stuck it out.

Our wandering gang back in those days included Duke and his pals; James (The Brute) Johnson, looking like a bear in his racoon coat; Corky Williams, a pianist who was the first guy to sing "Christopher Columbus" with its original bawdy lyrics; Alberta Simmons, the dark-skinned pianist, who could drink and pound a piano like a man; and Raymond (Lippy) Boyette. My boy Fatso (Waller), or Filthy as I called him, was always tagging along. We didn't give him much chance to play back then. I'd tell Duke, "Yeah, he's a yearling, he's comin' along and will do all right one of these days." By this time Fats had a regular gig playing on the ten-thousand-dollar Wurlitzer organ at the Lincoln.

We all dug Alberta Simmons. She could read, improvise, and memorize to beat hell; a real strider and shout player of the first water, who could give any man a fit on those keys. I called her Madame Society because she always wore eyeglasses.

There was usually lots of action in Harry Pyle's speakeasy up on Fifth Avenue. If there wasn't, we'd keep making the rounds until we found some life—sometimes it would be in some cat's apartment.

When we found a lively spot we'd get a fast session under way that would sometimes last until noon. This was a frequent occurrence during the 1920s and 1930s when we met in cabarets, speakeasies, or at the house-rent parties.

Some of the greatest stride piano ever heard in New York City was played at those rent parties. They still have them once in awhile and will as long as there are high rents in Harlem.

14

Payin' the Rent with Chitterlings

> *Get up off that piano*
> *Leave it there*
> *'Cause I'm here.*

WILLIE THE LION SMITH

A lot of folks have asked the Lion about those house-rent parties in Harlem. They were really something! Now, here is the real lowdown on those internationally famous affairs.

First, we had what they called parlor socials back in the old days. Sometimes they were put on by a church to raise money so they could pay the preacher. They'd charge you a quarter to get in and then sell you, for a low price, all the chicken or barbecued ribs you could eat. For an added attraction, they usually had some musicians and singers to put on an entertainment. All the money they raised would be used to help pay the church's expenses or to aid a needy member of the congregation. That was how the house-rent-party idea got started.

When the politicians got hold of the plan they turned the parties into election rallies to get themselves in office. A politician who wanted a job would stage a party featuring music and entertainment with free food. They'd put on gumbo suppers with New Orleans-style gumbo and fish fries. I can remember seeing Governor Al Smith and Mayor Jimmy Walker at those uptown affairs—they always seemed to be too busy politicking to enjoy the food.

An entire family would work for days preparing for one of those socials: there'd be piles of hog maws, pickled pigs' tails, pig's feet, southern-style fried chicken, mashed potatoes, chitterlings, potato salad, corn bread, red beans and rice, crab soup, and sometimes they'd even come up with a Chinese dinner with piles of chop suey. There'd be just about everything you could think of in the way of food served with plenty of vinegar, pepper, and hot sauces.

When Prohibition Days came along they had another excuse to have a party. Gallons of gin, beer, wine, whisky, eggnog, and brandy were made available to wash down all those vittles. Yeah, man, the party business sure did pick up when they made drinking illegal. Folks would get big quantities of liquor from the night-club owners and there always seemed to be enough business for everybody. The cabaret bosses had enough customers and they didn't worry about the private functions, especially when they got a big order for booze.

Then, even before the Depression, Harlem citizens having a hard time meeting their high rents latched onto the gimmick of having a party and charging anywhere from twenty-five cents to a dollar for admission. Sometimes when loot was scarce they'd get a hot shoplifter who'd go out and pick up a few hams, chickens, or some spare ribs. Fact is there were several sharpies in the business of furnishing food for these parties, which were now being called house-rent functions, and they'd stock a party for as little as twelve dollars. The people in charge would then sell portions of the food to guests for fifty times the cost. The hosts would take in plenty early in the evening and by the time they were good and loaded they didn't care if the rest of the food was given away free—if there *was* any left. It got so some of these party hosts wound up keeping liquor on hand for sale all the time. That's how a lot of beer flats got started.

It got to be a big business. They would advertise a house-rent party for a month in advance and have circulars printed up and distributed around the neighborhood telling who would be playing and entertaining at the party, as well as plugging the eats. They even built up mailing lists to which they mailed regular announcements. During the twenties, the admission price went up to a dollar.

Piano players called these affairs jumps or shouts and we would get substitutes to play our regular jobs for us. It wasn't always easy to do this because a lot of the shouts were on a Saturday night and the bosses frowned on us getting off. We made a lot of them after our regular jobs were over for the night.

The regulars at these rent hops included the Lion, James P., Beetle Henderson, Corky Williams, Lippy Boyette, Fats, Duke, Claude Hopkins, Abba Labba, Cliff Jackson, and others.

At the peak of the house-party days in the late twenties, the Big Three, who were most in demand, were the Lion and Jimmy Johnson with our shadow Fats Waller. It got so we never stopped and we were up and down Fifth, Seventh, and Lenox all night long hitting the keys. We even had a booking agent—old Lippy. He'd say, "You boys wanna jump for ten or twenty?" This meant he had a couple of parties paying from ten to a double sawbuck each. On a single Saturday he'd book as many as three parties for us and we'd alternate between them.

On occasions these sessions would start early in the afternoon and keep going until far into the next day. When I saw one of these long hauls coming up I'd eat ten eggs and a couple of steaks to get in shape. In addition to our fee we would get all the liquor we could drink and since I was drinking raw brandy with no chaser in those days I made it a point to be sure my stomach had a good firm lining before taking on all the fire water.

There were, of course, some of the chitterling struts where a bunch of pianists would be in competition. Lippy was a great promoter and was always trying to steam up the guests to argue about who was the best. It sometimes got annoying, especially when you had your eyes on a good-looking chick, or wanted to take time out to get in the games they always had going in one or two of the back bedrooms. But you had to stay by the keyboard to hold your own reputation for being a fast pianist.

Sometimes we got carving battles going that would last for four or five hours. Here's how these bashes worked: the Lion would pound the keys for a mess of choruses and then shout to the next in line, "Well, all right, take it from there," and each tickler would take his turn, trying to improve on a melody.

There was actually more arguing going on between the listeners than there was jealousy between us. Hard cash was bet on the outcome and more than once they'd get ready to fight between them as to who had won.

We would embroider the melodies with our own original ideas and try to develop patterns that had more originality than those played before us. Sometimes it was just a question as to who could think up the most patterns within a given tune. It was pure improvisation.

You had to have your own individual style and be able to play in all the keys. In those days we could all copy each other's shouts by learning them by ear. Sometimes in order to keep the others from picking up too much of my stuff I'd perform in the hard keys, B major and E major.

I had my own attitude and way of working at the piano. My way was to get a cigar clenched between my teeth, my derby tilted back, knees crossed, and my back arched at a sharp angle against the back of the chair. I'd cuss at the keyboard and then caress it with endearing words; a pianist who growls, hums, and talks to the piano is a guy who is trying hard to create something for himself.

Pianists today don't mingle with each other enough and it

shows in their playing. They should get around, be on the scene, play it clean, be seen, be keen, and be over eighteen. If you went to bed in those fast days back in the twenties you were sure to miss something.

They would crowd a hundred or more people into a seven-room railroad flat and the walls would bulge—some of the parties spread to the halls and all over the building. All the furniture was stashed in another apartment except the chairs and beds. When there wasn't a crap game, or poker, going in the back bedroom, they'd use it for a place to rest up, or sleep off, or make love.

The rent party was the place to go to pick up on all the latest jokes, jive, and uptown news. You would see all kinds of people making the party scene: formally dressed society folks from downtown, policemen, painters, carpenters, mechanics, truckmen in their workingmen's clothes, gamblers, lesbians, and entertainers of all kinds. The parties were recommended to newly arrived single gals as the place to go to get acquainted.

Everybody was always in the best of humor—the eggnog bowl would get as many as twelve pints of whisky poured into it in an hour. Strangely there were very few fights; if one broke out there were tush hogs—rough-nut bouncers—on hand to keep it orderly. Many of the women in charge were capable of crowning an offender with an iron pot if it looked like trouble was brewing.

There were different types of parties that drew their own special class of people. Some of the dicty ones liked to have a subdued type of music so the guests could carry on romantic conversations. Sometimes a well-known comedian would give impersonations of famous personalities, or an opera singer would give out with arias, or poetry would be read.

Of course, there were also parties where there was such a racket all night long that the neighbors called the cops to quiet the joint down, and these would usually end with the law having a ball for themselves.

At some of the struts there was a lot of marijuana smoking, but you would never see the real dope being used like it is to-day. The big dope amongst musicians was years later in mid-town when Fifty-second Street was the place.

The best time of all at these parties came early in the morn-ing. Then we'd play in a slow-drag style with the drummer muf-fling his hides and stroking the snare lightly and politely with the brushes. Sometimes we would doctor the piano by placing newspapers behind the hammers and put tin on the felts in order to get an old-fashioned player-piano effect. This also gave us a guitar sound.

During these early hours close to dawn the dancers would grab each other tightly and do the monkey hunch or bo-hog.* Their shuffling feet would give everything a weird rhythmic atmosphere. The lights would be dimmed down and the people would call out to the piano player, "Play it, oh, play it" or "Break it down" or "Get in the gully and give us the ever-lovin' stomp."

Those were happy days. We still play a benefit now and then, and even an occasional house-rent party, but it is nothing like it used to be. The younger folks can dance to their rock 'n' roll and bebop, using the juke boxes, radios, or phonographs. It has been hard on live music for many years.

I've got a lot of pictures on the wall in my apartment down in the valley, where I do my practicing, teaching, composing, and relaxing. The memories all come back every time I look up at Fats, Jimmy P., Sidney Bechet, and all the others that are now gone. I get music on my mind from the past and have to pick up the phone to call Luckey Roberts to reminisce about those good old times when there was good music in the air and the good times were rolling.

* A dance where the male would squat down on his knees and come up shak-ing—then grab his partner and freeze.

15

The Lion Roars and Breaks Down the Door

I was born in the night;
Everything that happens to me,
Happens in the night.

WILLIE THE LION SMITH

Talk about Fifty-second Street—that wasn't the first swing alley. 133rd Street was IT. Things were swinging to beat all hell on 133rd between Lenox and Seventh avenues in the mid-twenties. They called it "jungle alley" back in those days and it was only two blocks from the place where late in the afternoon you could find all the big-time musicians gathered around the Tree of Hope. As soon as it was dark, the cellar joints started to open up for a long night which sometimes extended to noon of the following day.

It must have been the busiest street in the world. There were fourteen different cafés, at least. In that one block you had The Nest, Mel Frazier's small club where Luis Russell had the band; Tillie's Chicken Shack with Bob Howard playing the piano; an after-hours spot run by a three-hundred-pound char-

acter named Basement Brown and his pal "Gulfport" (you had
to knock three times and blow your nose to get inside; during
Prohibition, every place had its passwords and signals) both
ex-vaudevillian opium smokers; Mexico's, run by a fellow named
Gomez who was from one of the Carolinas and had never seen
Mexico; Harry Hansberry's The Clam House where Gladys
Bentley sang songs with lyrics like her famous "My Subway
Man" that couldn't be sent through the mails; and a short block
further uptown the first Rhythm Club was located in the base-
ment of the building next door to the Lafayette Theater.

OPEN DOOR AT THE RHYTHM CLUB

The Rhythm Club was a hanging-out place for musicians
around 1924 and 1925. They served food for reasonable prices
and jazz men could come in at any time and play whatever
they wanted without bothering with the usual singers or floor
shows. It became the place where young musicians would go to
learn and to be heard. Many jazz figures were first heard at the
Rhythm Club and leaders like Henderson, Ellington, Elmer
Snowden, and Charlie Johnson would go there to hire their
sidemen.

Usually the big action didn't start until 3 A.M., because that
was when all the guys playing in the commercial bands got off.
They had a house band hired to work the four hours between
3:30 and 7:30 A.M., but many times they were kept going well
into the new day.

After I closed at the Capitol Palace, I went over and joined
the Rhythm Club's house band. The leader at the time was
Sidney Bechet from New Orleans, playing clarinet. Young Louis
Metcalf from St. Louis came in on cornet. My old friend Tommy
Benford was on drums.

We'd start out and we needed no one to say "Go, man" because the place was soon filled up with guys getting out their horns or lining up to get at the piano. Just to give you an idea of what took place, let me name off the men who were always on the scene:

On one visit, you could hear playing, one after the other, the Lion, Luckey Roberts, Fats, James P., and Duke, all working on individual interpretations of some popular tune of the day, like "Tea for Two." There were cornet players like Metcalf, Johnny Dunn, June Clark, Harry Smith, Joe Smith, Rex Stewart, Louis Armstrong (he was in New York with the Fletcher Henderson band), Sidney De Paris, Bobby Stark, Bubber Miley, and anybody else you ever heard of in those times.

Trombone players were almost as thick as horn men: Jimmy Harrison, Tricky Sam Nanton, Big Charlie Green, Jonas Walker, Jake Frazier, Harry (Father) White, are the ones I can still recall.

In another line would be the reed men, the clarinetists and saxophonists—Coleman Hawkins, Buster Bailey, Andy Brown, and even the dean of them all—Wilbur Sweatman, who had his own band and had traveled in vaudeville for many years playing three clarinets at the same time. One of the young reed players was a seventeen-year-old kid from up near Boston named Cornelius Hodges. In later years, he became one of the greatest alto saxophonists of all time, Johnny Hodges, still a star in Ellington's orchestra, after a career of over thirty years. He idolized Bechet and in those days he played a soprano saxophone.

When Bechet went to Europe in 1925, I took over the leadership of the band and hired Hodges in Sidney's place. Everybody took solos at those sessions; there was very little ensemble playing and a man had to be good with his instrument to hold his own.

It was the Lion's policy to give the yearlings tips on how to make it in show business. I used to tell them to learn to sing and dance. They could starve if they depended too much on

just being a good instrumentalist. A lot of them that have tried
to be leaders through the years should have paid more attention to the Lion.

As time went on, the club became a hangout for all entertainers. You could find Bill Robinson playing cards there every
afternoon when he was in town. I guess the musicians wanted
to be alone more, because late in the twenties, the Rhythm Club
guys moved over to 133rd Street in a room back of the Nest
Club and the old place was renamed the Hoofers' Club.

It was my decision to stay and I had a good four-piece band
at the Hoofers' for some months. Hodges had joined Chick
Webb's band and so I got young Benny Carter to join me with
his C-melody saxophone. Carter has done fine through the
years and is now one of the best arrangers in the business. Recently, he made all the arrangements and organized an orchestra to accompany Peggy Lee on her personal appearances.
Through the years Carter has also become noted for playing
both a great trumpet and a great alto. But back when he was
with me, he was just a fair C-melody player.

It was kind of a relief not to have all that jamming going on.
Our little band included Bernard Addison on guitar and Dewey
Beasley on drums, and it began to get a little swing of its own.
With all that freewheeling at the Rhythm Club, things sometimes got disorganized. I used to have to holler at some of them
to get in the right keys or put their horns up. That little quartet
at the Hoofers' turned out to be one of the best little bands I
ever had. It is always hard to get a band sounding right. There
is always one man who upsets things by trying to be a big-time
star himself, or a guy who rides along for the ride without pulling his weight. Or, as frequently happens, you have to contend
with both in one group.

It was around this time that I started composing. Clarence
Williams, another one of the New Orleans natives then living
in New York, had a publishing company. He was always looking
for tunes to push and he encouraged all of us to give him what-

ever we came up with. He would guarantee to print up the sheet music and get the number recorded.

My first original composition was called "Keep Your Temper," and on November 5, 1925, Williams set it up for a recording on the old Columbia label. We had a good band with the Lion's piano, June Clark's cornet, Jimmy Harrison's trombone, Buster Bailey's clarinet, Buddy Christian on guitar, Bill Benford on bass, and Jazz Carson playing drums. They called us the "Gulf Coast Seven," for no other reason than Williams came from down around the Gulf of Mexico. First we did a tune by Clarence called "Santa Claus Blues" and then we bore down on "Keep Your Temper." The sides came out and I don't remember ever getting a chance to hear them. I recall damn well I didn't see any other money besides the regular recording fee at that period. Such things as royalties were unknown in those days for jazz men.

By the mid-twenties, New York City was getting jazz-band-minded. The old days when a cabaret had a piano man and a raft of girl singers were over. Every hole in the wall featured a jazz band of some kind. There was a lot of exchanging of musical ideas and by that time there was no question but that the headquarters for jazz in America had shifted from New Orleans and Chicago to Harlem. Jobs for jazz musicians were getting more plentiful and things were set to jump uptown, until the Depression put the clampers on in the mid-thirties. But before that, in 1927, the Lion got a chance to appear on Broadway in the legitimate theater.

"FOUR WALLS" ON BROADWAY

Many musicians can brag that they played on the Gay White Way. They were the leaders and the sidemen in vaudeville or members of the bands playing in the theater pits or cabarets.

The Lion was in the legitimate drama, which is considered to
be the real Broadway scene.

John Golden, the producer and owner of a playhouse on
Fifty-eighth Street, signed me for a part in a three-act drama
called *Four Walls*. It was written by Dana Burnet and George
Abbott. The story was about a young Jewish hood who returns
home from Sing Sing and tries to go straight. He gets thwarted
by a woman. Man, ain't it the truth!

For the leading part in the play, the ex-con, they got a young
fellow from the Yiddish Art Theater down on Second Avenue
by the name of Muni Weisenfreund. This was his first appearance on Broadway. One of the minor parts in the play was
handled by another young man, named Lee Strasberg. He's the
man who heads The Actors' Studio today. Weisenfreund—or
Paul Muni—played the part of a guy named Benny Horowitz,
the leader of a gashouse gang, who has just returned to his old
neighborhood after doing a five-year stretch up the river. He
is determined to remain free, both in body and in spirit, for the
rest of his life. It is his vow that he will never again belong to
any gang, or to any woman.

It turns out to be the woman part that eventually goofs him
up. He can't get away from his old girl friend. She gets him
involved with an accidental killing. He can keep himself out
of the old gang, but the broad really louses him up. This very
dramatic situation was played to the hilt by Muni and as a
result he made it as a big-time star. The climax comes when
Benny (Muni) decides not to try to lie himself out of the mess,
but to turn himself over to the cops.

Where yours truly came in was during Act Two. They have a
street dance out in front of Tom's Cafe and there were four
musicians playing for the dancing. The list of characters called
us "the first musician, second musician, third musician, and
fourth musician." Of course, William Smith, piano, was the first.
Then came a fellow named Harold Potter, saxophone; Steve
Jones, guitar; and a drummer by the name of Percy Arnold

from Boston. Since Potter was white, we had one of the first mixed bands to play together on any stage.

I learned a lot from that show. Strasberg only had a few lines, but what he said meant something. One line can mean as much as fifty lines if you say it important.

You can also learn from such people how to become a real performer. I had always sung, danced, and talked. Every individual has a depth of drama in his soul, but they can only get it out by watching great artists. It kind of rubs off on you. Bert Williams always said, "Life is a drama and we all have to learn how to play it." Performers today go around with their hands in their pockets. These are not real performers. A real one knows what to do with his hands. Like a ballet dancer uses her legs, her neck, and her head. And you've got to be an emotional character to become noticed.

I remember Muni doing a scene. The director, Abbott, interrupted him at one point. Muni was the nicest man, but he said: "You watch the box office and I'll do the acting." He had a quick tongue. All actors do. (I mean actors, I don't mean guys who sprout up by night.)

Our part in the action lasted from 9:30 to 10 P.M. every night and so I was able to keep up roaming around the Harlem joints after the show. All four of us wore derbies throughout our time on stage. During the second act, we played six tunes —"At Sundown," "Hallelujah," "It All Depends On You," "Magnolia," "Broken Hearted," and a fast chorus of "Poor Butterfly" in the key of A major.

While we are playing outside the bar we hear that a rival gang from the neighborhood is going to attack the dancers, all of whom are former gang associates of Benny's. This rumor brings on the action for our big scene that lasts for ten minutes.

Our quartet, which had been playing off stage, is brought into the barroom for a drink by one of the gang members. He says, "These are scared coons. Let's give them a drink." The gangster was supposed to think that we wouldn't play any more because we were all too scared about the coming fight in the street. In another place, one of the hoods refers to us as "black rats." The present-day National Association for the Advancement of Colored People would object like hell to that kind of dialogue, but this was back in 1927.

The Lion handled the one speaking line the musicians had. With my cigar clenched between my teeth, I said: "I'd rather be full of hop than full of lead."

The director, Abbott, was a good scout. He would sometimes furnish a quart of brandy for us to drink at the bar onstage; other times they used weak tea. It was his feeling that the real thing would help us to do our parts with feeling. No one in the audience ever knew we were imbibing of the McCoy right in front of everybody.

Our show opened on September 19, 1927, and ran for 144 performances at the John Golden Theater. When they took the show to Chicago (where it had a long run), the Lion gracefully bowed out. It was my preference to stay right in New York where everything was happening. Leaving the play caused me to lose the chance to appear in the movie version that was later filmed with Muni.

The main thing that I gained from the experience was a long friendship with him. In later years I took my mother to see Paul Muni in another play at the Broad Theater in Newark. After the show, I took her backstage to meet the great actor in person. She said: "I loved your play very much. It took my son Willie to get me down here, although his grandfather and grandmother were great performers. I hope he'll bring me again." To me, she said, "Son, you were wonderful." I had taken her in a cab; she had little feet, only wore a size three-and-a-half shoe.

It was the first and last time my mother ever went inside a theater.

16

With My Cubs at Pod's & Jerry's

. . . *Pod's & Jerry's, I felt this tiny joint,*
with its dim lighting, its small bar at one end of the room,
its sprinkling of red-and-white checkered tables,
was what I had been looking for.
Mainly, it was the music, for it was the Lion,
who dominated the joint with his piano playing.[*]

ARTIE SHAW[*]

When Jerry Preston, manager of the Orient, and later the Royal Garden, finally got his own place, the Lion agreed to help him get it started. I went in for a couple of weeks and ended up hibernating there for over two years. It was every night from midnight till seven in the morning.

It was a basement speak[†] with one room holding about seventy people at twenty-five tables and another thirty or so standing up or sitting down in the hallways. Officially, the place was called the Catagonia Club, but it became known as Pod's &

[*] From *The Trouble with Cinderella* by Artie Shaw, published by Farrar, Straus & Co., Inc., 1952.
[†] 168 West 133rd Street.

Jerry's. In Prohibition times it wasn't exactly smart to advertise with neon signs and most of the customers didn't know the joint as the Catagonia. They knew the two owners and it got to be their habit to refer to the dive with their names.

The two partners were both good fellows. Charles Hollingsworth, nicknamed "Pod" while in the Navy (he was a jovial, sweet-natured man who always said "Pod-ner"), was originally from Atlantic City. Jeremiah Preston, a fast liver and gambler, was known downtown as West Indian Jerry, because he came from there somewhere. Both of these men are gone now. Preston went down from throat cancer in 1952, and Pod was killed in 1956 when a truck ran him down, dragging him for a couple of blocks along St. Nicholas Avenue.

I worked on an old upright piano with yellow-chipped keys. The entrance door was decorated to make it look like you were going into a log cabin. Later, when Prohibition was repealed, it was called The Log Cabin. It was then that Lady Day (Billie Holiday) got her try out as a dancer and by accident wound up as a singer for Jerry Preston.

Yeah, the piano had the right kind of vibrations. Mink coats used to wind up on top of it; there was barely room for the small bar at one end and they couldn't waste space on a checkroom.

Everything at Pod's & Jerry's cost a dollar, until the place finally got overloaded with funky butts‡ and Jerry slapped on a cover charge. For that buck you could get a bottle of Madden's No. 1 Beer, or a Top and Bottom—that gin and wine drink—and an order of fried, boiled, or roasted chicken; hog maws and red beans; or just plain old ham and eggs.

I accompanied the three entertainers as well as playing long sets of solo piano. We usually had one girl, who specialized in high-class singing, like Mary Stafford or Mattie Hite, both showstoppers who came on like mocking birds. Our other girl would

‡ Squares from downtown.

be able to sing and dance, but where she was really good was in doing the ups. The third entertainer was "Little Jazzbo" Hilliard, a dark, humpbacked fellow, four feet tall. He was a fairy but you could hear his baritone voice a block away.

For a short time we had the delightful Mary Straine, a beautiful, light-complexioned gal, who tried out for the *Ziegfeld Follies of 1928*. Mr. Ziegfeld wanted her for a pony-girl spot in the chorus but it turned out she was too big. She was a fine-built girl, dressed like nobody's business, but she lost her great opportunity. If it had worked out, she would have been one of the first Negro girls to work in a white show as a regular in the chorus. They featured Negro girls, but they didn't use them as regular parts of the show. Several years earlier, the great Florence Mills had been a featured act with the *Greenwich Village Follies* and years before that Bert Williams had been a star of the *Ziegfeld Follies*, but those were treated as special cases. (The same thing happened later in the band business during the swing days. Lionel Hampton and Teddy Wilson traveled with the Benny Goodman band as featured attractions, but didn't really play in the band proper. But you have to give Ziegfeld and Goodman credit for being the first ones to give our people a chance to show their talents.)

There were times when we had sitting-in, but the Lion discouraged it at first so the place wouldn't turn into another Rhythm Club. To sit-in with me they had to be able to run chords or, in other words, play in all the keys. I wanted men who could transpose, memorize, and improvise. A good minister or lecturer doesn't have to use The Book—a good one can make it up as he goes along. If you want to hear improvising, get to a Baptist minister, a priest, or a rabbi.

THE SHAW CLARINET

When Sidney Bechet came back from Europe he used to come down and join in on soprano sax. At the time I had Arthur (Traps) McIntyre working with me on drums. And for several months a handsome young man named Shaw would bring his clarinet in every night and play along. He had just arrived in New York and was having a dickens of a time getting organized in music. Shaw was waiting out his New York union (802) membership card—a man who wants in can't take a steady job until he's been in town for six months—and so he came in to play with the Lion every night for free.

My boy Artie was a good student and the Lion was proud of him when we went out to jam after finishing our nightly stint at P.'s & J.'s. He wrote about our association in his autobiography: "Playing with the Lion was a brand-new kind of musical experience . . . and I would do my best to get with it, until after a while I began to get the drift, to latch on to what he was doing to the point where I could have some general predictability of where we would end up."

We would visit Basement Brownie's or Goldgraben's blind pig. Sometimes we both played in these places until both of us felt as though we couldn't stay awake another minute. One morning at Goldgraben's, a place where they had a tile floor and booths along the side, Pops Bechet, who was particular about clarinet players, came up to ask about Shaw. "Lion, who is the musicianer?"

"Artie Shaw," I said.

"He is a good blues man."

I said he was.

Artie used to encourage me to get my tunes written down and published. While at P.'s & J.'s I started to compose in earnest. At that time I wrote "The Stuff is Here and It's Mellow." Later when Artie had his first band, he recorded some of my numbers. He featured the introduction to my tune "Music on My Mind" under a new title, "I've Got the Misery."

Things started out slow, but it didn't take long before we had more customers than we could use. At first there were nights when I had to play by candlelight because Jerry hadn't gotten around to paying the electric bill. But by the time I had two years of P.'s & J.'s, I had acquired a 30 per cent interest in the place, a salary of $350 a week, and tips sometimes as much as $100.

Yeah, the Lion was making so much money he'd let other piano players take over for him now. Guys like Willie Gant, Gerald (Corky) Williams, Bill Basie, and one of the greatest pianists of all time named Paul Seminole—a half-Indian, half-Negro lad—who originally came from Philadelphia, Pennsylvania, and died in 1932. He had a great left hand in more ways than one—he could play the piano with his right hand as he picked his guitar with his left hand. When he worked with Luckey Roberts in vaudeville and Roberts' society bands, he was featured on the xylophone. Seminole was one of those great all-round musicians who died before he got a chance to record and leave his work for posterity.

It got so that there were so many piano cats wanting to sit-in that I could go home, and change clothes a couple of times a night. Man, I really had myself a good supply of duds in those days. I favored English cuts and I must have had twenty-seven suits hanging in my closet from which to choose and each drape had fancy shoes, ties, and silk shirts to match. Those were the days when every sharp guy carried around a bankroll of at least a thousand dollars in his pocket. You didn't have to worry so much back then about muggers and holdup artists. Instead of fights on the street corners after the cabarets closed, there would be people dancing the Charleston.

GOOD GUESTS

The customers at P.'s & J.'s varied from tush hogs up to the biggest names on Broadway. They kept good order, like they did in all the Harlem places, and if a guy got too much Prohibition poison one of the bouncers (they were *big* tush hogs) would waltz him right on out to the sidewalk. Or if a guy got fresh with another man's chick they would just miss him for a while.

The biggest kicks I got during this period was when the musicians from downtown started to stop in. I remember Bix Beiderbecke, when he was in town with Jean Goldkette or Paul Whiteman, coming up in the middle of winter without an overcoat. He always carried his own bottle of gin to keep warm. His custom was to sit on the floor next to the piano and when he took a drink out of his bottle he would always offer the Lion a taste. That Bix was a real nice boy and a wonderful trumpet player until the wild life hurried him away.

Hoagy Carmichael was a frequent visitor when he was a bank clerk trying to write a few songs. The boys from The Mound City Blues Blowers—Red McKenzie, Jack Bland, Eddie Condon, Josh Billings—spent a lot of time uptown when they were in off the vaudeville circuits.

After Artie Shaw got a job downtown playing in the radio studios, he would still come up for a chat and bring pianist Claude Thornhill along to dig the Lion.

Oh, there were a lot of them, destined to make big names for themselves. Things would really get crowded when the boys from Ben Pollock's band at the Park Central Hotel showed up early in the morning. Guys like Jack Teagarden and Benny Goodman. Goodman met the test one night when he played "I

Got Rhythm" to my accompaniment in the key of E major—I got him into a tough key just for the hell of it.

I could go on and on about the famous musicians—both the Dorseys made it a regular uptown stop at P.'s & J.'s; tenor saxophonist Bud Freeman, who always asked me, "Am I playing well?" Bandleader Freddie Rich and drummer George Wettling became my good friends and listeners. There was a lot of action across the street at The Nest. The entertainer and ex-bandleader Phil Harris used to like to sit-in on drums at The Nest and used to like to have me playing the box. The two of us used to go out and drink it up after dawn. Howard Dietz and Arthur Schwartz worked on the shows they were scoring by writing all over P.'s & J.'s tablecloths while listening to me at the piano. We found uptown that the bigger the men, the nicer they were—this applied to Mayor Jimmy Walker, the man who was going to be mayor Fiorello La Guardia, and Governor Al Smith.

Folks from show business downtown were always looking around in Harlem for ideas they could use: Texas Guinan used to come up to see how things were run at P.'s & J.'s; James Barton, who rose from burlesque to the Broadway drama in *Tobacco Road,* became a good friend of the Lion's; Mae West used to stop by with Johnny Carey, a partner with Mel Frazier in The Nest; and a long list of other names come to mind —Ella Logan, Frank Fay, George Abbott, Eddie Dowling (my pal from the Chicago days), Tallulah Bankhead, Martha Raye, Helen Morgan, ladies' man Harry Richman, Lucille Le Sueur, who gave up a classy name to become Joan Crawford, Belle Baker, Bee Palmer, Beatrice Lillie, and William Powell.

It was like that all over Harlem, especially at the Cotton Club on Lenox Avenue. Georgie Raft was a sharpie in those days and about the best dancer in New York. When he showed up at the Cotton women used to ask the headwaiter to ask Raft if he would dance with them to the hot music.

As always, we had a good share of the prize-fighting boys,

because Jerry Preston was a well-known sport and gambler. I recall both Jack Dempsey and Gene Tunney dropping by—this was the time they were battling for the heavyweight crown. Max Baer from Germany came up once in awhile with Texas Guinan.

Some nights before it was time for me to report for work at P.'s & J.'s—the Lion came on at midnight—I'd go down to Times Square to catch the first show at the Kentucky Club, where Duke Ellington was leading his eight-piece band. Two of my good drinking companions were still in the group—Sonny Greer on drums and saxophonist Otto Hardwick. It was another basement joint like the clubs uptown and the bandstand was up under the sidewalk in a corner. The bandsmen had to walk up three stone steps to get on the stand. Their dressing rooms were like "the Black Hole of Calcutta." It has always been the same: operators will spend thousands of dollars to decorate a cabaret and then forget all about the people who work in the place every night. Uptown—downtown, or all over the country, they offer you dressing rooms and bandstands that are a disgrace.

The stand there at the Kentucky only held six men and Duke had to play piano and direct from the dance floor. If you worked up on the deck long enough, you wound up with hunched shoulders for good because the stand was about five-and-a-half feet from the glass grill up in the sidewalk.

Once Duke said to me: "You ever heard an Irish woman sing "Eli, Eli"?

"No."

"You're going to hear it."

I've forgotten her name, but she was Irish and I could never figure the tongue she was singing the number in, because it sure wasn't Hebrew. She would sing "Eli, Eli" (O Lord, why hast thou forsaken me?), but I got in a fight with her because I told her she shouldn't be singing the song if she didn't know what the words meant. I talked Jewish to her but she didn't understand a thing. But being Irish, she had a soul. Also auburn hair and big green eyes.

One New Year's Eve, there was a big party for Ellington and his band at Mexico's after working hours. Around dawn, the buzzer sounded. In rushed the racket squad, knocking down the doors with their axes. (They were the only authorities in New York who were allowed to break up a joint with axes.) All the places on 133rd Street had open-air gardens in the rear and these really came in handy on occasion. As the cops came crashing in, I made it up to the patio and up a tree in the small, fenced-in back yard. I'd no sooner gotten settled in nothing flat when another piano player by the name of Mike Jackson was pulling on my leg, whispering for me to make room. We'd just gotten settled when the cops came out and flashed their lights all over the place. Luckily, we were up so high the lights missed us. Mexico must have gotten behind in protection payments because raids like this didn't happen very often.

It was rumored that there was a tip-off. The tipster later changed his name and today has one of the most famous restaurants in Hollywood.

Well, a short time after Mexico's was raided, we had the same thing happen at Pod's & Jerry's. We always wondered if the same tipster was in on that. Of course, everyone knew that there was booze in every basement on the street in those days. The doorman at The Nest was assigned to handle the Prohibition police. He was a noted sweet talker and con artist. Also, those agents never roamed around alone uptown and they would usually give themselves away by their numbers. Ordinarily, they would no sooner get into one place before The Nest's doorman had every other place alerted. Somehow, the Lion got vibrations about coming trouble a few nights before our big raid. Both Pod and Jerry were going to see the Dempsey-Tunney fight in Philadelphia. I told them they'd better not go as I smelled something was not right.

Sure enough, on the night of the fight, with both bosses down in Philly, a platoon of cops rushed in and started making a shambles of the place with their little hatchets. The Lion got out of the way again through the garden in the back. That raiding party even had one colored cop.

When the bosses got back from the fight the next day, they started another one. They really raised a stink with the "protection boys" because all the payoffs had been made. Our bartender, Craig, had offered the cops all a drink after they crashed in. But he wound up in jail overnight for his trouble. It was all straightened out, and Craig was back behind the bar the next night.

And it was while working at Pod's & Jerry's that I hit a nice piece of good fortune.

WILLIE'S NUMBER COMES UP

We had three big-money rackets up in Harlem since way before the Lion moved to the section after World War I. A lot of cash was—and is—taken from people who can't afford it by the numbers game, phony preachers like the late Daddy Grace, and the floating dice sessions.

A fellow named Casper Holstein, half-colored and half-Spanish, was running the policy game when I first came to Harlem. It was the same as in other businesses: the Negroes owned and controlled things to start, but they cheated each other, and outsiders moved in to take over.

I remember how it happened with the numbers. Around 1927, the notorious gangster Dutch Schultz had charge of a bunch of laundries uptown—that is, he furnished them protection. One of Holstein's busiest runners was a girl named Emma, who made frequent stops to collect and pay off the girls in the laundries. Schultz finally noticed and got the whole story from

Emma. It looked too good to pass up. Schultz managed to take the setup over and put his man Fred (Crackers) Buchanan in as the policy king of Harlem. From then on, the big money went to the same boys who were getting all the loot from the night-club operations like the Cotton Club.

The policy or numbers game is run by three kinds of operators. At the top you have the guys in charge of things at the headquarters or bank. They are called bankers or backers and they're the ones that make the big dough. Under them you have the guys known as controllers or collectors, who are responsible for certain neighborhoods to see that the money is collected and delivered to the bank, and finally you have the runners who pick up the individual plays and deliver the prize money.

People who play, select a combination of three numbers from 000 to 999. Pay-offs are made at the odds of five hundred or six hundred to one. If your bet was a penny, you'd get back five dollars if you had a winning combination.

Over the years, the source for winning numbers has been switched to horse-racing results published daily in the newspapers and announced over the radio. The winning combination is taken from the prices paid on certain races run at Aqueduct, Belmont Park, and other tracks around the country.

One way of determining the winning combination is as follows: Suppose the prices paid to win on the third, fifth, and seventh races are 45.50, 94.80, and 17.70, respectively. They take the first digit to the right of the decimal point in each price. You would then have my favorite combination—587. This was the number I played back in the Pod's & Jerry's days.

Another system for determining the winner is to take the totals from the pari-mutuel betting at a designated track. The first number is decided by the pay-off on the first three races, the second by the first six races, and the third by the total of the whole card of eight races.

The methods are changed from time to time. Whatever

method is used assures the hoods, who bank the business, against cheating on the part of the betters.

Yes sir, back in the late twenties, I always played good old 587 and put five dollars on it. I had a watch in pawn and 587 was the number on the ticket. A friend of mine wrote the numbers and there was hardly a day when I didn't have twenty or twenty-five dollars down. He asked one day whether I wanted 587 and I said I'd take it for five dollars.

"I'll be back later if you want any more," he said.

"No," I said. And it popped straight. 5-8-7.

That Saturday night, I didn't go to work. I got my watch out of pawn, left Pod's & Jerry's, and had the runner bring me the money at the apartment during the night. I wasn't taking any chance on having someone follow me home from P.'s & J.'s to clean out my pockets.

Winning is nice, but you've got to be plenty smart to get any of your cash back from those operators. They say that today there are as many as five hundred thousand people making bets from pennies on up to many dollars in the New York area alone. A recent newspaper article announced that the police raided and broke up a bank in East Harlem. It said the cops estimated the total play to be a hundred and twenty-five thousand dollars a day, or over thirty-five million dollars a year. And all that money comes from the poorest part of Harlem.

The name "Sharkey" is a cover for one of the biggest racketeers in New York City. When you bet with those boys, you might as well play against loaded dice. You don't have a chance in the world. Politicians know damn well there will always be gambling, so why don't they legalize it and let the folks win fair and square once in awhile? As it is today, all the cockroaches, polecats, and wildcats down on blood-and-thunder row—that's 125th Street—get all the hard-earned pennies.

The numbers craze has always been big uptown and in a way our people need something like it to put some excitement and hope into their lives. Poor people don't go too far wrong.

Whenever the ministers in Harlem churches announce the number of a hymn from the pulpit, half the congregation gets busy writing it down to play with the runners on Monday morning. It's the poor people who are lucky and the poor people who need the luck. Our most noted poet, Langston Hughes, who lives in Harlem, has called the numbers "the salvation of Harlem, its Medicare, its Black Draught, its 666, its little liver pills, its vitamins, its aspirins, and its analgesic balm all combined." The thing about numbers is that everyone can play, at anytime, any amount of money they can raise. Not everybody can throw away three dollars a ticket on the Irish Sweepstakes twice a year. The law of averages won't bring you a winner with a long, long shot like that.

Still, there is all sorts of crookedness going on today. Like when you hit one, it gets to be impossible to find the runner and collect. If too many people get the winning number, the bank is likely to just change the combination so it won't be hit too hard. And I have seen cases where a runner will swallow the slips (pieces of paper on which the numbers are written down) when a cop approaches him.

The way they've got the thing set up makes it hard to get your pay-off. The Lion has found you have to be sharp and alert to get treated right. You have to be a right guy and know enough to give a runner a good tip if you hit—although he automatically gets ten per cent of the amount won. They don't like to make pay-offs to cheap skates and squares.

It is always the same old story. A lot of would-be Christians and church people claim they are against gambling of any kind —for other people. They make so much noise about it that the politicians are afraid to legalize lotteries or off-track betting because they are afraid of losing votes. But they are also afraid of losing the graft and protection pay-offs.

Hell, I've seen the churches themselves running gambling booths to raise money. It's true the money won may be going for a good cause, but the poor man who loses his paycheck to the church has to go on relief just the same.

You just can't stop gambling. When it is against the law there are always certain people who will see to it that people can wager. But why buy Cadillacs for small-time hoods? In fact, up in Harlem, the runners don't bother with Cadillacs; they buy themselves Rolls-Royces because they're the nearest in size to a train.

Way back, the game was called "clearinghouse" because the winning number was taken from figures in the newspaper giving the amount of money spent for bonds by the government each day. I can remember my mother playing those clearing-house numbers in Newark.

Clearinghouse is a good name in more ways than one.

17

Silvertop

She's my ace in outer space,
With me she rates first place,
'Cause she's got good taste.

WILLIE THE LION SMITH

If you move me I'm as warm as fire, if you don't I'm as cold as the Atlantic Ocean. A man can know a thousand different women, but there will always be one who will know him better than all the rest. That's the one a man is forever looking for.

I found mine in a gal I call Silvertop, who knows exactly what to do for her man. She is an inspiration and reminds me of my mother mentally, physically, and spiritually. Jane has straightened and brightened my life for many years.

It all started back while I was at Pod's & Jerry's. Mrs. Jennie Williams came in one night with her husband. Mrs. Williams—or Jane—spotted the Lion in his silk shirt sleeves, battered derby over one eye, and a cigar butt clenched between his teeth. She said loud enough for me to hear, "Who's that nigger?" There's a way of using that word that does not offend us, especially when it comes from one of our own people, and that was the way she said it.

I was attracted right off the bat and started to lay some of my quieter and prettier tunes on her. She dug; soon she sent her husband over to the piano with five dollars for me to play a request. Before that night was over we were comparing notes and it turned out we had both been working in Atlantic City at the same time before the war. She was a waitress at the dicty Fitzgerald's when I was pounding the keys at Kelly's. I also learned that Jane's brother was married to the sister of my old friend Harry Souser, the Jersey City pianist, who had worked at McFarland's Hall.

Although I didn't realize back at that time of our first meeting that we would eventually be together, both Jane and her husband became close friends of mine and spent a lot of their time at P.'s & J.'s. Yes sir, meeting Silvertop was to become the turning point of my life and my days of living out of a trunk would come to an end on account of her.

The Lion has been around for a lifetime and has seen all the angles. There's an old saying, "That chick ain't walkin' no more." This means some sharpie has figured out what makes her tick and is able to keep her ticking.

It's not how good-looking a man is, but is he a guy who knows all the answers? He's the one who escorts the lady to the table and seats her properly; he won't give the other guy a chance to show his manners. When a sharpie winks, presses a button, and spreads the jive, the hip girls will surround him because they know their destination. They can tell whether or not they like a man before he even opens his mouth. They also know that the "Pardon me, have you a match?" routine, or the "Pardon me, haven't I seen you somewhere before?" approach are for the squares.

Believe me, working around night clubs and joints gives you a liberal education in the ways of the women. For example, I learned way back in Newark about hand grenades. It was said the guys on the make for some other fellow's wife or girl friend would throw her a grenade. This is how it worked: a guy would write a note to a gal he'd spotted and give it to the hat-check dame to pass on to the girl in charge of the ladies' room. The checkroom gal would point out the chick to the wash-room attendant and when the desired party went to the toilet she'd get the note telling her how to get in touch with the writer.

It got so guys watched the washroom door like a hawk. The original escorts would tell their lady friends not to tarry too long, while the hopeful ones would keep their eyes peeled for a signal from the girl when she came out.

In one joint I worked in during the early days the piano was placed right alongside the john and the guys would hang around me as if they were interested in the music. Sometimes they would buy me brandy to keep tabs on their broads. It was a laugh—one time they moved the three-card monte (shell) game close to the ladies' room so the players could watch the door to be sure the hat-check girl didn't go in with a note for their ever-lovin' gal while she was prettying herself up.

In all the places I worked they watched the piano player carefully because all the good pianists were ladies' men. The women always wondered if the piano man was as good in bed as he was on the keyboard. Playing music, fighting, and loving have all got to be done the same way to be any good. The way you feel while doing these things is what counts. You've got to put a lot of feeling into these activities to get favorable re-sults. In jazz today there is too much reading and not enough original feeling. The real artist thinks 75 per cent faster than other people.

The sharpies always went for the big gals, the well-built ones with the big bodies and the big breasts, because that's what forms that passion.

History gets made in the night clubs and cafés, anyplace where alcohol is present. It is there that one runs into all kinds —nags, fags, lesbians, pimps, and hustlers. As soon as a dame gets one drink, she wants to walk, just has to walk, and that's when the hawks start putting the eye on her. They comment. "Did you lamp that?" So, in order for a guy to be on Even Street, he has to be a constant companion to his doll and be able to give her all the answers. It's like Ethel Waters once said, doling out some advice to a guy, "Find out how they like it, when they want it, and how they want it—then give it to them and you'll have no trouble."

The hip guy walks his babe to the ladies' room and then waits for her to come out. Many a man has lost his wife or sweetheart by letting her stay in that ladies' room too long. There are always some chicks who'll steal their own sister's husband. You've just got to watch it.

When you've got the right woman, you're home free. I began to realize this after spending many years in the cabarets. Some of the women that showed up in the joints would go for anything with pants on and didn't care what was underneath. When they caused a ruckus, their pimps left them to straighten it out alone. If a pimp's woman insulted another one's gal, it was up to the two gals to iron out the situation while the pimps talked to each other like old friends.

Two of the most famous pimps in New York were regulars at Pod's & Jerry's. They were the two Charlestons I mentioned— Yellow and Black. Yellow Charleston doubled as a dope peddler working out of Barron Wilkins' place and he was also employed by the Owney Madden gangsters; when Madden decided to get rid of the Barron—as I said, it was little, tubercular Yellow Charleston who stabbed him to death one night as he was leaving his club. It wasn't hard for Yellow to do because he was always hopped-up on opium. He managed to die from tuberculosis before they got around to electrocuting him.

The other Charleston had a string of four or five women and always wore a five-hundred-dollar stickpin in his tie. All the girls in his stable were crazy about him and in spite of the many close calls he had—the chicks would get jealous and sometimes take after him with a cutter—Black Charleston lived to be eighty-three years old.

Yeah, both the Charlestons would just as soon kill you as look at you. And we also had regular visits from Chippie Mame, a good-looking yellow woman who used to come into Leroy's with her pimp known as Lovey Joe—another one whose real name was a well-kept secret.

So, you see, with characters like these around a lot, it was quite a treat to run into someone like Jane and her husband.

Through the years Silvertop has become my right arm and is the cause of me walking in the right direction. She calls me stinker because I'm a great thinker but we get along together just wonderfully. Both of us being Sagittarians means we fight like mad, but in the end everything always works out fine. What would I do without her?

I just wouldn't be here, that's all.

Nothing bothers a lady when she really loves a man, because a real man will sit down with his lady and tell her everything she needs to know. In order to get along with a woman, a man must talk to her about sex and life because that's where we all came from—the women! The great mistake the average man makes is that he doesn't converse with his soul mate. You've got to discuss the physical parts ahead of time to make her like you. There was once a phrase we used to have in the tenderloin, "Did you cop?" which meant, "Did you catch it?" When a guy said he had copped, it meant he had made the grade and his woman thought the world of him.

Jane and I are the same age. A man has got to be either a leader or a follower, and when he's married to a younger woman, especially a good-looking one, he has to always be on the alert. She'll spot a sharpie and remark, "There's a good-looking guy." That's when you've got to watch out. You're in trouble if a girl starts throwing her eyes around and he starts passing hand grenades.

A lot of men just don't know how to handle their women. A

woman can be good for a man, but if she's younger, she's liable to wear you down. The man gets weaker and the girl gets stronger as the years pass. So the Lion says, it's best to have someone your own age because the woman with the same number of years you have, is actually fifteen years younger in her actions.

Women outlive men, but men are stronger mentally. Usually a woman strengthens a man—they carry us—the Lord made them so they can carry. A smart man feeds his madam every day with knowledge. You talk to your wife for half an hour and she is strong as a lion.

Jennie Williams, my Jane, is a dynamic personality, able to do anything and do it better than a man. She is a first-class dressmaker by trade and at one time, shortly after she came to New York City from New Bedford, Massachusetts, she served as a seamstress in the Broadway theaters. Her first husband, who died in 1949, was connected with the railroad and banking interests. After her marriage she was the head of several social clubs and an expert bridge player. She is still a prominent leader in the Harlem community life.

Jane and I have been through a lot together over the years. To this day she drives me around in her seven-year-old Studebaker and looks after me all of the time. I have two places of residence—one up on the dicty shelf of St. Nicholas Avenue, where Jane's cooking keeps me in trim, and the other is in "The Valley" near the tenderloin on West 151st Street. My retreat down there in The Valley is a section that will change your complexion if you don't have the right connection.

Some years ago I wrote an ode dedicated to Silvertop entitled "Lament of the Lioness" because she has a good feeling for everybody and is good to all. Why, she even gives the decorators two quarts of whisky before they start to work on her apartment; its just to help them along with their work.

Willie the Lion, Pianist

BY GEORGE HOEFER

The status of Willie the Lion in modern American music defies easy categorization. Many so-called jazz originals are products of a single era or environment. The Lion has managed to assimilate and operate in different periods, amid many influences. He is a user, not a copier.

In jazz, we have had frequent examples of an artist who establishes a style of his own and thereupon makes it a lifetime presentation. This is encouraged by the audience, even though jazz itself is, or should be, unpredictably spontaneous and ever changing. Willie Smith, selecting, originating, "shifting gears" to move with his own ideas of melody and showmanship, has progressed and grown musically through the years.

In fact, there have been times during the Lion's close to fifty years in music when he has been avant-garde. Artie Shaw suggested as much when he wrote, "From a purely harmonic standpoint, he was far ahead of most of his contemporaries; for jazz in those days (1928), however rhythmically complicated it may have been, was fairly primitive harmonically."[1]

Willie demonstrates his perennial youth regularly. When taking Leonard Feather's "Blindfold Test" for Down Beat *in 1958, Smith described a Jelly Roll Morton record as old-fashioned and barbaric, while praising and admiring the work of Bud Powell and Dave Brubeck.[2] Yet in the jazz histories, Willie the Lion is always relegated to the Morton era alone.*

It has always been axiomatic for Willie that if music is to be of any importance, it has to give the listener something to appreciate and enjoy. He has no sympathy for musicians who create for each other. Art, to him, must communicate and to this end he has always given great emphasis to melody. As he says, "First I always demonstrate the melody because they've got to know what I'm playing; then I redecorate it with counterpoint."

Artie Shaw says that the Lion "had a talent for introducing a melody, a thread of a tune, and then sliding into complicated little modulatory phrases of his own, which always, somehow or other, managed to get back into the tonality of wherever they started from."

Unlike many jazz men, Smith never had one idol, a musician he looked up to or tried to emulate, nor was there any given style that he chose to conquer above all others. Willie Smith has wanted to do it his own way from the first time he began to play piano "by ear."

There was, of course, an over-all influence in barroom piano playing that had its roots somewhere in the classical ragtime that originated, it is said, in St. Louis around the turn of the century. This style had nearly run its course by the time Smith began in 1914. Already under way was a distinctive Eastern seaboard form of ragtime that would flower ultimately during the twenties as "Harlem Stride Piano." The melodic and harmonic structure of the stride form has been credited to Willie, Luckey Roberts, and above all others, James P. Johnson.

Along with their gaiety and sprightliness, clarity of form, and other attributes of classic ragtime, the Eastern striders added their own unique rhythmic accents and developments of syncopation. Their playing enriched jazz piano with new chordal commentaries, a looser phrasing, and the forceful striding passages that gave the style its name.

Smith, with his fluttering arpeggios from the right hand and his steady, unrelenting tenths from his left, contributed his share to the style. Yet it is not accurate to classify the Lion as a stride pianist alone. Again, to quote Shaw, "His style of piano playing was something altogether new to me. It was full of old-time idioms; authentic old-fashioned ragtime; but scattered throughout the ragtime were occasional incongruously modern, modulatory passages—these last all his own, for I have never heard anyone else play anything quite like them, with the exception of those who have since copied him and incorporated some of the Lion's little melodic tricks into their own style."[1]

The self-taught techniques made it possible for Willie to copy almost anything he heard. Even classical music, or perhaps especially classical music, seeped deliberately into his style. James P. said once that "—for fancy piano we would drop into someplace where the Lion was playing 'The Sheik of Araby,' using elaborate concert-style introductions based on Schubert's 'Marche Militaire.'"[3]

Early in his career, Smith used the boogie bass; a fillip said to have originated in the southwestern section of the country. The reader will recall Smith's references to Kitchen Tom in Atlantic City in 1914. His early fascination with the bass helped to inspire, right at the beginning, the possibilities for using both hands to maximum advantage. As he says, "too many young pianists leave their left hands home." It is also his belief that "The trouble with most piano players is that they don't play enough Bach. Bach develops the left hand." In reviewing "The Lion's Boogie," a Dot album, Guy Waterman writes descriptively that "Lion's boogiewoogie is novel, with the characteristic Harlem left-hand device of hitting the top note of the octave before the bottom note, reversing the usual order for boogiewoogie."[4] *This is still another example of the variations the Harlem pianists used when "redecorating" a tune.*

Willie Smith's moods are likely to fall into two general but separate categories. There is, on one hand, his feeling for the earthier connotations of jazz. As he puts it—"playing low, in the gutter, in the alley, low gravy." This mood seems naturally derived from his early years in saloons, "joints," and playing at rent parties. During the thirties, a more delicate and fragile Lion emerged. This was the period during which he composed a series of Debussy- or Ravel-like melodies, tunes that have been considered unique in the literature of jazz. Even the titles, "Echo of Spring," "Morning Air," "Fading Star," bring to mind an artist with a much more subtle finesse than the growling Lion of the twenties and earlier.

Hugues Panassié, the French jazz critic and long-time admirer of Smith, wrote of his Commodore album of original compositions (FL 30,003—The Lion of the Piano) in 1939, "Here we have one of the most original of pianists. His playing is entirely different from that of others, with an extraordinary mixture in it of power and delicacy. Although he can play very forcefully, with basses of terrifying strength, he constantly reveals a delicately charming melodic talent, deliciously fresh and full of moving sensitivity."[5]

Part of the credit for the appearance of the melodic and musically more formal Lion can be attributed to his years of study with Hans Steinke, an elderly German music professor in New York, who tutored Willie in theory, counterpoint, and harmony. The years with Steinke, during the thirties and forties, were the only regular formal study in Smith's long career. He went to the German teacher at the suggestion of Clarence Williams, the first publisher of Smith's music. The combination of playing by ear, what he picked up in informal exchange with vaudeville pianist Arthur Eck, and the years in the clubs and with Steinke, have helped him to become a composer of much origi-

nality. Not constrained to follow any iron-clad rules of order, his solos are not merely improvised, they are carefully worked out, with intelligent attention to harmony, counterpoint, and form. Yet he accomplishes this without losing the freshness and spontaneity that are essential to jazz music. The resultant music is both vigorous and subtle and makes no concessions to vulgarity and no studied appeal to commercialism.

Panassié wrote further, "More than most musicians, the Lion bases his style on harmonic innovations of a brisk, sprightly sort."⁵ These innovations continue to amaze the technically accomplished modern-day pianist. Some of those closely identified with the progressive piano of the fifties and sixties have been heard to remark, upon hearing the Lion, "Hey, Dad— listen to the modern chords this guy makes!" The Lion says, in response, "They talk about augmented chords, ninth chords, whole-tone progressions and all that. I've been using them for years but I didn't know what they were." Billy Strayhorn, a composer and arranger of note, said after listening that "Lion's style is a strange mixture of counterpoint, chromatic harmony, and arabesquelike figures as refreshing to the ear as spring water to the lips." This talent of Smith's to play things because "they sound good" is somewhere close to the essence of jazz music, even if uncommon.

There is considerable evidence that Smith's piano had a great deal of influence on many who heard him. Some of the Lion is discernible in Ellington's early composition, "Black Beauty" (1928). Duke has been quoted frequently about the impact of Smith's playing. As he said, "It was a middle tempo, just like a belly laugh, hah-hah-hah-hah."⁶ In 1939, Ellington composed and recorded his tribute to the Lion's middle tempo and that deep belly laugh. It was called "Portrait of the Lion" and Smith returned the compliment with his recorded (1957) but still unpublished "Portrait of the Duke." In reviewing the record, critic Martin Williams said of the Lion's "bread and butter" accolade, that "'Portrait' is an excellent example of adapting ma-

terials in tribute to another without copying them. . . . The Lion is the most harmonically interesting of the 'Harlem school' to my way of thinking."[7]

In his "Latin" composition, "Tango la Caprice," Smith shows that the Spanish influence on jazz, or at least its tinge, was not confined to the effects it had on Jelly Roll Morton. When the Lion performs the work of other composers, he usually embellishes them with his own interpretations.

"The musician never masters music," Willie says, "but learns something new every day." He is still progressing and learning. He practices longer hours today than he did back in the time when there were more demands on him. His piano, a fifty-year-old instrument made by Jacob Doll in Germany, is kept in tune and ready in his hideaway on West 151st Street. Daily exercises keep his muscles loose for his program of twice-weekly practice sessions. He feels that setting up a rigid daily schedule is likely to make him overtaxed and overtense. Hence he plays and composes when the mood controls him, rather than adhering to a routine that might take him to the piano when he isn't, as he says, old-fashioned for once, "in the groove."

Waterman's review of Smith's long-playing record, "The Lion Roars," gave the pianist and composer a generous but accurate tribute when he wrote: "There are rare musicians who seem constitutionally unable to sound a note without it coming alive. The Lion has this quality."[4] Because he has always been so alive.

18

The Lion Goes Downtown

Don't worry about the Lion,
He is always on time, feels fine, and stays in line.
And will be riding in a Rolls-Royce,
When the others are trying to hop a freight train.

WILLIE THE LION SMITH

After taking a rest for myself after the numbers hit, I heard that John De Luca wanted to see me downtown at his place in Greenwich Village for a conference. I don't remember the name of the joint, or if it had a name, but it was a pay-off dive in the basement at 189 Spring Street. The De Luca Brothers, John and Duke, had charge of the beer trucks operating down in the Italian section of the 40th Ward.

The Lion paid them a visit and agreed to help out because I needed a change of scenery. The job at De Luca's was easy and I enjoyed it. We had a trio and only had to work when we felt like it. The three bosses, Johnny Finelli and the two De Lucas were good guys to work for. The mobsters might drop in from time to time to make their pay-offs from the protection money they got covering the various rackets, but it went quietly. The bosses liked to have a little music to entertain their guests while they did business.

Before they got around to repealing Prohibition, I worked in two spots in the Village run by Jules Podell, the guy who runs the Copacabana in the East Sixties now.

The sharpest and most fancy speak I ever played in was a place called the Club Napoleon, in an old mansion on West Fifty-sixth Street, once owned by the Woolworth family. It was really fixed up. They used all three floors of the house, each one with velvet carpeting and looking glasses on the wall, and with a big revolving bar on the first floor. Owney Madden and Big Frenchy were back of it. They had everything going for them. There was a garden in the back where they played soft-ball or, if you preferred, tennis, and on one of the floors there were a lot of ping-pong tables. Man, people lived high in those days. Every place was like a country club.

They had a lot of singers around the place and I recall one group furnished by the Clef Club that specialized in grave-yard ballads. They would introduce them with corny an-nouncements. "The next selection is dedicated to all the morticians in the house—we'd like to sing for you 'Some of These Days.'" Then the people clapped like hell. Then there was al-ways some drunk who would holler back at the quartet, "Don't sing some of these days, sing now!" One regular customer took delight in aiming the corks from champagne bottles at the big chandelier full of electric-light bulbs.

Some of the best times I've ever had working in clubs and cafés were in the Club Napoleon. Things were more relaxed down there and you didn't run into too many phonies. They were relaxed, that is, if you got along. The big shots were kind and considerate to the entertainers they liked. You had to know when to talk, when to kid, and when to keep your mouth shut. If you knew how to conduct yourself properly you had a chance to get in on some of the good money and the better jobs. The Lion knew and worked for most of them—Jack (Legs) Dia-mond, Larry Fay, Tommy Guinan (Texas' brother), Frankie and Alonzo Uale (Yale) of Brooklyn. I saw and knew some-

thing about Arthur (Dutch Schultz) Flegenheimer, Big
Frenchy DeMange, and Vincent (Mad Dog) Coll. I was also
on good terms with Arnold (The Gambler) Rothstein. He was
always on the make for a fast buck and I recall that, shortly
before he was taken off with a fast bullet at the Park Central
Hotel, he put up the money for Flournoy Miller and Aubrey
Lyles to put on the show *Keep Shufflin'* in 1928. (My pals Fats
Waller and Andy Razaf furnished the music for that revue.)

I used to see Lucky Luciano in the Club Napoleon frequently. He was a quiet man, but those vibrations were deadly.
When Lucky said go, you were gone. He used to take me
around the corner to the Club Epicure and command me to
play when he was feeling my music. He was a cold cat but he
came up with the tips. I think the Lion must have reached
some of his inner feelings. I remember a girl singer who used
to hang around without being regularly employed—she used to
stand at the stairway to the second floor and just sing. It wasn't
long after that I recognized her in the movies. It was the Sa-
rong Girl, Dorothy Lamour. And when Harry Richman and
Morton Downey came in, they always wanted to take over the
piano. I fought it where I could. Pat O'Brien, the movie actor,
was a regular. He used to stuff my pockets with twenty-dollar
bills. People got dazed by the atmosphere. Guys like Ray Bolger
and Fred Astaire made the scene at the Club Napoleon.

There was one thing about the Lion—he aimed to entertain.
That was my business. I never played the sporting houses.
They were interesting but they weren't for me. You bought a
drink of hooch worth ten cents and you paid a dollar. Out of
the different rooms came the ladies, dressed in nice gowns. The
houses were licensed and things were run carefully. There was
a fine for operating a disorderly house—fifty-two dollars and a
nickel. The madam was backed by the Big Men. She often had
a private house, where the madam lived alone, and the men
could call on her. They say that New York has no red-light
district. That means that every other street is. But when the

raids took place there, the piano professor had to go out the window with the rest of the staff. To me, that wasn't dignified.

Very few people have ever considered the Negro's feelings about the things he is asked to do. And the Lion found that the same things went on downtown that went on uptown and even more. If you wanted to be *in*, you had to know the chef, because if he didn't like you, I'm sorry. You had to be known by the waiters, the headwaiter, the checkroom girls, the cook and bottle washer, the doorman, the bartenders, and all of them— because if you didn't, you were square and they'd lay a bomb on you for sure.

They used to say there were seventy thousand speakeasies in New York and I'm going to tell you that the Lion must have been in damn near all of them.

While I was downtown, a lot was happening uptown, too. We learned in Harlem to "bottle-it," an expression that means the same as today's "cool-it." Both mean shut up.

In those days you went along with what was happening. The boys had the say. Those who crossed them were quietly banished from the scene. And each remembered with a headstone, providing their corpses could be found. Oh, there were few fights right there in the speakeasy. They all happened outside. Some genius from the square world would want to make it for nothing. Many a customer of the Harlem joints used to wait outside to get back at the people who had rushed him out because he had had too much to drink. He got it. Most of them wished the one-punch bouncers had crippled them. The women shills for the party flats got hold of some of them and took them to the crib joints where they really got taken for something they couldn't go back to their wives in Akron and holler about.

Yes sir, the old night-club circuit could kill you or make you. The only people who got made were those in the know. The suckers fell off to the right and to the left.

With the coming of the gangs, the real Harlem cat learned to put his money in his shoe—in the toe, not the heel, where he could get at it for himself when he ventured into a speakeasy, after-hours club, or sporting house. The Lion made double use of his cane in those days. I carried it for stance and protection. The end of the stick was hollow but it could hold a knife or even a slender flask of whisky in its head. Just a little idea I picked up from a sharpie that had made it to Europe.

When the Club Napoleon closed early in 1932, it wasn't long before it reopened as the Casa Blanca, run by my boy Larry Fay. But it wasn't long before Fay fell in the front entrance because some ex-doorman had a grievance with him.

He got mowed down with a blast of lead and the Club Napoleon was no more.

THAT ROAD AGAIN

In 1931, the Lion stopped thinking again and wound up on another theater tour—this time to the South!

The deal was an act featuring Nina Mae McKinney and they wanted "The Lion of the Piano"—that was my billing—to go along and see that she got a good start in vaudeville.

Nina Mae had started as a nineteen-year-old dancer in the chorus of Lew Leslie's *Blackbirds of 1928*, the big revue on Broadway that featured Bill Robinson and "I Can't Give You Anything but Love" (sung by Adelaide Hall). Miss McKinney was a classy looker. The people who were making the all-Negro talking picture, *Hallelujah,* dug her and assigned her a leading part. The picture, which did all right and is still shown on TV today, came out in 1929; like always when someone makes a name for themselves, some booker comes along and wants to dump them into a hall down south.

Well, movies are one thing, stage shows are another, and I tried to teach Miss McKinney to sing and how to walk out on the stage. When you appeared in the all-colored theaters of those days you had to grab 'em fast. You had to show more than just a reputation as a movie actress. A lot of the customers hadn't seen the movie.

Before we started out on tour they added Charles Ray, a singer and dancer, whose specialty was tap dancing while talk-singing the tune "Sweet and Lovely."

So out we go—first stop the Lincoln Theater in Washington, D.C. The act opened with the Lion at the piano playing his own compositions. After the audience got good and warmed up, Charlie Ray came out and did his specialty to my accompaniment. Then we brought on Nina Mae singing "I Must Have That Man" and "Sleepy Time Down South." Then after Miss McKinney had given her plug, "hope everybody has seen *Hallelujah,*" we went into our closing number—Nina Mae and Charlie performing a vocal duet with me trying to create some excitement and enthusiasm by banging away on the piano behind them. This routine, where I was on the stage for forty-five minutes, was repeated four times a day.

We did a week in Washington and then took the Potomac River steamer to Norfolk, Virginia, where we had another week at the Attucks Theater. After that second week, I figured I'd had enough. And anyway, the show was bombing.

As I mentioned above, the Negro theaters, both in the north and south, are hard to play. The audiences are real tough and very slow to show their appreciation. It is a lot easier to get a white audience to applaud and this inspires the performer to work hard at putting on a good show. In my time I've seen many an act that brought the house down at the Palace on Broadway, fall on its face at the Lafayette or the Apollo in Harlem. Bojangles once told me he refused to play the Apollo because the audiences talked and failed to pay attention while he was on.

I remember talking to Count Basie when he returned to New York from Kansas City with his first big band. He had just received his first booking for the Paramount Theater on Times

Square and was worried to death about how he was going to
go over. "Count," I said, "the white theater audiences are going
to like your band and show their appreciation. You'll think
those T.O.B.A. houses you've been playing were mausoleums."
He told me later, "You were sure right!"

Another thing I noticed in theater work was you had to always be on the look out for the upstagers when playing the
colored time. When you traveled and played on the bills with
white acts, they were inclined to leave us alone and let us do
our stuff. But when you got out with a Negro troupe there was
always someone trying to steal your fire and draw the audience's attention away. There's a lot of jealousy in show business.

While I was at the Lincoln in Washington, a booking agent
came to see me about getting a band together to play on one of
the Potomac River moonlight-cruise boats. So after our act
closed in Norfolk I went back to New York to get a band together for that riverboat deal—another big mistake!

Man, what a hassle the next few months turned into. The
Lion's five-piece jazz band really took a ride. People would
save up so they had the admission—fifty cents—to a moonlight
boat ride with dancing. Since they'd saved up so long they
wanted to get all the excitement they could for their dough—
and that included brawling.

One night while I was conducting the orchestra, a riot broke
loose. The guy sponsoring the boat ride had his head opened by
a flying bottle. With bottles flying every which way, we kept
on playing just as though nothing was happening, in the true
tradition of show business. The Lion just sat at the piano and
pounded out the music as the glass whizzed past us. We just
ducked and kept the jazz going because we figured sooner or
later they'd be tired and want to resume their dancing. And,
after about a hundred bottles had been broken on the floor of
the ballroom, that was what they did.

The Washington booking agent came to me and said he had

a one-nighter booked for us in Lynchburg, Virginia. I had to scramble around and get together a sixteen-piece band. We picked up the extra men around Washington and started south on one of those trains where the windows were so dirty you couldn't see out of them.

This brief dip into the land of cotton was to be my last foray down below the Mason-Dixon Line. The weather down there just didn't fit my clothes.

We got down to this mountain town in the southwestern corner of Virginia late in the afternoon and took a bus to the hotel we had been told to go to by the agent. The way the cracker bus driver was acting made me suspicious of what might happen. That place was a hundred years behind the times. Hell, the name of the town—Lynchburg—was enough to scare the wits out of us. Anything can happen where a lot of people can't read or write. The hotel turned out to be a crib joint, meaning it had a fast turnover, out on Main Street and was run by a Geechie woman.

Most of us were put up on the third floor. The horn men took out their instruments to practice for the night's engagement. The place was full of girls and there were some bottles floating around but everything seemed calm.

About 8:15 P.M. when we were getting ready to leave to play the gig, a crowd of cops in shirt sleeves came storming into the place. They wanted to arrest the whole band on a disorderly charge. It was a frame-up by the old biddy who ran the house. She said one of the girls was complaining because one of our musicians had hit her over the head with his horn.

We called the guy who was running the dance and he came over and made a deal so we could get to his dance hall to play the job. He did it by promising that he would guarantee we would all be in court the next morning. This didn't help our spirits because we expected to get turned over to the chain gang before we got out of town.

It turned out that the complaint had originally come from a white pimp who'd been hanging around the place the previous afternoon. He was known as the biggest stool pigeon in town and wanted to see that there band made up of "nawth'n niggers sent down by the Yankees" thrown in jail with the key thrown away.

They didn't have much evidence to pin on us, but where a Negro is concerned they could make almost any charge stick in the South.

We got in touch with the agent in Washington. After a lot of hemming and hawing the case was dismissed. The sentence? We had to promise to get out of town! As if we had eyes for staying there and finding ourselves in jail sleeping with the horses.

When we got back to Washington we figured up the whole deal. It cost us around two thousand dollars. This included transportation to and from Lynchburg, expenses at the house, salaries for the band, and the pay-offs to get it straightened out. We got five hundred dollars to play the date. I told the agent I would be missing for any more of his dates and headed back to New York City.

Experiences like that are a good reason why I gave up the idea of leading a big band around. You are bound to run up with sidemen who light up,* act like tramps, and are just generally going to get everybody in trouble. I never did find out exactly what happened in Lynchburg, whether or not anybody actually hit somebody over the head with a horn. It looked like a frame-up all around—and probably was.

One of the big problems in racial matters, not only in show business but in everything, was that the Negroes did not stick together like they should. During the few times I was down below the Mason-Dixon Line, I had more trouble with my own people than I did with the white folks.

* Smoke marijuana.

When I got back to New York, the time was fast approaching when Prohibition would be repealed. Some of the joints that had been undercover speaks would put out their signs and become legit. It was just an official thing. During the last of the dry years most of the places were operating with their doors open. You could see the bars from the street.

19

Fifty-second Street Beat

> How do you want it,
> Groovy, moovy, sad,
> Or after hours?
> Get me in the mood
> And keep me in the mood,
> and I'll play some happy music.
>
> WILLIE THE LION SMITH

There was one beat-up speakeasy that I used to drop in on quite often because it was a hangout for the musicians working at Radio City.

In those days the two long blocks on Fifty-second Street from Fifth Avenue to Seventh Avenue were packed with those old-fashioned brownstone houses. Damn near every one had a blind pig or speakeasy hidden away somewhere. Some of them were fancy while others were just a one-time bedroom without beds. You got the same bad whisky in them all.

Several of the musicians who used to visit me at Pod's & Jerry's were working in the big radio studios. They couldn't wait to get loose from the job and run over to a speak for a taste. They made one place their second home, stashed their instruments there, took telephone calls from chicks that they didn't dare receive at home, and even used the place for a mailing address.

This place was only a short block north from the studios. It was a second-floor joint but you had to go down to get up. You got in by going down a couple of stone steps to a basement door that was always open. After you walked down a short hall you came to a dark staircase and climbed two flights to another hallway. It was so dark you couldn't see in front of you or behind you. Up on the second floor was this doorway with silver paint all over it. You'd knock. A guy would look out at you from a peek hole in the door—they used to call them the Judas hole —and say, "Who's there?" That's where they got that game "Knock, Knock, Who's There."

Once inside you were in another hallway. Off of the hall were parlors, called "drinking rooms." In the back was a room where they had a beat-up bar, a push-ball game, an old upright piano, and a few shabby wicker chairs and small tables. You couldn't get more than twenty-five people seated in the place at one time.

The guy behind the bar was named Joe Helbock and he was the owner. He called the setup, "the joint," a club for musicians. He liked music.

The Lion got in the habit of stopping by and giving the piano a workout once in awhile. One day Joe said, "Lion, why don't you stop by every day around five and I'll give you a little salary for your trouble?" *That deal*, the engagement of the Lion for the cocktail hour at Helbock's in 1930, was the beginning of Fifty-second Street as "The Cradle of Swing." That was long before they had all those jazz traps on the street and called it Swing Lane.

Helbock's got to be quite a meeting place for famous musicians, especially piano men. For the years 1930–33, regulars at the piano included Joe Sullivan; Charley Bourne; Artie (The Baron) Schutt; Walter Gross, one of the real greats as a composer-arranger; Howard Smith, who was later featured with

Tommy Dorsey's band; Milt Raskin; and in 1932, when Art
Tatum came to New York as accompanist for singer Adelaide
Hall, he joined in every chance he got. It was the first time any
of the New York musicians heard the great Tatum from Toledo,
Ohio.

This was a lively gang and everybody had fun. Red Mc-
Kenzie would sing and perform on his kazoo (a comb covered
with tissue paper). His favorite tune was "Four or Five Times."
Del Staigers, a wonderful technician on the trumpet, would get
his horn out and try to show off. He claimed he could play
three notes at the same time on account of his phenomenal
technique and although it was the middle of the Depression he
was getting a grand a week as a legitimate trumpet player. My
good pal Teddy Bunn would sit in on guitar. There was one
guy who used to hang around and mystify everybody as he was
not a professional musician. He was Martin Block, who later
became the most famous disc jockey in radio with his *Make
Believe Ballroom* record programs. During this time I formed a
lifetime friendship with the two Dorsey Brothers, Jimmy and
Tommy, who were still sidemen.

Things were going along so well with Helbock I told him he
ought to bring in more entertainment and really go into the
business of furnishing music later in the evening. Up to that
time Helbock's place was busy in the afternoons but nothing
happened at night. The musicians who hung around there to
cash their checks and have a taste between broadcasts usually went home to their wives after supper. But his place was
replacing Plunkett's, the musicians' speak on Fifty-third, and
that meant he was getting a lot of cats from the dance bands
around town who had to be in midtown until late at night.

Just before Repeal, I suggested to Helbock that he hire the
Spirits of Rhythm, a group that included my friend Teddy
Bunn on guitar, Virgil Scroggins drumming with whisk brooms
on a suitcase, and scat singer Leo Watson performing on a
home-made instrument that looked like a ukulele.

The new policy worked out fine. When Prohibition went out in 1933, Helbock moved downstairs and across the street into larger quarters. The Spirits went with him and it was the true beginning of the famed "Fifty-second Street era" that lasted for over twenty years. He decided he needed a fancy name for the spot, so he called it the Onyx. Later that year pianist Joe Sullivan composed and recorded "Onyx Bringdown" and "Gin Mill Blues" in honor of the new club.

At first the Onyx was the only music on the street. There were a couple of other famous places that had converted from illegal to legal, but they didn't feature music. One of them, Leon & Eddie's, wanted the Lion to help, but after twenty minutes in the joint I knew it was wrong. The place was owned by Leon Enken, a headwaiter, and Eddie Davis, a singing comic, and it was always noisy and crowded. Davis had about twelve hundred songs in his repertoire and one of my friends had tipped me off that he was looking for a new piano player. I called up the joint and they told me to just drop around and try out the piano while Davis was on. I couldn't get to the stand it was so packed. The vibrations didn't come in good at all. The guy was singing about a "virgin sturgeon." I failed to recognize it as any song I'd ever heard. I thought I'd better get out of that slumming trap fast, and did.

The other place on Fifty-second Street that was destined to become big was at 21 West Fifty-second. It is still there today as "21," a famous restaurant, but back then it had been a speakeasy run by a guy named Two-Trigger Jack Kriendler. His partner was Charlie Berns, and during Prohibition we knew the speak as Jack & Charlie's. It was noted for its collapsible bar —in case they had a raid.

By 1934, three places on Fifty-second had music—the Onyx, the Famous Door, and the Hickory House. It was in that year that the fur coats from Park Avenue began to take notice of what was going on in the way of music. They started to pack the places and they had the cash; it forced a lot of cats out that came to listen seriously. The musicians had to get their shot and a beer from Reilly's bar because they could no longer afford to drink in the places where they worked. Helbock and the others raised their prices when they saw the mink.

The Onyx burned down during 1934 and didn't reopen until sometime in '35. The center of activities then went over to the Famous Door, where Wingy Manone from New Orleans had a band. The Lion performed on intermission piano. Regulars on Fifty-second at this time included Louis Prima, Red McKenzie, Joe Marsala, Eddie Condon, and Mike Riley, the guy who made "The Music Goes 'Round and 'Round" world famous.

Yeah, you could find all the jazz musicians on Fifty-second Street. Guys like Bud Freeman, Stuff Smith—the jazz violinist who opened the Onyx after the fire—Pee Wee Russell, Jonah Jones, and my boy Fats. I remember one night Fats was at the new Onyx sitting in with Stuff Smith. Cab Calloway came in and started hi-de-hoing with the band. They got a number going for a half hour without stopping. There was an ex-lightweight fighter, Al Singer, in the joint at the time, and Cozy Cole's drumming made him flip. He went running out of the place holding his head and screaming.

When you hung around the street in those days you were likely to pick up some good gigs, either from customers who wanted you to entertain at private parties or from other musicians who had arranged a recording date.

The Lion signed for a famous date in May 1934, put together by clarinetist-alto saxophonist Milton (Mezz) Mesirow (Mezzrow), a white boy who had arrived from Chicago. We had Max Kaminsky on trumpet, Bud Freeman on tenor saxophone, Benny Carter on alto, the Lion on piano, John Kirby on bass, and the great Chick Webb on drums.

With a line-up like that we couldn't go wrong. We did four sides for the old Victor Company: James P. Johnson's "Old-Fashioned Love" and three originals by Mezzrow and trombonist Floyd O'Brien titled "Apologies," "Sendin' the Vipers," and "35th & Calumet." Mezzrow always got a kick out of the tea smoking and that accounted for the tune about the vipers.* The street corner, Thirty-fifth Street and Calumet, was a location in Chicago where there were famous cabarets with jazz bands.

It was a very historic session for several reasons. It was one of the first recording dates where the band was made up of both Negroes and white musicians. It was also one of the first recording dates where the musicians were allowed to play the way they wanted. Mezzrow's arrangements called for what they call "freewheeling jamming." Up to that time the companies didn't want to make any records where they couldn't easily hear a simple melody. This was almost five years before the small jazz labels like Commodore and Blue Note got in business.

Starting around 1934, jazz musicians began to get more and more chances to record where we were permitted to jam and improvise rather than stick closely to a popular-hit melody. The record moguls soon began to look toward Fifty-second Street for musicians who could record swing music.

The Lion recorded again with Mezzrow in another all-star group in 1936. On that occasion I was responsible for the vocal chorus on a novelty hit called "I'se a Muggin'" that had rocked Fifty-second Street.

CLARENCE WILLIAMS' RADIO RHYTHM

Negroes have always had difficulty in radio and television. The people who run the shows are always afraid of the South. During the 1930s our people were depicted over the air by two

---

* The musicians of the day called marijuana "tea," and the smokers were known as "vipers."

white men masquerading as Amos and Andy. They didn't seem
to mind *that* down below the Mason-Dixon Line.

But once in awhile Negro entertainers would get a break
and get on a show because they had the talent—sometimes they
did this when it wasn't necessary to announce the artists. One
fortunate performer who got considerable air time was my old
friend Clarence Williams from New Orleans.

Williams was mostly interested in getting exposure for the
musical compositions he published and was always trying to
swing deals for recording and broadcasting. The key to his
success on getting on the air was through his wife Eva Taylor,
whose pretty style of singing was quite popular. She was known
as "The Dixie Nightingale" and for several years performed on
sustaining programs from nine to nine-fifteen every morning
over radio station WOR in New York. She made three hundred
and fifty dollars per week and turned every cent of it over to
Brother Clarence.

My Louisiana friend was a much better composer than he
was a pianist; he played the piano as if he was wearing mittens.
Everything came out heavy-handed. He also was good at making all the wrong chords. But when old Clarence got around
to writing tunes he was all right. He composed some pretty good
numbers in his time—"Sugar Blues," "Royal Garden Blues,"
"Baby, Won't You Please Come Home," and others that everybody has heard.

He knew he wasn't too great as a piano player so he decided
to use two pianos on his wife's show. He got James P. (The
Brute) Johnson to play one and he played the other. But then
Williams would push James P. around and get the men in the
control room mad at the both of them—Williams for badgering
Johnson, and Johnson for letting Williams boss him around. It
was The Brute's contention that as long as it was Clarence's
show he had a right to have things done the way he wanted.
This was another example of the way Negro musicians, The
Lost Tribe, have of never reaching their destination. They re-

fuse to fight for their rights. This applies to getting good book-
ings, clean dressing rooms, and a large enough fee for their
services. All too many of them let themselves get pushed around.

Well, James Johnson finally did get sick—sick of Clarence's
piano playing. He asked me if I would like to substitute for him
until he was feeling better—it turned out he never did feel better. He called me on the phone, "Come on, Lion, go on down
and make the gig for just this one day."

I must have been out of my mind to do it. The job only paid
fifty dollars a shot and they started the rehearsals at *six-thirty
in the morning.* But I arrived down at the studio in Jimmy's
place. Then I spent the morning babying Clarence, trying to
make the same chords he was making accidentally. Every time
he made a clinker on the piano which was every other note, Eva
would look away from Clarence and at the guy who was playing
the right note—me. This would make Clarence, the cat with the
club hand, think he was playing things right and I was messing
up.

Finally I exploded. "Eva, why are you looking in this direction? Your old man is the one playing those wrong chords."

Then I got a sudden idea. "Let's have Clarence play the jug."
In fact, he was a damn good jug player†—I'd made quite a few
recordings with him on the jug. We tried it on the show and
it helped. Until he got winded.

I stuck out the program for several weeks. James P. had
gotten himself real busy and so to get off the hook I recommended young pianist Herman Chittison to finish out the *Dixie
Nightingale* series.

Yes, Clarence was a great publisher, but as a piano man he
was nowhere. In all fairness I want to point out that he was an
inspiration to all of us, including Fats Waller and James P.
Johnson. He inspired and helped us to get our original com-

† A jug player makes a buzzing sound with his lips and holds the jug's narrow mouth up to his lips to make the earthenware jug act as a resonator for the
sound.

positions published. For many years he had his office in the
Gaiety Building on Broadway. It was once rumored around
Harlem that he had cleared over a hundred thousand dollars
in one year. Most of the numbers he had were old and from a
past era of show business. He always was a good man for getting his name on everything in sight.

I'll bet he is still collecting plenty in royalties. He might not
need the cash because he was always very careful with money.
I remember one of those cold, snowy mornings back when we
were doing the early morning show for WOR, I was standing
alongside Clarence when Eva turned her pay envelope over to
him. He broke down and said to her, "Do you want a cup of
coffee?" I broke in and hollered, "Man, it's snowing outside. She
needs some food!" His reply was, "We ate at home." That had
been almost six hours before and I knew she was hungry, but
she wouldn't open her mouth and say so.

I always got along pretty good with both Clarence and Eva.
In fact, after those days at WOR they hired me again to play
with them on another radio program over the National Broadcasting network. Everybody liked Eva Taylor and many people remembered her from the time she was a featured singer in
the show *Shuffle Along*.

It was around 1933–34 that Clarence and I got mixed up in
the recording of a jug band for the old Columbia-record people.
We made a lot of sides with Clarence playing a hot whisky jug.
The band included in addition to the Lion on piano and C.
Williams, jug and vocal: Eddie Allen, trumpet; Cecil Scott, clarinet and tenor saxophone; Ikey Robinson on banjo and flute;
and Willie Williams, Clarence's half brother, on washboard.
On some of the sides we were accompanied by what Williams
called his "choir." The record company called them the Low-
land Singers and the outfit usually included Clarence and his
wife, Eva Taylor; plus Clarence Todd, a guy who could give
out with a wild scat song.

Yeah, our jug band got off some numbers like "Wipe It Off,"

"The Shim Sham Shimmy Dance," "Organ Grinder," and a hot number called "You Ain't Too Old." There were many others and these are collector's items today.

Clarence Williams is still alive and lives in his own home out in Jamaica, Long Island. He has two grown-up children, a son Clarence, Jr., who is a policeman; and a daughter, Irene, a fine vocalist, who had a leading part in a recent revival of *Porgy and Bess*. Williams was the first New Orleans musician to have an influence on jazz in New York.

JELLY ROLL

While my man Williams is in my mind, I get to thinking of the late Ferdinand (Jelly Roll) Morton, also from New Orleans, and quite a piano player and composer in his own right.

It was in the early thirties that I really got to know Jelly Roll. He was living in New York City by that time and used to hang around the Rhythm Club.

Morton was a man with strong spiritual and magnetic forces; when he sat down to play he could hold an audience by the strength of his strong personality. He was a sharpshooter and had always traveled in fast company. He was intelligent, had something to offer, and as far as I could tell, he was always able to back up what he said. He had a story to tell you about any and every place he had been.

In this world if you give something you'll receive something in return and Jelly would make it a point wherever he went to meet the people of value. When you talked to him he could tell you a lot of things he had learned from the people he met in his travels.

It used to make me mad to hear the New York cats who hadn't been out of Harlem making fun of Morton. Like myself, Jelly

Roll had played in all kinds of places, and that was the way you learned about life—playing in all the different back rooms.

Some people used to put me on by asking whether jazz was born in New Orleans and whether or not Jelly Roll invented it. I said once that that was one of the worst things I ever heard. What I meant was that most of the jazz I knew was, in the beginning, from the brickyards. And another thing, jazz comes from the person's soul and not from a state. But Jelly Roll was a guy who always talked a lot. He used to be around the Rhythm Club every day and stand out on the corner and he used to bull and con all those fellows. He had his twenty-dollar gold piece on and he'd stand out there with a bankroll, meaning money, so every time I'd come around, almost all the guys who used to play the piano kept quiet. Sometimes I'd lay for Fats and Jimmy. Sometimes I'd even lay for Tatum. But I used to come around especially on Friday and Saturday looking for Jelly. I went around this one Friday and he was standing on the corner.

"Look, Mr. One Hand," I said, "let's go inside and let me give you your lessons in cutting." So Jelly and I would go inside by the piano. I was the only one he would stand and listen to and then he didn't open his mouth. I must have played nearly everything you could name and when I got through, I said, "Well, Jelly, you'll keep quiet now." And, true as I'm sitting here, Jelly would be quiet.

20

The Climate Doesn't Fit My Clothes

A lot of cats call this the right alley,
But I call it down in the valley.

WILLIE THE LION SMITH

When they got around to repealing that Prohibition law, things were already in a sad way. People no longer had the money to buy all that bad booze. The big Harlem clubs were rapidly going out of business and the smaller ones were all switching to juke boxes. There was hardly a joint left where a piano player or a trio could settle down—and the steady gigs didn't pay enough to make them worthwhile. Tips had disappeared entirely. It was the Depression blues on St. Nicholas Avenue.

My last job in Harlem had been at Pod's & Jerry's and toward the end of my long stay there I had used Sidney Bechet on soprano saxophone and Arthur (Traps) McIntyre, a lame guy who was a fine drummer. To help these guys out I fixed it so we split all the money down three ways even. This impressed Sidney because the leader was entitled to double money. After that time Bechet and I were the closest of friends.

Around 1933, I was still living at 580 St. Nicholas.*

Bechet was living close by and every time I'd run into him on the street he'd invite me over to his place to stay all night and have a ball.

So I'd ask Sidney where he was living.

He would reply, "I'm at 129th Street and St. Nicholas. I'm the proprietor of the Southern Tailor Shop."

That would gas me. I couldn't figure out what a good jazz clarinet player was doing playing "tailor."

So I said, "How many suits you got in there?"

"Oh," he said, "I've got up to about twenty; but we don't make them, just press 'em."

Then I asked, "Who's we?"

He replied, "Tommy and myself."

Well, I knew Tommy Ladnier from Chicago days. He was a good trumpet player. I found out later that Sidney would press and repair the suits, while Ladnier specialized in shining shoes. As Sidney said later in his book, "We were pretty easygoing with the money part of that business, but we got along."

Bechet mentioned they had some good sessions in the back of the shop. So one night I agreed to come around to see what was happening.

But first, I wanted some information. "How much you charge to press a suit?"

He replied, "Oh, the regular fee."

You see I figured if nothing was going on I could at least get my suit pressed. Then I wanted to know, "What do we sleep on?"

He then said, "I've got a couple of cots in the back. But usually there's a bunch of musicianers playing back there."

"You ain't gonna press any clothes tonight then," I said.

"No, man. I cooked up a batch of red beans and rice to add to a lot of cold fried chicken. We'll have us a party."

---

* At 139th Street. Other musicians made this apartment building their home—Wilbur Sweatman, Benny Carter, and in later years, drummer Jo Jones were neighbors of mine.

That night I found myself down in a dark, damp, beat-up cellar with a dirt floor in the back that Sidney called the Southern Tailor Shop.

After I'd had time to get a couple of shots under my belt—he had some redeye corn whisky—the place turned into a hornet's nest. It was the headquarters for working and nonworking jazz musicians. Some of these guys wore their tuxedos night and day so that they would be ready whenever a job of some sort came up. They all had long hair, and I mean their hair hadn't been cut for months, but they kept it plastered down with Kink-No-More. I wondered how any of these guys expected to get a gig with my old friend Luckey Roberts, whose society band was one of the few groups getting any work in those sad-eyed days.

It turned out I stayed down there in Sidney's dungeon, hanging out, for around six months. There was some damn good music comin' from that back room and Bechet was one fine cook with those Southern specialties he was always fixing.

After six months it began to get to be too much. Sidney had the women chasin' him all the time and he never got much chance to press the suits brought in by the customers. Bechet, trumpeter Bobby Stark, and trombonist Jimmy Harrison were three of the most wanted men by the women I ever did see. So, he wanted everybody else to take up tailoring.

But the main reason I hurried up to cut out was Bechet's announcement one day that he thought, "It might be a good idea if we convert the place to an undertaking establishment."

"You can't lose in that racket," he said.

I moved around the corner to 32 Macomb's Place, where I stayed until 1946. My Jane was always concerned about the way the Lion lived and when I left Sidney's dump she was so pleased she gave me a beautiful present—a two hundred and fifty dollar blue overcoat.

No sooner had I moved in with my new coat than trouble

came to Macomb's Place. I came home from work one morning at seven-thirty to find the coat stolen and the apartment ransacked for other clothes.

I suspected the superintendent because he had mentioned to me that his son didn't have an overcoat. Jane insisted I go out and get a watchdog. I told her that wouldn't make sense because the super would know the dog was there and stay away so I couldn't catch him and get my coat back.

Jane insisted. In order to keep the lady happy I went out and bought a bird dog. When I went out I left him sitting by the window watch-dogging. Nothing happened, until one night Jane cooked me a great big pot of chicken. Before going out that night, and before eating, I tied the bugger so he'd have to stay near the window and be unable to get at the chicken. I don't know what happened but when I got home the chicken was all gone—all eaten up—and the dog was sitting by the window quietly and the rope was lying loose on the floor.

When I took the dog back to the man who had him originally, Jane was so mad I had to go back and get him again for a second try. So we stationed him by the window and chained him up. The same thing happened again—when I got home the dog was free and he had been raiding the kitchen.

This went on for several days. I finally decided I would really fix him and tell Jane he'd run away. I took the dog out on a snowy night and walked him way up to the George Washington Bridge area. Then I pushed him into the hallway of a rooming house and rushed out to catch a cab home. That dog hadn't even seen what direction I'd gone in.

When I got back home in that cab, the mutt was sitting by the entrance to 32 Macomb's waiting for me.

I called Jane in the morning. "That dog has absolutely got to go," I told her. "He still has to go!" So this time we both took him back to the man who had him first. The pest cried like a howling wolf when we left but I won out.

A few nights later the robbers came again and ransacked the place. But I still didn't bring that dog back.

One time I ran into Bechet again on St. Nicholas Avenue. He had a new idea that was pretty good. We should make some West Indian records because everyone was laughing and enjoying the calypso songs.

Sidney and I got a band together: Kenneth Roane, trumpet; Bechet, clarinet and soprano saxophone; Olin Alderhold, bass; Leo Warney, drums; and the Lion. We called it The Willie (the Lion) Smith and Sidney Bechet Haitian Orchestra and we made over a dozen assorted merengues, rhumbas, and original melodies from Haiti. The album was good musically but no one bought it.

We were just about twenty years early. Look what happened later to Harry Belafonte when he switched from jazz to the West Indian tunes.

Back then a Cuban or Spanish band couldn't get to first base but today the whole country is crazy over the Bossa Nova. Those records of Sidney's and mine were another first. Seems like the Lion always got on the scene with those firsts too soon.

I RECORD AND STRAIGHTEN OUT
MR. HERTH

After making the first blues recording in history back in 1920, I tried to keep from getting too closely involved because they were always taking advantage of the musicians. They just wouldn't pay any decent money in those days. Today they reissue all those jazz records; the guys who led the bands, wrote the tunes, and played the solos do not see a single cent for all their creative efforts. There were no such things as contracts back then—you made a side and got a flat twenty-five dollars, regardless of what happened.

But by the thirties when records began to come back, things began to look a little better. The record firms were all looking for the guys who could play hot music—it was the start of the swing era. We'd run into record guys on Fifty-second Street every night with a proposition.

It has always been my opinion that the only way to do one-self any good with records is to make discs of your own compositions with a band under your name. I've stuck to that idea all through the years. Some say you cheat yourself out of a lot of money by not doing everything that comes up. A lot of big names have been cheated plenty by not being careful about doing business. The most important thing is to have a good contract in writing and be able to select the men you will work with on a job.

It was time for the Lion to get on records with my own band playing my own compositions. In April 1935, when the swing era was beginning to go full blast, I signed with Decca Records, then a brand-new record company partly owned by Bing Crosby, who was their leading record maker.

I used the same guys that had been with me on those Clarence Williams jug band recordings—Ed Allen, Cecil Scott, and Willie Williams. The sides were issued as Willie the Lion and His Cubs—without the jug—who needs it?

We made eight sides, including my composition "Echo of Spring," and they were released on Decca's Sepia Series, records for distribution to record shops in Negro neighborhoods only.

As I've said before, many of our people have been against the blues. Some of the more religious folks have always acted as though they were ashamed of the blues. I pointed out to Decca that a lot of my fans on Fifty-second Street wanted to get my records but couldn't find where to buy them. So they finally put two of the sides, "Streamline Gal" and "Harlem Joys," into the regular series. *Then* we began to pick up sales.

You have to stay on top of people to get things done right.

Everybody wants to get in on the act and be a boss—the doormen, sweepers, and janitors even want to tell you how to make records. But when it comes time to get some action, you nearly always have to go out and do it yourself.

A couple of years later, in April 1937, I recorded under my own name again for Decca. This time I got the fastest little jazz band on Fifty-second Street to work with me, a combo under the direction of bassist John Kirby that had grown out of the original Spirits of Rhythm. The group was still working at the Onyx where I frequently worked opposite them.†

All I needed to give Kirby's bunch was a lead sheet and they took it from there without me having to show them the chord progressions. These men were good musicians, and all they had to do was take a quick look at the sheet and we were off. In jazz, the score for the number is like a guide to hold things together, with the soloists improvising their own choruses. It was a pleasure to play with those guys because, besides each man being a top musician and improviser individually, they could work together so beautifully. After running through a tune once, or twice at the most, they'd say, "O.K., we're ready. Let's make it."

The tension on the date was always low when you had that Kirby outfit with you. You didn't have to worry about doing sides over and over until they came out right. When they've got a recording studio rented for two hours, they want to get a certain amount accomplished. There is no time for muffs, clinkers, and ruined takes. That means you've got to have fast musicians who know what they are doing and are able to do it right the first time around. The Lion always insists on playing with the best. In life the mutts always want to play with the good dogs, but the good dogs won't play with the mutts.

† Kirby had Frankie Newton, trumpet; Pete Brown, alto saxophone; Buster Bailey, clarinet; O'Neill Spencer, drums; and himself on bass. These boys, who later went on to make some of the best small-band jazz sides during the swing craze, were just right for the kind of jazz I wanted to put down.

We made eight sides for the regular Decca popular series, including a swing lament I wrote called "The Old Stamping Ground." After Charlie Shavers replaced Newton, most of those men played together as the John Kirby band.

YOU CAN'T MAKE A RACE HORSE
OUT OF A MULE

One of our favorite hangouts during the swing years was the Hickory House on the south side of Fifty-second Street near Seventh Avenue. Joe Marsala, a clarinetist, was the leader of a jam band there and many of the musicians that used to sit in became big names in show business—guys like Gene Krupa, Pee Wee Russell, Bud Freeman, Buddy Rich, and little Joey Bushkin. The latter was one of my piano pupils around that time.

You frequently saw a woman named Polly Adler sitting at a table in the corner. She used to say she had enough material for a book. But a lot of us said that. Polly made it work when she later wrote *A House Is Not a Home*.

The boss, John Popkin, was a good friend of mine and I introduced a lot of musicians to him. The Lion brought in a singing quartet, The Ink Spots, to meet Popkin who hired them for thirty dollars a week. That was before they had a hit record. Hazel Scott was another star who had her first important jobs at the Hickory. The Lion used to sit in often with the band for kicks. Popkin couldn't pay enough to have big names working there regularly. The pay was in uppercuts only.

Today, the Hickory House is the only jazz club left standing on Fifty-second Street, and John Popkin is still running the place. You can usually find Duke Ellington hanging around in there during the afternoons—it's his midtown headquarters.

To get back to the old swing years, one afternoon in 1937

I arrived at the Hickory full of brandy. I was in great shape for a business deal, but many a contract in show business gets lined up while the party of the first part is leaning against a bar.

Bob Stephens, an executive at Decca, came over to where everybody was buying a round and put his arm around my shoulders to start sweet talking. "Lion, my boss, Jack Kapp, wants to talk to you over yonder at his table. He's got someone he wants you to meet."

So I go over and shake hands with this guy. He's Milt Herth, an organist from Chicago, who's in town to make some records for Decca. Jack and Dave Kapp, the brass at the record company, decide they'd like to get some swing into Herth's music. Before we'd had two rounds the pens and contract forms were on the table and everybody was signing.

That's the way things happen. I'd stopped by the Hickory House looking for Joe Marsala to recommend a young drummer to him by the name of Gene Krupa and walked out with a hundred-dollar bill in my pocket and a new recording deal.

The next day you read your copy of the contract over and wished you'd insisted on more money. It was getting to be around the time that an artist with a name could get a flat guarantee per side; Artie Shaw told me that on his first record agreement he insisted that it be down in black and white that he got paid one thousand dollars per side.

That's the way it was in those days—easy come, easy go. Have a drink and wind up with a legal document that binds you. The next day I got a better offer from the Columbia people to make some sides, but it was too late. I was too busy living it up in those days, getting high with James P. and Fats, to tend to business properly. So I was tied to Decca and Herth for a year with an option.

We got together a trio, the Milt Herth Trio, with Willie Smith, piano, drummer O'Neill Spencer from the John Kirby group, and Herth on the Hammond electric organ. While Herth —I called him "Mother Hearth"—was knockin' himself out on the organ, Spencer and I tried to play loud enough so we could be heard. I had to holler at the guy all the time: "Play pianissimo! Play pianissimo!" I don't think he knew what the word pianissimo meant.

That off-key outfit was really giving me a fit. Herth not only played over the rest of us, but wanted to take all the choruses. Talk about hypertension. . . .

After the first couple of sessions I got them to add Teddy Bunn on guitar, in an effort to overcome that loud organ. They wanted me to sing some vocals but I couldn't sing through with that sound wave behind me. Spencer took the vocals. We went to town on all those swing things so popular around 1937–38; hit tunes like "The Dipsy Doodle," "The Campbells Are Swinging," "The Toy Trumpet," "Flat Foot Floogie." Man, we had Decca's Fifty-seventh Street studios rocking and cracking with that big organ sound. One of the Kapp supervisors used to scream at Mother Hearth to riff. That cat thought a riff was a broken windowpane.

Stephens had what you might call an uneven disposition. It almost got him into bad trouble on one date when he was riding Spencer. He kept telling him to tone down the drums. Spencer screamed back, "Why, why, tone down? So you can hear that organ?" and reached for his knife. He was going to leave the recording director's head in the studio. We smoothed it over.

Herth was a nice guy and we got along fine together when he wasn't exercising his ear on that organ. (The average musician has a tin ear.) He could play fairly well especially when everything was written down for him on the paper. Sometimes I'd straighten him out by switching to another key when he'd start blasting and he would have to slow down to get himself into the new key.

We recorded about twenty-five numbers with the trio and quartet. Some of the tunes were too cornball—"Looney Little Tooney," "Home Cooking Mama with the Frying Pan," and

"The Shoemaker's Holiday." The records weren't too bad, considering that in those days everything that went into the recording horn went down, but today they have devices like tape that permit them to doctor a bad side.

It was experiences like that that made me prefer to work as a single. To get the best results from a record date, it is important to get a bunch of relaxed guys and let them have their whisky, their brandy, let them light up, or do anything else they want to do so they can get in the groove. Nobody gets in the groove where some square is around making noises or faces; that stuff goes on the stage, but on records you concentrate on getting a relaxed swing. Artists live in another world and there has to be someone around who understands how to get the best out of a man. I've sure made my share of records and my motor hasn't run down yet by a long shot.

Looking back now on those Herth records it comes to my mind that this was another first, in a way. Herth was the first jazz organist on records.

Actually, Fats Waller was first, but the sides he made for the Victor Company weren't released for almost twenty years. Back during the twenties, Waller, who loved to play organ, made a bunch of tunes in that old church studio down in Camden, New Jersey. When Jesse Crawford, the organist, who had a regular recording contract with Victor, heard about it, he threatened to quit if the Waller sides were put on the market. Crawford, who played for the bouncing ball at the Paramount Theater on Times Square, knew what he was up against.

As Sidney said later:

"And maybe there's another thing why so many of these musicianers ended up so bad. Maybe they didn't know how to keep up with all that was happening to ragtime. If it could have stayed where it started and not had to take account of the business it was becoming—all that making contracts and signing options and buying and selling rights—maybe without that it might have been different. If you start taking what's pure in a man and you start putting it on a bill of sale, somehow you can't help destroying it. In a way, all that business makes it so a man don't have anything left to give."

I always said, like Chopin, that 60 per cent of the musicians and 90 per cent of the record men should be hod carriers.

21

Partying on Park with Fats

Come out of your hive,
and learn to jive.

WILLIE THE LION SMITH

Piano players are always welcome at parties even when unin-
vited. That's when the host or hostess figure they can get for
themselves some free entertainment to make their parties
popular.

I've talked about the all-night parties we used to play for
up in Harlem. There were so many of them that a good piano
man could make a living just playing the rent-party circuit.
Jimmy, Fats, and the Lion also received a lot of invitations to
play for parties downtown and over on Park Avenue.

There was one big one, around 1924, given by a socialite to
celebrate George Gershwin's new composition "Rhapsody in
Blue." It was one of those fancy cocktail shindigs, behind closed
doors, of course, because it was Prohibition time; all three of us
were invited. It was in one of those luxury hotels on Park
Avenue.

We all knew Gershwin because he used to come up to Harlem
to listen to us and he was the one who got us invited. It looked

for a while as though he was going to stay seated at the piano all night himself and hog all the playing. We three were standing at the bar getting up our courage and the more we imbibed the more anxious we became to get at those keys.

I finally went over and said to Gershwin, "Get up off that piano stool and let the real players take over, you tomato." He was a good-natured fellow and from then on the three of us took over the entertainment. In those days I had to almost push Fats down on the stool to get him to play. Young Waller was really a very shy kid, and I think it was that shyness that eventually turned him into such a heavy drinker. But at that Gershwin affair the brandy took effect and he not only beat the keys, he started singing his comedy songs. It was the first time I'd heard him vocalizing for the public. He made quite a hit.

From that time on, Fats and I made a lot of those parties together. We used to get bugged by some of the people we'd wind up playing for, but they always kept the juices flowing. A lot of the people we met thought they'd have to build a bridge in a day—after a few hours they would start to run out of gas.

They were always asking us silly questions. "Do you play by notes? Can you read music? Where were you born? How did you get into the music racket?" It would get you; they'd ask too damned many stupid questions. We felt like a couple of whores being interviewed by a high school reporter.

These parties were all shapes and sizes. Many of them turned into brawls. You sometimes wondered how the hell some of them were able to acquire or hold big money with their bird brains. Actually a lot of them didn't—they got the money as a gift when they were born. They'd get tight and tell stories about their best friends. Of course, behind the victim's back. Some of the things that made them laugh like hell would make me want to cry.

We played for Jack Philbin, who is now a big-time television man; Mrs. Felix Warburg, whose husband was a big-time banker on Wall Street; Mrs. Harrison Williams, who always invited all the songwriters and publishers; Ella Logan, the singer—her apartment was quite a hangout for artists; Sherman Fairchild; and many other famous people whose names I've forgotten.

At Mrs. Harrison Williams' parties we felt more like teachers. Show-business celebrities would study our work and try to get our music-arranging ideas. I saw people like Harold Arlen, Gershwin, Vernon Duke, Roy Bargy, at those affairs in Mrs. Williams' shack on Park.

Sometimes the artists who tried to pick up on some of our stuff had a hard time of it. They couldn't get much out of James P. because he wasn't a talker at all. He just played but couldn't explain what he was doing. They always thought they could get a lot out of Fats if they kept the jug handy, but when Fats got swinging he would sing and play for hours without saying anything sensible. We usually made fifty dollars apiece at Mrs. Williams' and all the food and liquor we could consume.

At one of the Williams' late-afternoon parties I met Gene Austin, who wrote and recorded a lot of fine tunes during the twenties. His recording of Walter Donaldson's "My Blue Heaven" was one of the biggest hits of all time. He became one of my best friends and drinking companions. It was Austin who introduced me to Sherman Fairchild and both Fats and myself became regulars at his frequent afternoon-party sessions in his apartment off Fifth Avenue. The highball brigade that made these affairs were always cheap with the tips to the musicians. This was a crowd that spent all their money on the chicks. Man, these afternoon crawlers were really suckers for the gals on the make.

Roy Bargy, a former featured pianist with Paul Whiteman's band, decided to have a stag party to end all stag parties. He invited all his buddies and there wasn't a woman in the place. The shindig was given at his house on the East Side in the middle of winter with the town covered with ice and snow. The

idea was to drink and we did. For several days. They had everything going from champagne to back-room hooch. Drummer
George Wettling and I stayed on the premises for the duration
and when it broke up we left together sliding on the ice looking
for another place to drink.

There were quite a few times I played for gatherings at Toots
Shor's old place on Fifty-first Street. One of the best was in
honor of Tommy Dorsey and his third wife. Tommy was for
many years a close friend from the Onyx Club days and my
favorite trombone player. He was one of the greatest of all the
bandleaders because he was a strong man. He insisted on dis-
cipline in his band, held frequent rehearsals, and was able to
keep his crew in line at all times.

One of the most unusual parties for a jazz pianist was Helen
Decker's wedding reception in a small Pennsylvania town
where the Lion got to roar on a hundred-and-ten-year-old organ.

Fats and I got in on every kind of party you can think of,
ranging from society on Park to the United States fleet at
Brooklyn. The Navy party was given in a club on Fulton
Street and we had to leave through the back window when the
sailors got in trouble with the local boys because they were
taking over the home-town girls.

My boy Filthy was one of those June people, a Gemini—very
restless. Unlike James P. Johnson, Fatso was always on the go
and never stopped clowning. He was truly a "cheerful little
earful" and everywhere he went there was a ball in the making.
He was the kind of guy who would give you the shirt off his
back, a good-natured alley cat, and he was show business all
the way through. He'd go to work sick, but when that curtain
went up, man, that was it and he turned on the Waller light.

Underneath his constantly devil-may-care appearance, Fats
was a deeply religious man, always so busy living he didn't
know exactly what he wanted. He was sure of one thing, he'd
always say: a man's best friends were his woman, car, and

bankroll. He didn't have time for doctors. And that was his big mistake. He overdid everything in the manner in which he overate and overdrank. He never stopped to think that a person's life depended on how he took care of himself.

Fats was born down on Waverly Place in the old Greenwich Village Negro section, where his father, Edward Waller, maintained a religious home with a lot of hymn singing and Bible reading. Father Waller was a deacon in the Abyssinian Baptist Church.

I've already talked about how I first met young Fats when he took over the piano chair at Leroy's during one of my short vacations. When we met, he wasn't born yet. He was wished on me. From that time on he followed the Lion and The Brute around. We both tutored him and I was the one who first told him to sing and make faces to draw attention. He was always mimicking West Indian talk; I could see where he was a natural as a showman. He had that magnetic personality with big brown eyes.

As I've mentioned he was shy at first and I would loosen him up with sauterne. Later he drank ABD's* and started traveling so fast through life he forgot to eat. He just never took the time to set himself in the right direction. When he jumped from the basement to five thousand dollars a week, I told him to slow down. "Lion," he would say, "one never knows, do one!"

Waller was the biggest eater around Harlem up until the time he started drinking heavily. He could put away a couple of orders of corn beef and cabbage at five in the morning. Whenever we stopped in at Fat Man's (Turner's) bar on our all-night rounds, Fats would take on a load of hog maws or fried chicken or anything else at hand back in the kitchen. After he'd cleaned up all the available food in the joint he would chant, "I'm a harmful big armful." These expressions he was always using—most of them he put in the vocal choruses on his records.

You couldn't hurt Fats's feelings if you tried. He was low

* Anybody's drink.

down to the ground; he would laugh about what you'd said until you felt sad. He didn't worry about anything as far as outward appearances went and I was always playing straight man to him. As soon as he started to perform, he took over, talking and playing. If a person or a spot doesn't look right, I freeze. But not Fats. He dug right in and made himself at home.

That doesn't mean Fats never had any troubles. He had nothing but trouble. Every time he came around I knew he was still living on Beale Street (a hard-luck, mean section). Part of it was because he was a mama's boy, at least when I first knew him, and his life got all jumbled up at the time of her death. Then he took himself off and got married while I was out in Chicago. They lived with the girl's parents—always a bad mistake for anybody. Those cross-vibrations in a situation like that really play hell with one's peace of mind.

When I got back to New York in 1923 and saw that Fats had himself a new chick sitting alongside of him on the organ bench at the Lincoln Theater, where he was working steady, I knew his marriage had gone plunk. His new gal, Anita Rutherford, distracted him so much the Lincoln fired him. He once played "Squeeze Me" when there was a funeral being shown on the screen during a newsreel.

Fats and Anita were together for over twenty years.

There was an older boy, Thomas Waller, Jr., the son he had with his first wife, whose support caused Fats trouble until he died. His wife was always running Fats into court, even got him put away in the lockup for six months, for nonsupport. He was always short of cash because he was busy living it up. But his last year or so, he was finally making it faster than even he could spend it.

Another companion he frequently had sitting on the bench with him at the Lincoln was young Bill Basie from Red Bank, New Jersey. After Fats left there, he went on his first out-of-town tour with Liza (Katie Crippen) and her Shuffling Six, a fast vaudeville act. When he decided to leave that group, after a few months, he recommended Basie as his replacement. It was with this show that Basie got stranded in Kansas City, eventually becoming known as a K.C. jazz man.

Fats was a great storyteller and a good press agent for himself. He used to tell me some wild stories about how he got the titles for his various hit songs. Once, out in Gary, Indiana, he heard two of the town sharpies talking about a dance. "Say, boy," one said, "you goin' to that dance tonight?" The other one replied, "Ain't misbehavin', podner, ain't misbehavin'." Fats liked the expression so well he got his lyric writer, Andy Razaf, to use it in the words in one of their compositions.

Fats and Andy were speeding through Asbury Park one day on their way to Bradley Beach, New Jersey, to play a date. The local constable pinched them and took them to court where the judge laid a fifty-dollar fine on them. They didn't have the money.

"Give me a break, Mr. Constable," Andy said. "My fate is in your hands."

Both Waller and Razaf claimed that the constable softened, took the twenty-four dollars they did have, and let them go. The next day, those two sat down and composed "My Fate Is in Your Hands," or so they said.

Fats, whom the newspapers called "The Rachmaninoff of Jazz," sometimes improvised original numbers right on a recording date, like Duke Ellington has done. He was quick to dig up a new melodic line and it came to him so easy he would sometimes sell his tunes for next to nothing. He once let Fletcher Henderson have a dozen or more tunes for around a hundred dollars.

We all had to know the dirty lyrics that got involved with some of the best-known popular tunes, because we had so many requests from the customers in the cabarets. It got so we had to be very careful to sing the right words when we were working in front of the general public. Eugene Sedric, a clarinetist, once told me what happened when he was on the road with the

Waller group. They had been using up the time on the bus improvising new barroom verses for "Blues in the Night" and Fats was having a ball. They opened at the Paradise Theater in Detroit after an all-night run on the highway. During the first show, Fats started singing some of the smelliest phrases from the night before into the microphone. The management banged down the curtain and called the cops. It took them all day to get Fats out so that his show could finish the week.

Yeah, Fats was quite a rounder, as we used to say; we all were in those days. Up all night, always on the go, happy-go-lucky, that was Fats, the Lion, James P., Carolina Rice (Sam Young) —a rice eater from North Carolina—and Andy Razaf. Sometimes the Lion only went along to please the others because he didn't like the atmosphere in some places where he just didn't belong, especially the locations where the taste was low.

But no matter what we said to Fats about taking care of himself, he wouldn't pay attention. Before he was forty, Fats's health was not at all good. He broke up his regular group in May 1943, and only took a few one-night engagements. The royalties on his songs were pouring in and he was riding around in a four-thousand-dollar Lincoln with a chauffeur at the wheel. But the years of running around all winter without an overcoat, eating like Richard the Lionhearted, and drinking like a fish were beginning to catch up. He should have tried to take off weight many years before and the last time I saw him, his ankles were swollen and he could hardly walk.

He had been getting attacks, like epileptic fits, for quite a while, and when he felt one coming on he would have to get up and walk around. These would act on him like a cramp, so he got one of his cousins to travel with him and whenever he felt an attack coming on, his cousin would turn him over on the other side and the cramp would disappear. Coming back from the West Coast in December 1943, he was traveling with his manager Ed Kirkeby on the Santa Fe Chief. Early in the morning, while the train had stopped in the Union Station in Kansas City, Kirkeby heard Waller make a choking sound and rushed in to him. The big pianist was trembling as though in a spasm and when his manager, thinking he was having a nightmare, tried to shake him awake, he wouldn't come to. When they got a doctor in, Fats Waller was gone for good.

An autopsy later diagnosed his death as having been caused by bronchial pneumonia. He had rushed himself off at thirty-nine years of age, at about the time he was really beginning to make some money. The show *Early to Bed*, for which Waller wrote the score, opened on Broadway at around the same time. It was destined to make a lot of money and ran for over a year. He didn't.

That was the end of our Big Three. The passing of Fats and, later, the illness of James P. Johnson made me stop to think about my health and how to take care of it. Man just can't try to do things too fast—it's better to live slow and get the job done well.

The three of us used to argue about reincarnation. James P. believed in it. Fats didn't believe that man's soul returned in any other form during a future era. It was Waller's wish that he be cremated and he was.

22

Camp Unity

You got to pass my house to get to your house,
So don't do anything wrong to me.

WILLIE THE LION SMITH

One day in 1941 I'm walking down St. Nicholas Avenue and I
run into Bechet. So he invites me over to his place for another
blast of that corn of his. He said he had a gift he wanted to
present to me. It turned out to be a deer-handled cane.

After I had admired and thanked him for the new walking
stick, he came on with the catch. "Lion, I've got us a job for the
summer up in the woods near Poughkeepsie. We play a little in
the dining room, before and after supper, that's all. The rest of
the time we swim, play tennis, take walks around the coun-
tryside, *and read pamphlets.*

"What kind of pamphlets?" I ask.

"Oh, stuff about welfare, social reform, stuff like that. You
know."

I said, "I don't know, Sidney, if we have to walk back, that
place is too far from Harlem."

Well, we knocked the idea around, back and forth, for the
rest of the afternoon, as we played ping-pong and enjoyed

our whisky. Before long I found myself turned into one of those mechanical musicians, all wound up and ready to go.

That's how the Lion turned up at Camp Unity near Wingdale, New York. We had Frankie Newton on cornet, Everett Barksdale on guitar, Arthur Trappier on drums, in addition to Sidney and myself.

I knew something was wrong right from the start. Soon as we arrived everybody was slapping us on the back instead of giving us a firm handshake. They kept asking us if everything was all right. How the hell did we know?—we'd just gotten there.

The Lion can usually smell funny business and this Unity place, billed as an "interracial camp," was beginning to remind me of an experience trumpeter Oran (Hot Lips) Page and I had gone through a year or two previous to this time.

We had been invited down to a large apartment on Seventeenth Street in Manhattan for dinner. The people in charge were a wife-husband combination with a flock of angora cats. They were weird people and at first I couldn't figure what the vibrations signified other than the fact they didn't know how to approach other folks right. They wanted to promote Lips and me by setting us up with new suits, a horn (for Lips), and a one-thousand-dollar advance for which we were to sign a contract where we agreed to return the grand after things got rolling. These are the kind of set-ups musicians have to keep leery of. They get your name on the paper and then they start to tell you what you have to do. I checked into that Seventeenth Street crowd before we signed and found out they were Communists. We never did find out exactly what they had in mind for us to do.

So, before the first night was over up there at Camp Unity, I knew we'd been hooked into something that wasn't good. They kept calling us cats and I decided if I wanted to work in a cat house I preferred a real old-fashioned one.

Yeah, it didn't take long for any of us to realize we were in a nest of commies. They kept coming up to tell me, "You'd be a lot better off if you were not so hardheaded!" It took that Sidney and James P. Johnson to get you mixed up with the damnedest people.

You had to have a flashlight to get back to your tent at night. It was wise to place a big rock by the door of the tent in which you were supposed to sleep. Everything seemed to be catch as catch can, and everybody slept in a different place each night. It was the most mixed-up camp I ever saw or heard about—the races, the sexes, and the religions were all mixed.

One night when I got back to the tent and turned on the overhead bulb I heard a buzzing sound I couldn't locate. When I finally lay down to sleep a big turtle crawled out from under my pillow.

At the end of our first week I had lost twenty-five pounds from all the aggravation and the bad food. I felt like we were trapped —like on the *Titanic*—and the only way to be saved was to jump and try to get away.

Sidney was mad too, because they were always trying to get us to attend meetings. He told me after he'd caught one of their sessions, "I told them I couldn't see anything in that Communism stuff. Instead of the early bird getting the worm, they wanted the early bird to cut up the worm and give away all the pieces."

On the first Sunday I told Bechet I was going to town for the day because the air at Unity was no good for me. I had to get away before I found myself in Sandusky.* He said, "O.K., but be sure and come back and get your pay."

When I got over to Poughkeepsie I grabbed a train for New York City and found another piano man to go up and take my place. That climate didn't fit my clothes.

During those Depression days, the people in show business always had a bunch of Communists hanging around them through no fault of the artists. I thought the experience at Camp Unity had taught me a lesson.

* An expression signifying "nowhere."

But I was to get hooked again in 1945. I went out to Detroit to play at a club some booking agent had lined up for me and found myself in another interracial operation. This one was run by a group of colored women who were mixed up with a Communist organization. This time I hurried myself away after three nights.

You'd think that would have been the end of my friendship with Sidney, but in September he showed up on St. Nicholas Avenue with another deal. He opened with, "Lion, we are going to make a record. No singers—just you, me, and Barksdale!" Before I know it I'm back in Sidney's basement apartment around a jug—not brandy, but that same old hooch (corn whisky) and we are rehearsing a tune called "Strange Fruit" over and over again.

"Where did you get this number?" I asked Bechet. "Did those cats up at that camp lay it on you?"

He denied that they had anything to do with it.

In fact, it was a good number. Billie Holiday had recorded a vocal version the year before for Commodore records. We were to be the first ones to make it for a major recording outfit—RCA Victor.

We got eight tunes ready, and at 4:30 P.M. the day after the rehearsal, we went downtown to the Victor studios. That day we made some real fine sides—"I'm Coming Virginia," "Limehouse Blues," "Georgia Cabin," and "Texas Moaner Blues."

After we finished, Bechet, Barksdale, and myself stayed on to do two sides as a trio. Besides "Strange Fruit," we did "You're the Limit."

Bechet on the soprano sax on "Fruit" gave us a fit—it was great, just great. He was at his best and added new ideas from the way we had rehearsed the number.

And to my knowledge, those two trio sides have never been released, in spite of the fact that the "Strange Fruit" was recorded without any vocal chorus. It is hard to understand.

23

On a Park Bench

Lion, let us hear some of your tunes.

MY CUBS
(Mel Powell, Joe Bushkin,
Howard Smith, etc.)

Composing music has fascinated me for a lifetime. I've wanted
to beautify the music I've heard from the day I first heard my
mother play "Abide with Me" on the organ during my child-
hood. When I hear a melody I keep thinking of melodies of my
own that would make a tune even more beautiful.

I used to follow all the tough bands. You know how it is, when
a band leaves the bandstand it gets very quiet. They usually
call it a lull. They used to have piano players who would sit
there and nobody would pay attention. So what I wanted was a
hot chorus to take that lull away. Every time it would be time
for me to get them back, I would say, "Bring on the band.
They'll really send you. Bring on the band." That gave me an
idea for a tune.

The Lion was at a party one night, listening to the people
talking and drinking. They were acting as if everybody had a
different emotion or attitude. I got to thinking of Chopin and

the right-hand triplets, and dividing up the music with motion, thought, and emotionalism, I wrote "Contrary Motion."

I wrote "Finger Buster" after doing an exercise one day, working with a scale. I happened to be sitting talking to Clarence Williams—it was in his office in the Gaiety Building one afternoon. I wrote the first thirty-two bars of it right there. We used to sit around after the places closed, noodle around with strains, trying to see how fast we could play. I was playing double forte, or as fast as you can play.

I used to get off on wild sprees with Fats and Jimmy and different fellows like Jack Teagarden and Georgie Wettling. One morning I came home about nine-thirty after having a good time and I was groggy, so I started playing the piano and fooling around. I got a weird strain in the bass and I looked around again and I got it over and over again and I got another strain. Being half high, I called it "Zig Zag." The bass goes like a drum, half a tone down, half a tone up.

There was one very important thing I learned way back at the beginning and that was to always search for a melody or a certain theme that will capture the people right at the start. If you want your listener to be with you and follow your music you have to grab their fancy from the first note on.

During the last ten years I've heard more rotten music than I've ever had to listen to before. The kids open their rock-'n'-roll renditions with a belch, while the modern jazz men seem to start a selection in the middle and just stay there without building anything in either direction.

In my songs I have always tried to tell a story that describes a certain mood. For instance on a dark dismal day you have a blue mood and if someone should ask me to go to the piano and compose a tune the result would be to show how it is outside.

One of my best-known numbers, written in the early fall of 1935, had such a beginning. The night before I composed it it had been one of those nights when I had raised a ruckus and had finished the night out by riding back and forth on a subway train; every time I went through my station I was sound asleep.

When dawn broke, it turned out to be one of those real mellow fall days—warm, yet breezy, just like in the spring of the year. It felt good spiritually, as well as physically, to get out in the morning air away from the underground roar. The city was quiet and one could hear the sounds of nature.

Before entering my apartment I sat down on a park bench in front of City College and relaxed, absorbing the atmosphere. Under the inspiration of this scene a melodic line began to run through my mind.

Later that morning I was scheduled to give one of my pupils, Mel Powell, a lesson; I had been rehearsin' him for six months on "Otchi Tchornya," to help him develop some speed. When we were through I was sitting at the piano modulating and fooling around while looking outside at the clouds and trees. It was then that I worked out the complete composition. That one, "Echo of Spring," has proved to be one of my most popular pieces.

Playing long hours of solo piano in the cafés gave me the ability to improvise and experiment. Some of my compositions were derived from the ideas and melodies that entered my mind during those long hours. In fact, the chance to dream up my own ideas was one reason I've often preferred to work alone rather than in a band, or to play jobs where it was necessary to always follow the written score.

In the old days the Clef Club used to have a lot of classy bands playing classical and semiclassical music, but the players got bored because they couldn't tear off and get loose on their own. That is why a lot of them would look at the sheet and say, "Give me a shot of ether so I can cut this score!" The younger musicians, like the Lion, were studs and wanted to race on their own.

As a result the colored people have a fine record of composers and arrangers with original musical ideas—Duke Ellington,

Mary Lou Williams, Don Redman, Billy Strayhorn, Luther Henderson, Sy Oliver, Ernie Wilkins, Benny Carter, Fred Norman, Count Basie, Lloyd Phillips, and many others.

All the composers, lyricists, and arrangers get help or inspiration from each other. I have been inspired and influenced by Cole Porter, Irving Berlin, Harold Arlen, Noel Coward, Jerome Kern, David Rose, Roy Bargy, and others.

Although Negro musicians have always had a hard time getting jobs with radio and TV studio bands, they frequently want to use our styles of playing. To do this, they have to use us because we are the ones who not only originated it, but are the only musicians giving the music authenticity.

In 1931, when Freddie Rich had a band, at the Columbia Broadcasting studios they had a program of all-Gershwin scores. Rich, who used to come up to Pod's & Jerry's often, wanted me to come to the studio to give them some gut-bucket piano on several of those Gershwin numbers.

It was a fine band with Tommy and Jimmy Dorsey and trombonist Jack Jenney, the fellow who played the beautiful trombone solo on Artie Shaw's "Star Dust," and the late Eddie Duchin as house pianist. Duchin and the Lion were to alternate solos with my parts open for improvised jazz piano. I noted that those musicians were almost going blind from reading the sheets. Guys that have to read all the time are nothing more than slaves.

Playing with that large studio band at 10:30 in the morning was an experience: I was still high from playing uptown until 9 A.M.

I've done quite a bit of radio work, but sometimes those walls feel like they are closing in on you.

We've got two big problems in jazz composition today. On the one hand we have the ultramodern mathematical cats and on the other the juvenile rock 'n' rollers.

All this mathematics in music gets to be too much for the Lion. There have been plenty of times where I've worked alongside a musician who makes a freak chord, way out of key, and he'll turn around to me and say, "Did you dig that one! Man, that's one of my new chords." Well, I've heard some weird chords, but how they can swear they're in key when they're a tone and a half out all the time, is beyond me.

24

Willie the Lion, Cantor

I feel so poker-hauntedish,
Slightly a bit tauntish,
If you don't blow your wig
You'll knock me out of a gig.

WILLIE THE LION SMITH

Early in the forties, the swing era was reaching its peak and the Lion was in the middle of the alley with his own twelve-piece orchestra. Yeah! I was enjoying a long run at the Man About Town, on West Fifty-first Street. A block north on Fifty-second Street the modern bebop cats were beginning to take over. My new headquarters, known as "The Mat" for short, was the nightly hangout for the studio musicians from Radio City and we kept the joint so crowded it was always hard to get in. We had our own arrangements, so we did not encourage sitting-in, but this didn't keep the NBC musicians from stopping by to dig the band and relax themselves.

Billed as Willie Smith, the Lion of the Piano, and His Cubs, we had a line-up of star jazz men.*

* Dave Nelson, the nephew of the famed Joe (King) Oliver, was on cornet; Eugene Meyers, formerly with the Spirits of Rhythm, was our bassist and it was his playing style that inspired Slam Stewart to become an outstanding singing

It was while working on this job that real tragedy struck me unexpectedly. The spirits will sometimes throw a hard jolt into a person when things seem to be going along too good to be true.

All through the years my mother had been an invisible spirit that was always with me wherever I was playing. Before starting a performance it was my custom to always say a prayer for her—I still do to this day. Whenever I felt the need to relax or to keep the tensions down, I would play one of the hymns she used to play on the church organ or on the piano at home. My favorite, we both loved it, has always been the beauteous "Abide with Me." I just can't explain how it affects me, but it is so peaceful and reassuring.

One night she suffered a stroke. My mother was taken to the Newark City Hospital. When I went over, she had told the nurses that she hoped her boys would come to see her, and that Willie would surely come and bring her a pair of skates so she could get out. She didn't like the place and felt she was not getting the best of care. She had said to me, "Son, I want to get out of here. Don't let me stay here."

It took me about a month to get her released from City Hospital. She had been delirious several times and it was all they could do to keep her from running out to go home. When she finally did get back home she said to me, "Son, I don't ever want to go back there again." I promised her, "Well, you won't have to go back there. It's not a good place."

A few days later I went back home to Newark to visit her and sat in the parlor with my brother Melvin, who had also come from New York City. We decided then and there that if she got another stroke we would sign her into Beth Israel, a

bass man; a fellow named Lang (not the famed Eddie Lang) was on guitar; Jerry Blake, a veteran of the Cab Calloway band, who had been in Europe with both the Willie Lewis and Sam Wooding bands, was featured with us on alto saxophone and clarinet. After Meyers left, we had Duke Ellington's long-time bass man, Wellman Braud, who originally left his home town, New Orleans, with King Oliver around about the time of the First World War.

Jewish hospital on the outskirts of Newark. I knew they would take good care of her.

It happened a week later and this time I feared it might be the stroke you never come out of, the one that takes you away. I rushed to Newark and had her placed in Beth Israel, but she was in a coma. As she lay in her hospital bed that day I saw a black fly keep buzzing around her—that is a very bad sign for a sick person. I knew when I saw the fly the time was drawing near. When I left to return to work that night, I told the nurse, "Here's my telephone number so you can call me if there are any changes." It was the number at The Mat because the spirits told me something could happen at any minute.

Around about midnight of that same day I was playing with the band accompanying me, and right in the middle of a selection my hands stopped; they lay on the keyboard without moving. I sat there unable to sound a note for minutes. Then the headwaiter came up to the piano and said, "You're wanted on the telephone upstairs."

I had known what they were going to say from the time my hands froze at the piano. The message was, "Your mother has just passed on, Mr. Smith."

She's been gone for twenty years, but my mother's spirit and the expression on her face are still in my mind, just as if she was alive today. Whenever I make a decision regarding a job of any kind I always stop to think of what she would have said was the best direction for me to take. There are so many jazz musicians walking in the wrong direction—to bad jobs, to too many bars, to bad managers, to the one-way trolley up the hill—or down it.

The people at Beth Israel were very considerate and I began to think more about religion. I had always thought about the possibility of becoming a rabbi, but the opportunity to get the right education didn't come up. After my mother's death I became a member of a congregation of Jewish Negroes in Harlem and started studying religion. I got as far as becoming a

cantor. Because of my devotion to Judaism, I was called The
Lion of Judea.

When I had a studio on Broadway to do modern piano teaching, I also included on my calling card that I was "The Hebrew
Cantor." At that time I was cantoring at the synagogue located at 122nd Street and Lenox Avenue, where I was as fast
as the rabbi with the singing and chanting. This work was en-
joyable but I still had to make a living by playing the piano
all night. During this time, the Lion collaborated with Cantor
Goldman on several Yiddish compositions. One of these was
entitled "Wus Geven Is Geven," when translated it means
"Gone—Never to Return," and it was written as a memorial to
my mother.

As I have said before, I have always been interested in in-
vestigating all the different religious beliefs. Although I remain
loyal to Judaism and won't answer my telephone on Yom Kip-
pur, I still attend other churches when there is something coming up of interest to me.

My curiosity regarding Father Divine's flock once got the
best of me. Jane and I used to occasionally have supper at
Father Divine's place when he took over Rockland Palace during the Depression to serve meals to his followers for pennies.
The father left Harlem ten years ago when one of his woman
followers turned state's evidence against him; he had the most
devoted following of all time—he had his flock hypnotized. At
those Father Divine dinners you could eat all you wanted for
fifteen or twenty-five cents, but you had to stand in a long line
to get to the food. The cult was always singing, and no dogs
or profane language were allowed in the line. He had church
services every day starting with the breakfast session at 5 A.M.
But getting to see the father in person was harder to do than
getting to see Europe.

When Jane and I went to dinner at the palace we had to sit
at different tables. If you joined the flock you had to forget
your family. They gave you a different name and you had to

live in one of the father's places where you paid room rent; in fact, the money you made working had to be turned over as a donation. He would give out names like Heavenly Dove and Glorious Illumination and, as I have said, the members of the flock had to forget all about their husbands, wives, daughters, etc. A mother couldn't even talk to her own daughter, if she belonged, about the insurance money—she had to make Father Divine the beneficiary.

It was Father Divine who first greeted everybody with "Peace"; long before Dave Garroway started doing it on radio and television. The Lion recorded a tune entitled "Peace, Brother, Peace," written by Clarence Williams, way back in 1937, as a tribute to Father Divine and his large flock.

Although they sometimes operated like confidence men, both Father Divine and the late Daddy Grace gave a lot of folks peace of mind during times of stress.

Harlem has always had colorful, religious movements and I've checked them all out—Holy Rollers, Jehovah's Witnesses and those Baptists, the ones that can sing and dance and jump for hours without getting tired.

The Depression years of the thirties and the war years of the forties kept things jumping in New York City. They were the years that saw jazz music come of age; everybody wanted a jazz band to bring customers into their bars and cocktail lounges. I worked in all the midtown and Village spots during those years.

Adrian Rollini, a fine bass saxophonist and vibraphone player, had his own place in the basement of the President Hotel. The place was hopping with singing waiters and the sporting crowd. Occasionally we had some old-fashioned excitement, like the night Max Schmeling knocked out Joe Louis and the German bartender hollered, "Hooray, Max smashed that nigger!" The Lion hopped the bar swinging his cane like a baseball bat and made the guy apologize.

One night I was in the middle of a free-for-all at Cafe Society

Downtown. I had on my derby and some drunk grabbed a bottle off the bar and aimed it at my head. It wasn't long before full bottles were sailing through the air in every direction. Another place where the atmosphere was bad for Willie the Lion, was Nick Rongetti's place on lower Seventh Avenue. I went to help out Eddie Condon, who had the band there at the time. I was to play the piano between the regular band sets. No sooner had I started than Boss Nick sat down at another piano for a little two-part harmony. He could only play in the key of G and the results were terrible. I kept changing keys to get him away from the keyboard but he wouldn't budge. That was all. I cut out after that first set.

I had a long run in the Venetian Room at the Hotel Forrest on Forty-ninth Street; that hotel has long been the headquarters for the traveling sidemen from the big bands. A few blocks away on West Forty-fifth Street was the Hotel Whitby, another place where members of the swing bands camped while in Manhattan. Harry James, Ella Logan, and others from these two hotels kept the Venetian Bar packed every night. We had regular parties going when a crowd gathered around the chipped piano to sing along with the Lion.

During the middle nineteen forties I had a lot of gigs in Toronto, booked by Canadian Dave Gerrard, a good friend of mine. In October 1945, we filled the Eaton Auditorium for a big concert. The Lion's jazz band at the time included Sidney De Paris, trumpet; Wilber De Paris, trombone; Budd Johnson, tenor saxophone; the Lion, piano; Al Hall, bass; and Danny Alvin, drums. The listeners of that day were amazed that we didn't use any music sheets. I've always enjoyed playing in Canada because the audiences up there have more appreciation for good jazz than the average American crowd, and they show it by their applause, which stimulates the artist to do his best.

I almost went back on Broadway, in 1947, when they wanted me to lead a band in the original production of Tennessee

Williams' "A Street Car Named Desire." We rehearsed with the
show for several weeks for the opening in New Haven, Connecticut. The band I got together had Eddie Barefield on
clarinet, Dick Vance on trumpet, and Denny Strong on drums.
Turned out we were supposed to play six tunes during the
show, not on the stage, but in a glass cage offstage. That deal,
and the fact I was supposed to teach one of the cast members
to sing the words of "Hesitating Blues" for no extra money, got
me mad at the whole affair. I dropped out a few days before the
New York opening and turned the chair over to a young white
pianist named Johnny Mehegan.

That same year of '47, I had a gig I'll never forget—the Lion
plays a sex show. A "Dr. Frederick Wilson" from out west
somewhere, who sounded like that old-time preacher Steam-
boat Bill, came to town to do a series of lectures in a string of
Brooklyn theaters. He would talk only to an audience of men
with this pitch: "All you guys think you're great because your
wife told you she was going to have triplets or twins. If the
truth was known, you haven't even satisfied the little woman.
It is simple for a woman to become pregnant without ever
getting satisfied."

When he came on with the above lines, Old Doc Wilson
made his male audience fidgety. The idea was to get the men
to buy Dr. Wilson's herbs, a concoction guaranteed to make
every man big and strong.

To build his show up, Dr. Wilson used five colored acts. They
were the Lion on solo piano; singer Leonia Williams, who
sounded like an old-fashioned preacher; a couple of jugglers;
a singing-sister duo; and a couple of comedians doing a boogy
(fade-out) skit.

In the middle of the entertainment Dr. Wilson would appear
on stage to sell his tonic for a dollar a bottle. That bottled-up
mess was supposed to build up a man's nervous system and it
was surprising how many bottles he sold after scaring his
captive audience about their virility. At the end of each day he

would split up his take with the acts. We soon learned he was not a bona fide doctor, but an ex-carnival barker. Although he gave the appearance of being a deep man, he ran things like they do in the traveling carnivals out in the country.

Leonia, who had worked at Connie's Inn and the Cotton Club, and I tried to enjoy ourselves to make up for the low salary. But opening at the Supreme Theater in Brooklyn, we played a flopping six weeks. When the doctor announced he was taking the show to Philadelphia, both Leonia and I decided it was time to get off the merry-go-round—eight shows a day for seventy-five dollars a week was getting us nowhere.

As far as I know, the doctor never showed up in New York again to peddle that crazy no-good tonic.

25

Cognac and Cakes:
Willie the Lion, Teacher

You don't have to sing,
Just keep on the run,
Have lots of fun,
And keep shaking that thing.

You see mothers lugging kids downtown every day to Radio City or to the studios on Broadway. They all insist, "My kid's goin' to be a singer, a dancer, or a comic. He's gonna be one of the greats. He'll be better than better yet—I tell you. I know, he's my child and he's got to be good. He'll pick it up right away."

A man studies and works constantly to build up his art and his name for forty years, but these kids today are geniuses. They start right out at the top—big top names getting three thousand dollars per week for making noise on a guitar and bawling into a microphone. Whew, a lot of them can't even talk yet, much less speak good English.

It's getting so the agents on Broadway hide from any woman dragging a youngster down the street. They've joined the music publishers who are hiding from everyone carrying a brief case holding a future "Yes! We Have No Bananas" or "The Music Goes 'Round and 'Round."

Before any entertainer can be any good he has to learn the basics. The problem today is that no one seems to know or care about the important things in show business. Then by accident one of them gets a hit record and when it is time for them to appear on a stage or in front of a camera, they are lost—don't know how to walk, or what to do with their hands, and in most cases they are unable to sing, dance, or act. No wonder they fade away after the record stops selling.

The places where the great entertaining artists, like Jimmy Durante, Eddie Cantor, Milton Berle, Bob Hope, Frank Sinatra, and Bing Crosby got their starts, no longer exist. There are no more old-fashioned saloons, vaudeville theaters, and big dance bands. The young hopeful musicians are in the same boat. The jam sessions, where many of the great jazz instrumentalists developed their unique styles, are a thing of the past.

If there are going to be any great stars in the future there will have to be teachers and trainers who are capable of making them into real stars.

The Lion has been teaching worthy students from time to time over the years. During the nineteen forties I maintained the studio at 1674 Broadway, where I taught piano, voice, and how to use a microphone. But with all due respect to young talent a teacher is lucky if he finds two out of a hundred kids who are naturals. By naturals I mean those who have the spiritual power to climb up to the big time. My teaching experience has taught me that if the pupil is high strung, emotional, and affectionate, there is some hope he might make it.

The first thing I impress on a hopeful piano student is that he can't be anything that he is not. There is only one Lion, Tatum, or Fats Waller. If they try to imitate, then all they will get is headaches and they will start singing "Trees" when I knock them to their knees. They just can't act like a crazy man up a tree—they've got to be creative, mean what they play, and be able to perform with ease.

Today the big problem is that no one wants to work their left hand—modern jazz is full of single-handed piano players. It takes long hours of practice and concentration to perfect a good bass moving with the left hand and it seems as though the younger cats have figured they can reach their destination without paying their dues.

I have tutored prominent musicians in my time. Mel Powell was a student of engineering at the City College of New York when I first met him; he had musical ambitions and played in a Dixieland band up in Nyack, New York. He was short on money but long on talent and I could see he really wanted to be a professional pianist. Instead of cash he used to bring me strudel cakes, a half-dozen cigars, or a bottle of absinthe with a lump of sugar in it.

It took me six months of constant training to get him to develop some speed and to use his left hand. In later years, when he got with Benny Goodman's band, his head got as big as a house, and he said Teddy Wilson taught him all that he knew. He is Swedish and for some reason has left the jazz world entirely to concentrate on composing classical music. I don't hear anything about him any more and I guess he's forgotten all about those days when he was breaking into music on a seventy-five-dollar, broken-down upright with Willie the Lion showing him the way.

Another one of my regular pupils who became equally famous was little Joey Bushkin. I introduced him to his left hand, too. He brought me cognac for his lessons and in later years always gave me credit for getting him pointed toward the right destination. You still hear Bushkin occasionally on a television show or playing a smart night club with his trio. Like the Lion, he picks and chooses his engagements.

A favorite student of mine with whom I was always arguing was Dick Wellstood, who has turned into one of the finest rag-

time pianists you ever will hear. His problem was fighting the
piano too hard; I used to tell him to relax and let the music flow
out. Wellstood was the nervous type, always limbered up his
fingers by cracking his knuckles. He was very sensitive and set
up very high standards for himself; so high, that he was always
having trouble when he had to play with musicians who were
unable to keep up with him.

Howard Smith, a swing pianist with the Tommy Dorsey
orchestra during the thirties—he was the soloist on TD's best-
selling recording of "Boogie Woogie"—studied with me when
he first started out. I still see him frequently, as he works in
the studios with Garry Moore. Smith once made an arrangement of "Nola," using my riffs. Other students of mine who did
well were Milt Raskin, pianist with Gene Krupa's orchestra
during the swing era, and Walter Gross, the composer of the
beautiful tune "Tenderly," who now lives out in California.

They talk about the fabulous Peck Kelly, the Houston, Texas,
piano player, who refused to leave home no matter how much
money he was offered; one of my charges was just the same.
Jack O'Brien, of Hartford, Connecticut, a terrific piano man,
absolutely refuses to leave his home town. Every time I am
playing in Hartford we get together and he picks up on what
I'm putting down. It's a shame he has never come to the Big
Town—he'd be a sensation!

Bob Wilber, a one-time student of Sidney Bechet's, introduced me to one of my favorite pupils some years back. His
name is Dick Levy of Philadelphia. He is a cousin of the late
Manie Sacks, the discoverer of Frank Sinatra and a former
record executive at both RCA Victor and Columbia. Young
Levy would come to hear me on a job and then take me home
in a cab. I would teach him the piano and how to score music.
He is still active in music and has composed in all the various
idioms from popular songs to classical music, including jazz
and ballet. In the summer of 1961, Jane and I made a special
trip to Philadelphia to attend a musical play called *The Elegant*

Witch at the John B. Kelly Playhouse. The show, staged by the Children's Theatre, featured a score written by Levy and the book and lyrics by Samuel Rulon, a prominent chemical engineer. The Lion is very proud of this student.

Currently I am working with another young man of whom I have great hopes. His name is Mike Lipskin and he comes from a highly intellectual family out on Long Island. Mike's mother is a painter and his younger brother Sam is studying to be a classical concert pianist. Lipskin comes regularly for lessons and is at present attending Bard College up in Annandale-on-Hudson, New York. He is already an authority on the Harlem piano style and has written articles for the music publications on the various stride pianists.

In addition to pianists I've tried to instruct all musicians along the same general lines regarding showmanship and learning their trade. This includes the many bands that I have led —I'd always tell them the band is as big as the leader and the arrangements. I could take a church orchestra and after an hour's rehearsal turn it into a jazz band if the men in the band had music in their souls.

Negro music is based on soul. Take the gospel singers, they are all highly emotional and have plenty of soul and feeling. They are physically strong people, like bulls, but when they play New York's Apollo Theater the management has nurses standing by to look after them when they come offstage. They always have to take a long rest after a show.

The Lion can make a star if the student has music in his soul and will practice.

26

Slow Down, Lion

Every time I took a drink,
I'd say, it's later than you think,
So why kick up a stink,
Just try to keep in the pink,
Yeah, I'll do if I don't mildew.

WILLIE THE LION SMITH

An old friend of mine, a blues singer named Trixie Smith, used to say, "Man, you keep missin' your couple of meals a day, you'll run out of gas!" Trixie knew what she was talking about, but the Lion, James P., and Fats just couldn't be bothered back during the twenties and thirties. Then came the forties; Fats Waller died in 1943; James P. suffered a stroke in 1940 from which he never completely recovered; and the Lion, without knowing it, had a seat on the last trolley.

Lillie Johnson was going to follow James P. in a short time. She died taking care of him. She had to take him around and her hearing was going wrong while he was getting to the point where he couldn't speak. She had to get close to him to talk. There were complications.

The last time I saw my old friend, he was in a coma. For two weeks he hadn't spoken to anybody. I thought to myself: Old Fats, the Gemini; James P., the Aquarius; and Willie, Sagittarius. There was an old piano in the room and I sat down. I played the "Carolina Shout." It was his tune, his piano selection, and I played it like he played it. It was stride piano, guys playing with two hands. Then Jimmy opened his eyes and smiled. He managed to write out a message. LION, it said, THEY WERE TOO GOOD TO THE PIANO PLAYERS WITH ALL THAT FREE BOOZE AND RICH FOOD. IT CATCHES UP WITH YOU.

* * *

I thought back to Fats's funeral. It was a full church and Adam Clayton Powell was the preacher. He could preach. But I wasn't satisfied. He knew who was in the audience, and how close Tom Waller, James P., and myself had been. But there they were, all of them, all talking about how good they were to Fats. Yet they used to toss him around before he got a name.

James P. Johnson's private name for the Lion was "Cuz" and I usually called him The Brute or The Bear Cat. He was a worrier and it seemed like he was always getting into trouble over some little thing that didn't mean anything. All he wanted to do was just play the piano; other things he didn't care about. He wasn't much of a showman because if he could manage it he always sat at the piano with his back to the audience. He was soft-spoken Jimmy, rarely talked above a whisper, and he would let people take advantage of him. He just couldn't be bothered by anything that didn't have something to do with playing or composing music. A sort of shy, retiring type that I would have to pump and wind up.

We bummed around together a good deal in the early days and worked in most of the same places in The Jungles and uptown. It was our policy to be dressed sharp and we both liked our little taste. There was many a night we never made it to bed and later on when young Waller started to hang out with us, he set us a fast pace with the capacity he had for the juice.

Johnson and his wife Lillie lived on 140th Street. Lillie took quite a fancy to young Fats. He spent a lot of time practicing on James P.'s piano around four and five in the morning. It got so Lillie was losing sleep and she'd have to run him home.

It is my opinion that James P. was a better composer than Fats, although Waller's tunes have had much more success. Johnson started to invent his own melodies back in 1914 when I had just met him. His most famous rag was the "Carolina Shout," a number that all the New York ragtimers used to feature. Ernest Green, who is still alive and playing a Wurlitzer organ with forty-four keys up in Albany, New York, got Johnson interested in classical music and it was Green who taught him to read and write music.

The tune that James P. wrote that I was most fond of was his "Caprice Rag." I recorded this number for Blue Circle records in the early 1950s, along with Johnson's "Carolina Shout," "Porter's Love Song" (To a Chambermaid), "Stop It, Joe," "If I Could Be with You One Hour Tonight," and others. The last tune, a great popular composition, got Jimmy into the American Society of Composers, Authors, and Publishers. Millions of people know the tune, but how many could tell you who wrote it?

The Lion recorded this special long-playing record of Johnson compositions at the same time that I held a benefit for him at Town Hall in 1953. He was completely paralyzed from 1953 to 1955. I was in business with Neil Lawrence in Blue Circle records and we staged it. All of the old-timers, including Clarence Williams, Luckey Roberts, and Ethel Waters, were there to pay tribute to a good friend. We had a wonderful long list of sponsors, including Duke, Cab Calloway, Count Basie, Lionel Hampton—it did a lot to bring up his spirit.

James P. started to devote most of his time to writing show scores during the early twenties. He also got on an arranging and conducting kick. It was his hope he could become a symphonic conductor. From then on he had no eyes for clowning or showmanship. I used to tell him that when we ran into pianos with the keys broken you had to mug your way to entertain the people. His reply was, "Lion, it just ain't dignified." In later years Danish concert pianist Victor Borge came along and proved he was wrong.

During the twenties, Johnson wrote the music for such shows as *Running Wild*, which featured his "Old-Fashioned Love" and "The Charleston." He also toured the vaudeville circuits and conducted the orchestras playing for the tab shows at the Lafayette.

By the time the thirties rolled around, he was all wrapped up in orchestral writing for concert groups. He produced his "Yamacraw," "Symphony Harlem," and his "Piano Concerto." I remember he performed his "Piano Concerto" with the Brooklyn Symphony Orchestra at the Academy of Music.

James P. and Luckey had a sort of rivalry going for a time during the thirties. Roberts had a Carnegie Hall concert where he featured his compositions. Then Johnson did a Carnegie concert. Roberts did a Town Hall concert, but James P. couldn't get one lined up. I did it for him when I played that benefit in 1953.

Illness began to bother James P. as early as 1940 and as the years went by he kept getting worse. He spent most of the last ten years of his life at his home in Jamaica, Long Island. A second stroke in 1951 left him unable to speak and he was confined to his bed.

For years, going all the way back to 1914, I was drinking for kicks. Drinking, I found that I could play for longer periods without getting tired. During Prohibition, the underworld guys never took a drink from any bottle that had been opened; when I sat down with them between sets they always ordered a fresh bottle for the piano player. The booze helped me to pace myself through the long night. My schedule was to start at 9 P.M., eat a big meal at midnight, and revive myself for a second and third wind with a large taste. It wouldn't have been so bad if I had then gone home to bed, but there were the after-hour spots and the party flats to be visited. There were nights when my head never touched a pillow and days when my stomach never felt food. We lived fifty years in five years' time, BUT WE WERE ALL MAKIN' AN EARLY DATE WITH THE CEMETERY.

Yeah, many a morning I found I had been sleeping in a taxi, a subway train, or on a park bench. Back in the days when the subway turned into the elevated up on 110th Street I used to get a big thrill when the train, way high up over the street, would make a sharp turn at the bend over 110th; but when I was cold sober it would scare me so much I couldn't look out the window. So when I was goggle-eyed from the ether I'd make a special trip just to ride that train.

I inherited the Bertholoff traits from my real father—a love for wine, women, song, and gambling. In my younger days I was a great one for being around when the bottle was passed, especially the brandy—my favorite was brandy—only drinking whisky for its strength-giving value.

The Lion usually carried a heavy load and as the years went by it began to be the other way around—that load was carrying the Lion. Every conductor on the Sixth Avenue subway line knew my station and used to wake me up so I wouldn't ride back and forth the entire length of the line. There were many cab drivers in Harlem who would stop and pick me up from a park bench and drive me home. Every guy who's worth a dime has taken me home at one time or another.

Along about the mid-forties I found I was having a hard time shifting gears. My legs and ankles began to give out and I found it necessary to ride the rest of the way home.* There had been a time when I always walked from Times Square to Harlem (from Forty-second Street to 110th Street). My

---

* The Lion wrote a tune in 1948, called "I'm Gonna Ride the Rest of the Way."

strength was giving out and the strain was beginning to tell. I had always fancied myself as being like those characters on the Bowery—those guys are stronger than bulls and after they get three shots of canned heat they can lift a truck.

It was a saying in the old days that there was good booze and bad hooch; the booze never killed anybody but watch out for the hooch. We used to think booze was good protection against the cold, damp weather. It took some of us a long time to realize that when you drink it opens your pores and the cold goes right through you, resulting in pneumonia. My good friend, the drummer, Kaiser Marshall, rushed off overnight in 1946 when he caught pneumonia.

That business about forgetting to eat hit me hard when Tommy Ladnier died in 1939. He was living with Mezz Mezzrow and passed away suddenly one afternoon. They said he died because he kept on drinking hard while he was undernourished.

The way I was feeling began to worry me a lot in 1946. If I stayed away from the stimulants I found my playing would suffer as I would get tense and tied up inside. Finally I went to see a German doctor over on 138th Street. At the time I weighed 220 pounds and had a mouthful of gold teeth. The doctor gave it to me straight in the eye. "My friend," he said, "you have high blood pressure, and you'd better start taking care of yourself. Get those infected gold teeth out and lose some weight. Slow down, or you are going to fall out one of these nights."

It was the doctor's word that the main thing was for me to learn to relax. He was a German Catholic and he gave me some incense to take to my apartment to help me create a restful atmosphere. It was around this time that the Lion moved into his new lair at 300 West 151st Street. It has always been my feeling that the apartment where one lives is sacred and it is necessary to have a place where the vibrations are right and you can sense the spiritual forces at work.

For over fifteen years now I've had the same apartment. I

frequently burn incense and sometimes light white candles to give me the proper setting for complete relaxation. This gives me the opportunity to think things out and find out about myself by looking at both my mean and good sides. My den, located in the valley off Eighth Avenue four blocks south of the Polo Grounds, is also where I practice the piano for many hours. My old music professor, Hans Steinke, had taught me how to relax while playing. He showed me that when you sit erect you become tense, and he pointed out how to stretch the legs out for relaxation, while at the piano and at home in an easy chair.

I did the other things he told me to do. My dentist, Dr. Williams, removed the bad teeth and I lost around twenty-five pounds.

But the Lion still had to let his hair down once in awhile. I kept on working in those smoky night clubs, night after night. One morning when I was paying my respects to my many musician friends in Greenwich Village I had the big scare.

It happened at the Village Vanguard on Seventh Avenue where I was batting the breeze at the bar with two piano men, Cliff Jackson and Hank Duncan. As I got ready to leave I had a dizzy spell and collapsed into a chair. Now, I knew for sure I was on the list—that trolley was getting to the end of the line.

Cliff Jackson took me upstairs and started to put me in a cab, but I insisted I could make it myself on the subway. He helped me over to the station and after he left I got out on the platform where the blind staggers hit me again. Somehow I finally managed to get home. That early-morning experience was something I'll never forget. It was a nightmare. And it was the beginning of my long siege of weekly treatments, as well as the ending of my wild period.

Several days later I ran into Duke Ellington on the street and told him what had happened. The Lord sends us to friends when we are in trouble and Duke insisted that I immediately go and see his doctor, Dr. Arthur Logan, who makes his headquarters at the Health Center, 152nd Street and Amsterdam Avenue.

Taking Ellington's suggestion was one of the smartest moves I ever made. Dr. Logan, the finest physician in Harlem, takes a personal interest in musicians and I would guess he, along with Dr. Kenneth Wilson, a dentist, has been responsible for keeping over two hundred artists and entertainers alive since I've known them. Ellington phones him the minute he has any aches and pains, regardless of where he might be at the time. Yes sir, everybody has their cycle.

Doc Logan has been my best friend and adviser now for over fifteen years. His lovely wife, Marion Bruce Logan, has also been a great comfort to the Lion. Before she became Mrs. Logan she was an entertainer at the Cafe Society Downtown.

The doctor told me straight, right off the bat, "Lion, you can't take that trolley ride yet for a while, but you've got to get some ventilation and proper food to survive." He meant that when you get up there at the top, you have to stop spending those long hours in the cooped-up joints full of liquor fumes and smoke.

Yeah, the doctor changed and preserved my life, by insisting I take vitamins, eat good (steaks, broiled chicken, lima beans, corn, and I use a little brandy with milk), and get plenty of the staffs of life—music, sleep, and affection. He told me, "It takes four years for an individual to learn to breathe right, but if that person is not careful he can unlearn in four seconds." It is very important to have peace of mind because, as the doctor says, "If the mind is not right the legs will falter—keep smiling and keep eating."

Dr. Logan's sign is Virgo, indicating he is a person who will finish whatever he starts, believes any person will live long and well, providing he learns to have spiritual control—the mind over the physical. When you are emotionally upset, you can age five years in two hours because that emotion is more powerful than all the whisky in the world. He suggested that I stay in New York City as much as possible, not only to take regular treatments, but in the big city I would run up against less aggravation. When the doctor is out of town, his sister Dr. Myra Logan takes care of his patients and whenever one of us needs medicine at any time of day or night the pharmacy at the Health Center, under the direction of Dr. Howard O. Reckling, will deliver it immediately to our homes. The center is officially known as the Upper Manhattan Medical Group. In a tribute to their good work Duke Ellington and his orchestra once recorded an original composition titled "U.M.M.G.," on which Dizzy Gillespie made a guest appearance featured on trumpet. There is none better than the entire staff of the U.M.M.G.

There are a lot of musicians still around that should stop and take inventory before it's too late. Every day you read of one of them dropping out. They can't forget the joints after they play a gig and you can walk into the bars frequented by the older jazz musicians, like Beefsteak Charlie's or The Copper Rail any time of day or night and see them acting like winos. It's the life of the alley cat that shortens your time.

Don't you worry, you can't worry, or you'll die in a hurry. I know now if I had tried to keep a band going the last ten years I wouldn't be around to talk about it. Too much aggravation. You have to beg the guys to play, to get them on the stand, and after they are finally up there you have to beg them to play right, while you inhale all that foul air.

You can't keep rushing or they will know where to find you on Decoration Day. So many of my close musician pals are gone—Fats Waller, Tommy Ladnier, James P. Johnson, Tricky Sam Nanton, Bubber Miley, Bix Beiderbecke, Jimmy Blanton, Charlie Christian, Paul Seminole, Mamie Smith, Tommy and Jimmy Dorsey, and many others—all of them too young to die.

Between the doctor's guidance and my Jane's cooking, the Lion has fared pretty well. They say you are reborn every twenty years and I'm now going into my fourth span. There is no more of that meeting myself at the door when it's time to go to work.

To enjoy a long and worthwhile life a person must put faith in religion, astrology, and the medical sciences. AND STAY OUT FROM UNDER THE ETHER! A brandy a day keeps the black fly away.

Why, the Lion might have been dead.

27

Jupiter in My House

> *You're not taking a chance*
> *when you're riding Air France,*
> *because the women are nice and the men are fine,*
> *I've ridden all kinds of planes,*
> *but that never worried my mind,*
> *Once you ride Air France, You'll ride with them all the time.**

After the Lion had been away from the night-club routine for some months, keeping busy with concerts, recording, composing, and one-night engagements, Dr. Logan made a suggestion. "Lion, why don't you think about making a world tour? The change will do you good."

It wasn't a bad idea. Europeans liked jazz and had taken note of its importance as an art form before our countrymen over here got around to it. My friend Hugues Panassié of France wrote the first book on jazz, *Hot Jazz*, in 1934. I have corresponded with M. Panassié for many years.

In America during the early days everyone kept jazz a secret from everyone else. Even the musicians tried to hide the music from each other. A guy who worked for a club owner who

---

* Lyric from "What's My Name—Trains and Planes" by Willie Smith (unpublished).

liked jazz sometimes didn't want other musicians to know about it for fear they'd get his job.

When World War II was over, there was a big push on to get American musicians to go over and perform in France, Sweden, England, and Germany. Both Panassié and Charles Delaunay (author of *Hot Discography*) came over here from France to make records and to line up artists for European tours. The trouble was they couldn't offer the money we could get playing right here at home during those boom days after the war.

After they got back to Europe, Panassié and Delaunay continued to set up concert tours and would send women over to sweet-talk the American jazz men into making the trip. There always seemed to be some chick around Jimmy Ryan's place on Fifty-second Street trying to sign up artists. You never knew how certain a deal you were getting into; some of the guys got hung up after they got on the other side.

One night a girl offered the Lion three hundred dollars a week to play a series in France for Delaunay. It was turned down later that same evening when I learned the same person had gone down the street to the Famous Door and offered Coleman Hawkins, the tenor saxophonist, one thousand dollars per week for the same tour. I decided that if I ever did go over, I would work for Panassié.

In fact Panassié had been insisting for some time that I come to Paris for a visit. I had not been back since World War I, but my health was such that I didn't quite feel up to it. Besides, like Duke Ellington, I don't care one little bit about that flying jazz.

When December 1949 came along, Jane learned that Dr. Logan was in favor of my taking a European journey. I told her I didn't like to fly and wasn't going to go. So, like our lady friends very often do, she went out and bought two tickets to Paris by Air France. That did it. Now I had to go, poor health and all. My weight had dropped to around a hundred and sixty,

which meant I was as far underweight as I had been over-
weight a couple of years before.

As Jane and I walked up the gangplank at Idlewild on a
windy dismal night, my wide-brimmed hat blew off and rolled
on down the runway. Jane ran after it and got it back to me so I
could pose with my cane, hat, cigar, and bottle of cognac for
the photographers from the New York press.

When I get into a plane I usually take a couple of stiff belts
of brandy before I start praying; as I've already told you flying
is not my favorite form of travel. The overnight hop to Paris
makes for a long session and I wasn't going to wait for them
to serve cocktails after we had arrived above the clouds. The
getting up there is the nervous part; that, and getting back
down.

There was a rabbi sitting in front and he kept turning around
to look at me. Finally I spoke to him in Hebrew and got started
on a long conversation with him. He kept asking me, "What's
your name?" While I was studying on how to say "What's my
name?" in Jewish, the lyrics for a song started to run through
my head.

Except for a period of a half hour, used for conversing with a
Catholic priest, another fellow passenger, I spent the rest of the
long night working on my ditty, which I called "What's My
Name—Trains and Planes." When it was finished I talked to
the pilot and the hostess before singing it for everybody. It
helped all of us to forget the long monotony of the flight. It
was a comedy novelty song dedicated to Air France.

When the plane landed in Paris all the lovely French people
were there to greet us. Panassié and his Madeleine (Gautier)
had a gang of brandy on hand and we all took four or five nips
as we toasted each other. Then, after having something to eat,
we drove straight to the broadcasting studio, where I started
making records for the Vogue label. They sure didn't waste any
time getting the Lion to roar.

Late that night we checked into the Hotel Ronceray, on the

Boulevard Montmartre, which became our home for the entire time in Paris. The next day the Lion and his Lioness started to have a ball up and down the Champs-Elysées. Everybody was so fine.

Panassié, Madeleine, Jane, and I went to Inez Cavanaugh's place in the rue Pigalle for dinner. It was a small downstairs night club known as Chez Inez; at that time Inez was married to the Baron Timme Rosenkrantz from Copenhagen, Denmark. Both Inez and Timme are well known around New York in jazz circles. In 1955, Miss Cavanaugh ran an exclusive small club in the Wall Street section. The baron is noted for being the first man to record Erroll Garner.

"How big is this joint?" I asked her.

"Oh, this is a small bistro," she replied, "where all the stragglers hang out."

"In other words you've got me in a place where all the bums congregate. It's like those joints on Eighth Avenue."

"Yeah, exactly," she says, fast, "we get a bunch of downhearted guys who meet here to talk about the past."

We had our fine-tasting chicken on those high benchlike tables you find in France. When it came to be time for the entertainment to start, an old friend of mine came out on the floor to sing French songs. It was Charlie Beal, a piano player who once played in Louis Armstrong's big band, but left the States many years ago to live in Europe. He's still there and is now working in Rome. He is now back to playing the piano, but when I saw him in Paris he was concentrating on his singing accompanied by a French pianist.

Jane and I were on the go from dawn to sunset to dawn. The French were still warm people and they idolized jazz stars. Bechet was treated like a king of France in Paris, when he lived there from 1952 to 1959.

It was always "be my guest" with those folks over there. On my recording dates they would spread out all the sandwiches, caviar, and booze I could handle. In New York you are lucky if the recording supervisor sends out for coffee.

The European teen-agers have made American jazz musicians popular in the various countries. Just this past year I received a letter from a young Swiss boy in which he said that he admired my "swinging and melodious piano playing really very much." This is just one of many that the Lion gets out of a clear sky.

It was over ten years ago that I was in Paris. You sometimes think you will be forgotten if you don't go back regularly. A friend of mine returned from the French city not so long ago. "You know I walked into a small bar in Montmartre one night and there was a young girl sitting at the piano playing—she didn't work there—and do you know what she was playing, Lion? Your 'Echo of Spring.' "

After concert performances in Europe I was surprised to have seventy-five-year-old ladies come up to shake my hand. Some would ask all kinds of questions about how jazz musicians fared in America. I didn't have the heart to tell them that the cruelest and coldest audiences in the world are right in New York City.

My European tour lasted a bit over a month; after leaving Paris I played the French provinces; Antwerp, Belgium; Barcelona, Spain; Switzerland and all over North Africa—Tangier, Algiers, Casablanca.

Everywhere we went the music was well received. I had a frightening but funny experience. The program in France called for me to open the concerts playing "La Marseillaise," the French national anthem. When we hopped to Zurich I didn't change the routine and opened with the French song. When no one stood up, clapped, or hollered, I got mad. I thought they were being unpatriotic. After blowing my top with what few French words I knew, I was told that we were in Switzerland and I had been playing the wrong anthem.

It was a wonderful trip. I hope to do it again. Panassié keeps in touch with me every year and makes me an offer and when the planets are again in the right position, Jane and I will wire Panassié to line up the dates.

Jupiter, the money planet, was in my house at the time of my last trip. The Lion may not wait until 1967 when Jupiter is again due.

28

Those Everlasting Saints

Don't think I retired,
I just retired from Central Plaza,
Before it retired me.

WILLIE THE LION SMITH

Shortly after returning from Europe, the Lion was called upon to help get the jazz at the Plaza sessions under way. This Plaza turned out not to be the famous hotel; it was the Central Plaza, a Jewish catering hall at 111 Second Avenue on New York's Lower East Side. They specialized in wedding receptions and bar mitzvahs.

They had tried renting out one of the ballrooms for jazz concerts. Much to everyone's surprise those Friday and Saturday night affairs drew customers like flies and for a while they even added Sunday-afternoon jamfests. That was over ten years ago and the weekly bashes were still going on in 1962. But I got tired of dodging the waving arms by 1958.

The top man in charge was Bernie Birns, who didn't know the first thing about jazz. To manage the operation, Birns brought in Jack Crystal, then the manager of Milt Gabler's Commodore Music Shop, to handle the music end. Crystal put me in charge of the musicians and I would get my friends like trumpeter

Roy Eldridge and drummer Jo Jones to come down and play for kicks. Guys like Roy and Jo dug the scene as long as they had good men to play with in those freewheeling get-togethers. The bread,* which was low, didn't matter if they were free for the night.

As I said, things started to go well right from the beginning, and it was a ball. Even Bernie Birns's father, who had been seriously ill for a long time, came down and he claimed the happy Dixieland was making him well.

The sessions were held in a fifth-floor ballroom—a place that was probably called a grand ballroom during World War I—with red and blue neon tubes lighting the room up in place of the old-fashioned chandeliers that were still hanging from the ceiling. With a little crowding they could get around fifteen hundred people jammed into the place.

On the dance floor they placed tables and chairs like in a regular cabaret, with a spot left vacant in the center for those who wanted to dance. And there was dancing of all kinds, from the wildest jitterbugging to the lovers' knot.† Some of the characters that used to show up from the Lower East Side, dressed and danced like the apaches I had seen in the Paris cellars.

The admission started out at around a dollar and eventually rose to two bucks per person. They sold pitchers of beer for a dollar and bottles of Imperial whisky were available for six dollars a fifth. Many brought their own bottles.

At first we attracted jazz fans, but as time went on they began to be replaced by hell raisers from the Bronx to Brooklyn. You would also see a smattering of college and high school students, parties made up of Ivy Leaguers and society folks from Park Avenue, and quite often there would be big-name celebrities. Regardless of who was there it could be classified as a motley crowd.

* Musician's word for money.
† A dance where the couple stands and embraces without moving from the one spot.

THE CENTRAL PLAZA BLUES

Between the heat, the crowd, the booze, and the jazz there
would be times when all *hell* would break loose. The management had to beg them with table placards and speeches to re-
frain from breaking the glasses, bottles, chairs, tables, and
lights. One night they ripped the floor indicators from above
the three elevators. Birns figured out there was no profit operating on New Year's Eve because the breakage expense was far
greater than the net profits could possibly be. He told me, "On
an ordinary night our audience breaks half the beer pitchers,
at least fifty chairs, and a dozen tables." Once the joint got to
jumping, nobody was satisfied unless he was dancing on a
table that was not built for the purpose. You have a problem
when you mix together nitwits, morons, and tush hogs with
their own cheap wine.

The musicians who worked the Plaza called themselves the
Foreign Legion. The marching song got to be "When the Saints
Go Marching In." They used to turn out all the lights and play
the "Saints" at midnight, but it got so rough they had to reverse
the procedure by turning every light in the place up and ringing
the crowd with cops. There was always a slew of cops on hand
to collect their payola, eat frankfurters on the house, and to
keep the "Saints" from causing a riot.

That "Saints" ritual was something to behold. From the
opening note at 9 P.M. the audience would start hollerin',
"When are we gonna hear the 'Saints'?" By midnight the tension was really built up. We would start playing the number
while still on our three-foot-high bandstand against the back
wall; at about the fifth chorus one of the horn men would start
leading the parade off the stand and around the hall. Big Chief
Moore, the Pima Indian trombonist, was the favorite leader—

and by the time the band returned to the stand the crowd was in a frenzy. Everybody was screaming, wriggling, and throwing glasses. It was a good thing I couldn't carry the piano around or they would have had *me* snake-dancing around. I always turned my back to the crowd while pounding the piano, so a flying bottle wouldn't hit my glasses and put my eyes out. There were usually five more choruses after the band returned to the stand. This was when things would get *real* rough, as everybody joined hands and played crack-the-whip. Some of those dancers knew judo and it was sometimes hard to tell whether they were dancing or practicing their judo. You'd see a guy throw his partner in the air and then run like hell to catch her when she came down. You can easily see why it was necessary to turn up all the lights—to guard against someone getting killed, that's why.

Then one night a fellow named Roger Tilton arrived on the scene and decided he wanted to make a movie of the Central Plaza activities. He wanted to show everything exactly like it was happening. First he brought in some professional moviemakers. They told him it would be impossible to catch it as it really was. They presented him with a lot of road blocks: the dancers would stumble all over the sound cables, they would have to use real actors because the kleig lights would goof up all the hams and they wouldn't act natural, plus about a hundred other problems and excuses why they couldn't make the picture.

This fellow Tilton was real stubborn. He decided to hell with Hollywood and he went ahead and figured out ways to do it on his own. He set up a tape recorder and got about four cameramen running all over the place, taking pictures under the tables, lying on their backs, from a balcony, standing on the chairs and tables, and they even went down and took a picture of Pee Wee Russell getting off the subway on his way to the session. He had special light reflectors built for the job in Chicago so they could do away with the kleig lights.

After they got about an hour of our music on tape simultaneously with all the picture taking, they went into a laboratory and "married" the sound to the pictures as they were run off on a screen. By that I mean they watched the action while editing the tape to get the appropriate tune going on the sound track for what was going on in the pictures. Some of it was easy to do—like when the camera caught the Lion in a close-up, they picked out a part of the sound where you heard solo piano. There were other scenes where they had to do some guessing—like what sound to use for a close-up of a pitcher of beer sloshing and bouncing on a table as the jazz fans beat their hands to help us keep time.

All the dancers and listeners were Central Plaza regulars. The film was actually made on a Wednesday night with all the regulars who showed up admitted free. The only pros on hand were the musicians—Jimmy McPartland, trumpet; Jimmy Archey, trombone; Pee Wee Russell, clarinet; the Lion, piano; Pops Foster, bass; George Wettling, drums—and the Jazz Dancers, Leon James and Al Minns. The last two did a couple of specialties for the film, but were made to look like they were just weekly customers. James and Minns were prizewinning dancers back in the jitterbugging days at the old Savoy Ballroom; they can do every jazz dance from the cakewalk to the twist.

Well, Tilton and his helpers did what they set out to do. The finished film, called *The Jazz Dance,* was a twenty-minute talkie shown at the Paris Theater in New York City. They also took the sound track and put it in a long-playing record album.

Up until then, things weren't too bad at Central Plaza. We had some devoted fans; when I would take the wrapping off a fresh cigar some joker would rush up to retrieve the cellophane as a souvenir. But as time went on, the money didn't get any better—regardless of the size of the crowds.

They started mixing up the bands willy-nilly so you never knew who you were going to be playing with. And then they brought in the off-key kid, Conrad Janis and His Tailgaters, who drove the crowd wild playing his trombone while standing on top of the piano. Yeah, he terrorized the place, everybody would stampede—Conrad's so full of emotion and nothing happens. This appealed to the younger squares. Some of them don't care as much about jazz as a monkey cares for watermelon. For their admission they were zooming for a free ride on anything and having a ball without hearing the music.

The Lion was usually frustrated. The only time you could hear the piano was early in the evening before the ruckus got under way. My boy Dick Wellstood, who played for a while with the Janis band, used to go all to pieces in a half hour. I'd catch him when he came off and say, "Don't try to fight it, don't fight the piano! Bad music is like poison to the real musician." It was madness in 110-degree temperatures—they didn't have a cooling system of any kind. When you've got a thousand people crammed into one room, the tempers are all short. You had to fight your way in and way out—fight everyone from the doorman to the manager, who wouldn't get the piano tuned, or even fixed when the foot pedal was broken. Another thing we had to contend with was a bunch of show-business hambones, who'd come out of retirement to perform at the Plaza, and we had to accompany them. Some of the gals would shout, "Hey, let me do a number. I think my key is C." After forty years in the business they *think* their key is C.

We always split into two groups, to give the joint continuous music. For instance, there would be the Fancy Five made up of Max Kaminsky, the Lion, ex-Ellington drummer Sonny Greer, Jimmy Archey on trombone, and Cecil Scott, clarinet and saxophone.

Oh, we were great, a bunch of Dixieland guys. We'd open up with a tune like "I Found a New Baby," and each guy would be so tense that each one was playing a different tune. Man, oh, man, I've had experience playing on bad pianos but this was too much. The only places where I ever had good pianos was in the recording studios and the big-time theaters. So—that taught me to play on bad pianos. The man said, "When the keys are broken, learn how to do a trick, sing-sing, or dance, or make faces. So there at the old C.P., I really made use of what I'd learned. I'd do a great deal of mugging. It would get the customers when they couldn't even hear the piano. I'd sing a blues song without taking my cigar out of my mouth. They liked that, too.

We all had a fine laugh one night when Cole Porter showed up. He had been rehearsing a show called *Can-Can* in the same building all afternoon and when they continued into the evening, Porter and some of the cast heard music coming from upstairs. They arrived in our ballroom to take it in. Hot Lips Page, the trumpeter, was featured that night. Lips was out to make an impression, so he announced, "The next number I'm going to dedicate to its great composer, Cole Porter." So then he takes off on "Embraceable You." I kept waving at him and shaking my head, but he didn't notice; he was too busy with the tune. When it was over Porter stood up and said, "Thank you a heap, Lips, but that's not my tune." When I told Lips the tune was written by George Gershwin, he turned seven shades of purple.

We had all the celebrities you could think of down there. Tallulah Bankhead, Trevor Howard, Bert Parks, Robert Preston, Patrice Munsel, Gene Lockhart, Hoagy Carmichael, and Carol Bruce, the actress, who came to me and said, "Willie, I'd like you to teach my daughter the piano." I told her, "It would be a pleasure—with no fee!" But, nothing ever came of it. Everybody used to show up in the back room. It was magnetic. All the cats would go in there and hang their things up on the hooks and then the clatter would begin. You couldn't hear yourself think. The back room was supposed to be for the musicians only but it became populated by the fans, buffs, and celebrities, while the waiters would start sounding off on the dishes and other guys would tap a keg of beer or stomach a couple of swigs of ether, and the bedlam became a mess. I had to go downstairs to sit quietly after I came off the stand.

Another gag we had at Central Plaza was the birthday-party pitch and it helped to drag in customers. For instance, we had anniversary and birthday parties for such famous music personalities as W. C. Handy, and Fletcher Henderson. Even one for the Lion on his fortieth anniversary in jazz.

My night we had a load of different stars. Dizzy Gillespie showed up, and Inez Cavanaugh (Paris) and my good friend Luckey Roberts. It was a wonderful testimonial. Yeah, the place was lousy with trumpet players—Wingy Manone, Jimmy McPartland, Sid De Paris, Wild Bill Davison, Muggsy Spanier, Red Allen, Bobby Hackett, plus Dizzy.

It was a night in November as I recall. A few nights later I went to the Pennsylvania Hotel as a guest of Tommy Dorsey and he bought me a ten-dollar dinner. He played four of my tunes that night. The next day he died. It hit the Lion hard. He was one of my best pals.

The grind at the Plaza finally got the best of me and I cut out in 1958.

29

Get Me a Cab

I'm only going to be here a hot moment,
What you want, I got. . . .

WILLIE THE LION SMITH

When I gave up night-club work, I determined to stay in New York, the Big Apple, where everybody rambles and scrambles to find the handle. The days of parlor social playing were over, but there were a lot of other things for a good piano player.

Some were band jobs at places like the Pied Piper down on Barrow Street in the Village. I appeared there a lot with Max Kaminsky (1944) and at Wilbur De Paris' "Swing Soirees" once a week at the Piper. Then there were Helen Decker's afternoon affairs (she is a writer and the musicians' great friend) at the Hotel Brittany and the Hotel Van Rensselaer. I would stop in the Club Riviera frequently; it was across from Nick's in Greenwich Village and there was always a crowd of good musicians and sessions to play in.

I don't mean to say that I refused to travel out of town; when the spirit moved me I did take a few selected jobs in various cities away from Manhattan. I had a band with my old friend Ernest Elliott on clarinet, Andy Pendleton on guitar, and June Cole on bass, for a long spell at the Casa Blanca in my old home town of Newark, New Jersey. One August I went up to Saratoga Springs with Herman Autrey, trumpet; George Stevenson, trombone; Eddie Barefield, alto saxophone; and Art Trappier, drums. We played in Jack's night club up there.

My favorite away-from-New York town was Toronto. When I took a band, or went up there solo, there was always a crowd of over three thousand listeners. One time, soprano saxophonist Sidney Bechet, trumpeter Rex Stewart, trombonist Benny Morton, and drummer Gordon (Specs) Powell went to Toronto with me. I played a solo set entitled "Turning the Lion Loose" or "The Lion Runs Wild," wherein I featured my composition "David in the Lion's Den." They really loved that show up there.

The Canadians are fine people, always been my friends, with only one exception. There was one time when Eubie Blake phoned and invited me and Luckey Roberts over to his house in Brooklyn. Luckey and I drove over and met this couple from Canada who were there with a tape recorder. They were French Canadians and were all set to have the three of us play piano while they took everything down on the recorder, for free yet. They wanted both our pianistics and our singing voices. Luckey played his "Junk Man's Rag" for them, but the Lion wouldn't budge from the chair. No sense making future trouble, and that was what there'd be if a few years later those records had come out on some kind of obscure label without the proper payment. As I say, musicians have to look out for themselves.

The only free work I did was for worthy benefits, and I did a lot of them. While I was appearing at Central Plaza I did a lot of benefits with Jack Crystal. Once in awhile, on Sunday afternoons, a group of us used to go up to the Tuberculosis Hospital in Beacon, New York.* Sometimes it was a real hot day in the neighborhood of ninety degrees and it took two hours to

* Other places we used to go to entertain were the Kingsbridge Veterans' Hospital in the Bronx; The Lighthouse, Inc.; Institute for Rehabilitation; the Halloran General Hospital (during the war); and the Abraham Jacobi Hospital in the Bronx.

drive up there. On one trip we had Eugene Sedric (Honey-bear), an ex-Fats Waller saxophone-clarinet star; trombonist Herb Fleming, and drummer Arthur Trappier. They put us on a real high stand and placed the piano in front so I could look down on the crowd. I was sensitive to height, whew, but I announced, "The Lion's here, any tune you want to hear, just start callin'." That group of patients were all elderly but they called one tune after another. We played one number for forty minutes without stopping. Then we struck up a coupla things for dancing. Man, those folks were in their eighties, and they all started to jump. Before I knew it, my Jane had grabbed up her dress and was doin' the Monkey Hunch with one of the oldsters. She's sure subject to jump music, goodness me.

One fantastic junket I took with Crystal was to Pittsburgh in 1950 or 1951. I didn't like the idea of flying around those mountains near Pittsburgh. I wasn't alone. Freddie Moore, drums and washboard, didn't go for it either. Before we started off I had a presentiment about trouble. I was sitting next to Big Chief Moore, the 300-pound Indian trombonist, and he was sitting next to the window. We had left LaGuardia at 8 A.M. and all hell broke loose forty-five minutes later. The pilot announced, "We are now cruising at twelve thousand feet and will be in Pittsburgh in forty minutes." Then they hit the air pocket. Big Chief almost broke out of his seat belt and the coffee which Wild Bill Davison was drinking, flew out of the cup all over me from across the aisle.

We hit a storm and it stayed bumpy and shook us all up. Freddie Moore was praying his head off, offering prayers for the protection of his wife, kids, aunts, uncles, grandparents, sons-in-law. The plane was being bombarded by hailstones as big as baseballs. When the bumping continued, Big Chief almost pushed me out of my seat belt.

It was pretty early in the morning for that kind of excitement. All I could say was, "I knew it." American planes fly too low compared to those in Europe.

When it was all over, Crystal asked Freddie Moore: "What's the matter with you, you're a bachelor. Why were you praying for all those people?"

"I know," Moore answered, "but while I was about it, I wanted to cover all the possibilities." He said he was reaching out for everyone.

Oh yeah, I played a lot of benefits, starting from many years ago when they had one for Eva Tanguay at the Palace Theater on Broadway. We had some real entertainers for that—Dancin' Dotson, Belle Baker, Blossom Seeley, and other stars of the day. In 1959 the Lion performed at the last appearance of Billie Holiday when we both played a benefit at the Phoenix Theater down on Second Avenue. I did "Finger Buster" for that one. Miss Holiday's untimely death came within two months.

The National Capitol is housed in a good town. It didn't used to be, but now it is good for Negro jazz men. A couple of years ago I went to do the Dixieland Jubilee. We played for two thousand listeners, at ten dollars a head, in the ballroom of the Sheraton-Park Hotel. Most of the audience were from Congress and the diplomatic corps. We had a Moth Ball Five made up of some big names like Willie the Lion, Dick Cary, Bud Freeman, Pee Wee Russell, Ernestine Anderson, Paul Barbarin from New Orleans, Buck Clayton, Jo Jones, and Willis Conover from the Voice of America, who did all the talking.

Mrs. Dwight D. Eisenhower was a patroness for the event but she didn't show up, and a lot of the political celebrities that did show, shouldn't have—for they talked during the music from a front table. After they got bored and left at intermission the large number of jazz fans who stayed had a chance to hear, and that helped the proceedings. The lady that did most of the work for the benefit, Mrs. Richard Bolling, wife of a congressman from Missouri, stuck it out. She told the Lion she'd loved jazz ever since the family maid had taken her out to hear some good music when she was a little girl. She especially liked a duet that Jo Jones and I did for fifteen minutes.

While in Washington, the Lion played at the National Press Club and presented a lecture program on jazz to the students at Howard University as a guest of my old friend Dr. Sterling Brown. This work at the various colleges and universities around the country became a regular activity.

For many years I had played for dances and entertainment at college affairs. New York jazz musicians are frequently invited to Yale and Princeton. Jo Jones and I recently made a special trip to the interracial college up the river to Annandale-on-Hudson, where Bard College is located, and gave them what Wingy Manone calls "the word, the truth."

Several years ago, Sidney Gross, a British guitarist, had a jazz-appreciation course at Columbia University for which I played and lectured from time to time.

There have been many radio and television shows that have used the Lion and his music. The one I enjoyed the most was Art Ford's old jazz TV show (1957–58) on WOR from Newark, where I appeared with Eddie Condon, Bud Freeman, Max Kaminsky, George Wettling, and Connie Boswell in an hour-long show; it was a ball.

Then, in 1960, Eubie Blake, Don Lambert, and yours truly, played an afternoon program at the Newport Jazz Festival—before the fuss.† The crowd at Freebody Park that afternoon loved our program of the jazz classics. I really had to extend myself that day in competition with my old contemporaries Eubie and Don (another New Jersey-ite born in 1904, the same year as Fats). I played Chopin's "Polonaise Militaire," the last thirty-two bars of which I rewrote. Then I performed James P.'s "Carolina Shout" and Fats's "Ain't Misbehavin'." On that day I also resurrected Tim Brymn's "Sparkles." Everyone said we gave the only decent concert at that ill-fated festival. We entertained on Friday afternoon; on Sunday they shut down the five-day festival on account of the rioting Saturday night.

† Riot.

Through the years I've managed to keep busy without suf-focating myself every night in a smoky night club. There have been repeat appearances in places like New Rochelle, New York; at the Westchester Country Club near Rye, New York; and up at Bridgeport, Connecticut, where Rocky's used to fea-ture clarinetist Tony Parenti and the Lion every weekend.

Then I went to the Westchester Country Club once with a ham drummer named Pop Eyes and we worked until 2 A.M. There was some brandy flowing that night and one woman there, a handsome woman, was hanging around the bandstand, asking us to have drinks. Near the end, when some of the other people had left, she was still there. I don't know whether the guys thought I was making a pass at the lady or not—it was a sneaky kind of place—but the bartender and a few sly guys took the other two players to the station and then they told me they'd give me a ride. I soon found myself in an automobile with a crowd of drunken white folks. We were riding about twenty minutes, and the roads were dark, and I could see that we were getting nowhere.

"Slow down till I light a cigar," I said. When the driver did, I opened the door and jumped out, then walked three blocks to a telephone and called the police to get me back to town.

When I saw the guys I had played the date with, they had the nerve to ask me how I had made out. I said I jumped out.

Nowadays I always take Jane along to keep tabs on the ar-rangements. And it proves another lesson I learned a long time ago: *Go when the others go.*

30

Always Play the Melody

*Hey swifty, you gotta get in the mood
and stay in the groove,
If you're once a turkey,
You're always a turkey.*

WILLIE THE LION SMITH

It's never too late to reach your destination. You should never doubt what is in front of your eyes. These days I put flowers by my mother's picture so that I can get my concentration and expect to live to a sober 102. To recuperate, I slowly play her hymns—maybe a little "Abide with Me." My mother is in Newark at the Evergreen Cemetery, while the rest of the family are buried at the overcrowded Fairmount. I believe in psychic perception or reincarnation. When we are asleep we are born over again. I'm a tough man for facts, but I do feel that people come back to inhabit the earth in other forms. The main thing is to live with righteousness and don't be afraid.

Just live right—that's the answer. But the average human being is like a piece of meat. He'll clean his house, car, rugs, and glasses, but sometimes he won't go to the doctor and clean himself.

I had trouble only until I was fifty. There were ups and downs and I had some scrapes, but it says in the Bible that life is sacrifice, love is sacrifice. Most of all, I knew how to perform. And when I performed, it was for the audience. You had to be ahead of them, they had to be with you, and sometimes if they knew what you were thinking, they'd never clap. All artists are religious people at heart—that's what carries you to an audience. I always say a silent prayer before I go on. ("God, give me the wisdom and strength and knowledge to please the people and to do what you think I should do. You are the only one who can help me.")

But struggle? No—I was versatile. I could play, sing, talk, and dance. Even before the Lion, they called me "Technique." That was when the artists, as I said, had a nickname to suit what they looked like or the way they played. Duke grunts. Jimmy used to sing like a bird. I talk and fight. A booking agent once said to me, "Man, *sing*. Sing and talk, express yourself." He was right.

As for music—60 per cent of those playing today shouldn't be. They've got everything in their favor. They've got good parents, a good education, but forget to listen to the teachers. The young musicians of today have strayed too far from the old masters. You can never outpoint the dean of the college. Why, they forget everything. They can't remember where they parked their cars. When you mention one of the older men's names to the youngsters, they say, "Oh, he's been around a long time." Sure he's been around a long time—it takes a long time to learn anything. You just can't pop up over night and think you know something like they do today.

A career in music is like an automatic elevator: a man has to push the right button at the right time. The Lion has learned after a half century that an artist has to think for himself to take the right direction, and the best way to stay out of trouble is to stay away from trouble.

Personal managers and booking agents can break you as

fast as they make you. They can even break you if they don't make you. That makes it important to be cagey about the guys a musician gets hooked up with. In jazz, it is frequently true that a jazz man can do better on his own. The big agencies, like the Music Corporation of America, for example, or the William Morris office, are no help in my opinion. Some big organizations have never cared or known anything about jazz music. All they have ever cared about was a buck—for themselves. They'd send Big Joe Turner out to sing the "Whisky Blues" (I've Got to Have My Whisky) to a bunch of bluenosed old ladies at an antisaloon-league meeting if there was a commission in it.

A man should be hired on his merits, not because he's got a hit riding on the record charts. I've rarely signed with a big office. If a musician gets around and makes the right kind of friends, he'll play in a place where he belongs.

Romance without finance is no good. When they want the Lion to put on his show, they have to donate me some bucks. A lot of cats walk up and down Broadway, go up in elevators, eat hot dogs, and wind up without carfare back uptown. When an agent comes up to me to talk, I tell him: "Give me some brandy if I've got to talk to you." And then, when they want to talk terms, I say, "Man, you've got to pay me to sneeze."

Another thing you have to watch—maybe it's not so true any more—is to guard against Uncle Tomism. All the managers and bookers used to know, they thought, that a Negro performer was a lazy no-good loafer. They would give you this Uncle Tom talk before they sent you out on a gig. Then those cold turkeys would send out stool pigeons to keep tabs on you. Yeah, man has learned to choke his fellow man and the hard knocks dished out by money-mad managers and bookers will catch you every time if you are asleep.

There's a guy I admire who can't be pushed around. That's Cab Calloway. I wrote a tune with him once and got to know him well. Nobody takes advantage of his good nature. He's a take-it-or-leave-it guy, plain-spoken. A natural and lovely man.

The agents have always been afraid of the sophisticated Negro performer with the "keep cool, fool" attitude. They don't know how to handle that jive and as a result bookers hire the worst types of performers, while the guys who've got something to offer are often kicked around. There are good artist-manager relations. Joe Glaser (Associated Booking Corporation) and Louis Armstrong; Sam Berk and trumpeter Jonah Jones; Martha Glaser and Erroll Garner; Helen Noga and Johnny Mathis; but I can't think of many more.

For the most part the music business is a jungle where dog eats dog. It's all based on money, like the apartment situation in Harlem. You can get anything with a little taste, like three hundred dollars under the table.

The town is full of agents. You look in the union magazine these days; I've never seen so many booking licenses. And half of those guys are starving to death right in New York. I get as many as two or three calls a week offering me some half-assed deal. You've got to know how to bide your time and wait. They've got to pass my house to get to theirs, and it pays off to take time to look them over. A musician has to know that he can get sick from doing a forced performance and he is a sucker to go for a left hook just to please some agent.

It don't mean a thing if you don't pull that string. Producers today try to tell you how to play your music. Not so long ago they asked the Lion to go to Pittsburgh to film a TV *Route 66* segment. I wanted to go because the show was featuring Ethel Waters. But while talking to the agents in New York I could tell they didn't dig what they were trying to do. When I saw the show later, they had (trumpeter) Roy Eldridge playing drums and (drummer) Jo Jones on trumpet.

Ethel is a good or a sad case in point. They only made one Ethel Waters. She played all the benefits. Now she needs benefits but she won't accept them.

Jazz gets the worst shuffling of all. Take the Arthur Godfrey show. Godfrey comes out laughing and giggling, then a ham act comes out introduced by some lady who says they are good, like this. "Well, ladies and gentlemen, this act is fine because this guy used to drive a truck down in Tennessee and this is his first time in front of the public." You can hear, but you can't see, because he's off to the side, a big-time bandleader with his real musicians. Most of the time they don't even introduce them. That's why Ray Bloch, a man who has studied music all his life, stands up and giggles too. He's found out that in order to get credit for what he is doing, he has to learn to be an actor.

The biggest stars are always cool and collected. They know that to stay around with peace of mind these days, they can't live on champagne and no sleep. The slide to the graveyard is greased. The Lion insists that the check be made out, a taxi sent for pick up and delivery, and the piano placed downstage where the lights are.

If you can hold and entertain a large audience, you've got a right to fight for good working conditions. The union specifies that we should have decent accommodations—but who fights for it? The cafés and theaters spend fifty thousand dollars for fancy furnishings and then come up with fifty dollars to buy a piano painted purple. Ever since I can remember, night-club operators have hated to pay money to get anything repaired. Or take the old Apollo Theater, here in Harlem. It ought to be torn down. The dressing rooms and toilets are a disgrace. It's getting worse than the old T.O.B.A. days—a circuit the Lion refused to play partly because you had to make up in a toilet. I worked a club once in New Bedford, Massachusetts, a brand-new place expensively decorated, but it had a ten-dollar piano on a ten-dollar stand. That stand was so small the player couldn't breathe. The guys who play lounges like that are cockroaches and are hurting themselves. Operators should try to keep the talent happy and inspired if they want to see the public crowding in. I can recall when the smart owners always had a bottle of whisky in the dressing room, waiting for the artist. Today they spend their time beefing about how bad business is and asking you to go down to a table to extract money from a good customer who is rolling in his cups. If you don't hop, skip, and jump, the operator starts to bawl you out and asks you to play "Beer Barrel Polka." When they bawl out the Lion, they are missing a piano player.

We all miss the big bands. Since they've been gone, show business has been in the clutches of a lot of unmusical, whining young rock 'n' rollers, a bunch of screaming kids unfit to walk on a stage. It isn't all their fault. A big part of the blame can be put on the record producers, the bookers, the managers, all those cats I've been talking about who can't see anything but a green dollar. They should all be put on a desert island with nothing but thousand-dollar bills to eat.

Another reason why the bands got lost was the same old thing about musicians not standing up for their rights. Too many leaders let the agents and bookers tell them what to do. When the war was over, the managers all thought they had to bring Glenn Miller back. The country was flooded with dog bands playing Miller arrangements. The younger generation, the ones who—twenty years ago—made the big bands, wanted something new. The band managers didn't give it to them. Then they went out and dragged in untrained talent off the streets to make recordings. I was on one date when the recording supervisor complained as we tuned up: "I don't want these records in tune, damn it!" he shouted.

The musicians began to forget that they owed a lot to the arrangers. And the leaders let the managers dictate to them. Dorsey was an example of the right kind of bandleader. He refused to take any guff from anybody and he ruled his band with an iron hand. He wasn't like other leaders who let prima donnas rule the crew. One man can upset an entire band. One saxophone player can wreck the reed section.

I once got booked into a famous theater by Joe Glaser for a week. It wasn't Joe's fault, but each man in the band was supposed to get a hundred and five dollars for the week and then I found out that we were expected to kick back fifty-five dollars to the owner of the house. They said it was the usual deal— the theater had to show the union they were paying scale in spite of the fact they couldn't afford it. I blew my top and went to the union right away.

The union, whose motto is "Keep Music Alive—Insist on Live Musicians," was headed by Jake Rosenberg and he, along with a delegate, Ralph Redman, stuck by me. Redman saw to it that my men got their hundred and five bucks at the end of the week. The result of my complaint was that the house quit the grafting.

But let's look at the musicians for a moment. Young pianists do not know the keyboard. They hammer away at their pet keys instead of learning every key in the piano and "running chords," as they call it. And the young entertainers lack showmanship. We don't have many of the kind of people who could hold an audience in their hands, people like Harry Richman, Sophie Tucker, and Eva Tanguay.

But there are some. There's Hope, Sinatra, Jack Benny, Danny Kaye, Judy Garland. There's even her daughter. She can tie an audience in knots and what's more, she can dance. The giants are gone. But they will come back. Their forces and their souls return to guide others.

Some things survive. The barbershop chords will survive, and the melody will predominate. I've always been tough on that. I mean melody. The public doesn't have to guess what I play. Like I've said, piano playing is like walking. You either walk good or you walk bad.

Spirit means a lot, too. Look at the performers you find in the rough dives where the pay is poor. They've got spirit. Even the gangsters have a lot of spirit. Your spirit or subconscious talks to you every day. There is counterpoint in life as well as in music. You have to listen to the thoughts from the spirits for they will tell you what to do. We've got to get bands back in the theater pits and get rid of a lot of the canned music. In corn music, where the performers can't make a chord, it's pitiful. We have to keep up dignity. Concerts should be formal affairs even if they are not easy on the musician. Take the Lion —putting on a full-dress suit in May with all my hypertension. Why, all I've got to do is to put the collar on and I'm up.

And the righteous shall survive.

When I am alone, the spirit comes to me in the night and tells me how to write. When something is going to happen, my psychic perception informs me of it beforehand. I still use incense and keep holy water in the house. They say I'm a hobo with the heart of a king. But I've had five hundred chances to go ahead of my time and if I had taken them, I wouldn't be around to enjoy them. I'm not mad at anybody. This is the happiest time of my life. I love flowers, eating, playing the piano, and little children. I've got time for children and elderly people and if I had my life to live over again, I would do it exactly the same way. You have to be around where you are seen or can be seen. If you hide yourself, you can become a corpse.

This means going out, but not only to help yourself. It helps to call a shut-in and do a good turn daily. Life is a stepping-stone to a higher destination and you have to stop and lend others a helping hand. As Dr. Logan says, "What good would it be living, Lion, if we didn't give something to somebody?" Everyone should belong to an organization, like a lodge, and not depend on his neighbors because those next-door folks can soon forget his address.

In my life, I've been all over the country. In the last ten years I've really lived. I've been able to do something I really want to do and smart enough to get out of the clubs, out of the basements. Two more years there and I wouldn't have been able to tell the story. When you play there, the clubs become a prison.

You're traveling on a cloud and when you wake up, your mind is not clear. Now I go out, inhale fresh air, and play with more ease. I still like to hear a choir. Great singing is in the choirs. Anytime you hear a choir, you hear it all. It's like the blues. The Baptist people are still crying and shouting the same thing they have for the last hundred and fifty years. White people made the blues. I was playing some pretty things and people would say to me, play some more blues. They notice a lot of things the Negro has that he doesn't know he has and they can help him to put it to good use.

With our music, first we put it in the alley, then swung it, grooved it, and now keep it cool. But let's not cool it so much it freezes up.

The nice part is that the planets are out there. And anyone who doesn't live by *that* universe ought to have his head examined. I believe the spirit still lives. You can hear a man's voice on a record after he has passed and it is not just a recording. When we sleep, we're practically dead, and yet rest is the most important thing in life.

I want to say one more word to the jazz writers. They can also be the kind of character who is inclined to follow the dollar sign. Sometimes they'll say anything if they think it will bring them a buck. They should learn to govern their tongues and look at the water before they jump. All writers who take the career of a man in hand by criticizing him should visit their victims beforehand and at least check their information.

My first idea for a title on the book was "Phonies on Parade." Sometimes I think that eight people out of every ten are phony. They lie; they're not truthful from the soul.

But in spite of all the troubles one comes up against, there is no business like show business, like the song writer said. It may be no business, but it's show business and it's my business. Rex Stewart, a trumpet player who used to be with Ellington, said to me the other day, "Willie, they can't buy my soul. They can't even make me feel sad. Because I'm gonna blow my horn at all costs—that is what keeps me alive."

People say to the Lion, "You look good!"—that's how old I am. The truth is delight.

Notes and References

INTERLUDE ONE

1. *The Story of Jazz* by Marshall Stearns—Oxford University Press, New York City, 1956.

2. Article on "Ragtime" by Guy Waterman—*The Record Changer*, edited by Bill Grauer and Orrin Keepnews, 1955.

3. *They All Played Ragtime* by Rudi Blesh and Harriet Janis—Alfred A. Knopf, Inc., 1950. Revised edition published by Grove Press, Inc., 1959.

4. "Conversations with James P. Johnson" by Tom Davin—*Jazz Review* magazine, July 1959.

5. "The Jazz Panorama" by John S. Wilson—*Hi Fi Review* Supplement, published by Ziff-Davis Pub. Co., April 1959.

6. "Supreme Tickler" by Whitney Balliett in *The New Yorker*, May 11, 1963.

INTERLUDE TWO

1. *New York Holiday* by Eleanor Early—Rinehart & Co., 1950.

2. Article—"Garvin Bushell and New York Jazz in the 1920s" by Nat Hentoff—*Jazz Review* magazine, January 1959.

3. *Jazz—A History of the New York Scene* by Samuel B. Charters and Leonard Kunstadt—Doubleday & Co., Inc., 1962.

4. *His Eye Is on the Sparrow* by Ethel Waters with Charles Samuels—Doubleday & Co., Inc., 1951.

INTERLUDE THREE

1. *New York City* by the editors of *Look, Look at America* series—Houghton Mifflin Co., 1956 revised edition.

2. *Amsterdam News*—1921.

3. *Jazz—A History of the New York Scene* by Samuel B. Charters and Leonard Kunstadt—Doubleday & Co., Inc., 1962.

4. *Harold Arlen—Happy with the Blues* by Edward Jablonski—Doubleday & Co., Inc., 1961.

INTERLUDE FOUR

1. *The Trouble with Cinderella* by Artie Shaw—Farrar, Straus & Co., Inc., 1952.

2. "Blindfold Test" by Leonard Feather—*Down Beat* magazine, April 17, 1958.

3. "Conversations with James P. Johnson" by Tom Davin—*Jazz Review* magazine, September 1959.

4. Review of "The Lion Roars" by Guy Waterman—*Jazz Review* magazine, December 1958.

5. Review of "The Lion of the Piano" by Hugues Panassié—*Hot Jazz* magazine, April 1939.

6. *Duke Ellington* by Barry Ulanov—Creative Age Press, Inc., 1946.

7. Review of "The Lion Roars" by Martin Williams—*Down Beat Record Reviews*—Vol. III, 1958.

CHAPTER 27

*Willie the Lion's European Tour December 20, 1949,
through February 7, 1950*

Paris, France—Vogue Records

Berne, Switzerland

Paris, France—First concert, Salle Pleyel

Tours, France

Zurich, Switzerland

Paris, France—Second concert, Salle Pleyel

Guéret, France

Marseilles, France

Cambrai, France

Limoges, France

Toulouse, France

Montauban (Hugues Panassié's home city), France

Bayonne, France

Pau, France

Montpellier, France

Casablanca, Morocco, North Africa

Rabat, Morocco, North Africa

Oran, Algeria, North Africa

Algiers, Algeria, North Africa

Tangier, Spanish Morocco, North Africa

Paris, France—Vogue Records

Antwerp, Belgium

Louvain, Belgium

Lille, France

Strasbourg, France

Zurich, Switzerland

Geneva, Switzerland

Lausanne, Switzerland

Paris, France—Third and Farewell Concert

Barcelona, Spain

LIST OF COMPOSITIONS
MUSIC BY WILLIE THE LION SMITH

TITLE	YEAR	LYRICS	PUBLISHER
A New Kind of Song	1948	Edwards	Edwards Music
Be True to the N.R.A.	1935	Hammed	Leeds Music
Boo La Boo	1936	Lawrence	Advanced Music
Bot Zot Zot Zu Zu	1942	Lawrence	Broadway Music
Bring on the Band*	1949	Edwards	Commercial Music
Can You Hear Me?	1952		Willie Smith
Concentrating*	1939		Leo Feist, Inc.
Contrary Motion*	1949	Norman	Dayton Music
Conversation on Park Avenue	1941		Shapiro, Bernstein & Co.
Curfew Time in Harlem	1938	Lawrence	Joe Davis
Cutting Out	1938		Irving Berlin
David in the Lion's Den	1946		Willie Smith

* Have been recorded by Smith.

TITLE	YEAR	LYRICS	PUBLISHER
Dreamy Rag	1945		Leeds Music
Echo of Spring*	1935	Hammed	Leeds Music
Fading Star*	1937		Mills Music
Finger Buster*	1934		Leeds Music
Fussin'	1937		Mills Music
Got to Think It Over	1939	Williams	Leeds Music
Happy Hunting Grounds	1935	Hammed	Leeds Music
Harlem Joys	1935	Bishop	Leeds Music
Hot Things	1935		Leeds Music
How Could You Put Me Down*	1945	Parrish	Mills Music
I Ain't Gonna Swing No More	1938	Adlam	Exclusive
I Can't Forget the Love You Forgot	1937	Razaf	Leeds Music
I Did It Again	1934	Edwards	Commercial Music
I Got Sugar, Plenty of Sugar	1942	Razaf	Broadway Music
If It's Good, You Gotta Buy It	1955	Edwards	Edwards Music
I'm All Out of Breath*	1937	Bishop	Exclusive
I'm Gonna Ride the Rest of the Way	1948	Edwards	Edwards Music
In a Daze	1940	Edwards	Commercial Music
In the Groove	1936		Mills Music
Is You Tellin' I?	1937	Bishop	Leeds Music
It's the Beat that Counts	1946	Edwards	Edwards Music
Just Lookin' Around	1942	Noel	Blue Circle, Inc.
Keep Fingerin'	1938		Mills Music
Keep Your Temper*	1925		Leeds Music
Lament of the Lioness	1940		Georgia Music
Late Hours	1940		Willie Smith
Let Every Day Be Mother's Day	1945	Hammed	Leeds Music
Let's Go Joe	1942	Palmer	Cherio Music
Let's Mop It*	1944	Edwards	Edwards Music
Lion's Boogie Woogie*	1957		Dayton Music
Love Remembers	1935		Leeds Music
Lullaby to an Empty Bandstand	1940	Jacobs	Irving Berlin
Mellow Moods	1942		Sharon Pease
Morning Air*	1938		Leo Feist, Inc.
Morning, Noon, and Night	1955	Elber	Willie Smith

TITLE	YEAR	LYRICS	PUBLISHER
Music on My Mind	1955	Ross	Willie Smith
No Local Stops	1939		Leo Feist, Inc.
Noodlin'*	1940		Irving Berlin
Passionette*	1935		Leeds Music
Portrait of the Duke*	1949		Dayton Music
Relaxin'*	1949		Composers Music
Rippling Waters*	1939		Leeds Music
Roll 'em, Rock 'em, and Weep*	1957		Crystal Music
Rushin'*	1940		Irving Berlin
Searching	1954	Edwards	Commercial Music
Searching Everywhere for You	1939	Mypels	Rialto Music
Sneak Away*	1937		Mills Music
Sneaky Pete	1943	Bishop	Walter Bishop
Spanish Rag	1938		Leeds Music
Streamline Gal of Mine	1938	Williams	Leeds Music
Sweeter Than the Sweetest	1941	Lawrence	Mort Brown
Tango a la Caprice*	1939		Leo Feist, Inc.
The Lion Roars*	1957		Dayton Music
The Lion Steps Out*	1953	Lawrence	Blue Circle
The Lion's Theme*	1953	Lawrence	Blue Circle
The Old Stamping Ground*	1937	La Freniere	Roy Music
The Romp*	1953		Blue Circle
The Stuff Is Here and It's Mellow	1929	Bishop	Leeds Music
The Swamp	1935	West	Leeds Music
Through for the Day	1942		Mutual Music
Trains and Planes*	1949	Smith	Willie Smith
Way Down Yonder on Bourbon Street	1953	Lawrence	Blue Circle
When You're Gone	1953	West	Leeds Music
Willie's Blues*	1953		Dayton Music
You for Me and Me for You	1940	Edwards	Commercial Music
You Know What I Mean	1949	Hammed	Leeds Music
You Let Me Down	1942	Razaf	Broadway Music
You Wrong Me More and More Each Day	1937		Leeds Music
Zig Zag*	1955	Edwards	Commercial Music

NOTE: Not all dates and publishers can be considered entirely accurate due to faulty files, contractual confusions, and failure of memories.

DISCOGRAPHY

NOTE: Capitalized tunes composed by Smith.

New York City, August 10, 1920
Mamie Smith and Her Jazz Hounds—Addington Major, cornet; Dope
Andrews, trombone; Ernest Elliott, clarinet; Leroy Parker, violin; Willie
(the Lion) SMITH, piano; Mamie Smith, vocal.

Okeh 4169 Crazy Blues[1]—It's Right Here for You

November 5, 1925
Gulf Coast Seven—June Clark, cornet; Jimmy Harrison, trombone;
Buster Bailey, clarinet; Prince Robinson, tenor saxophone; SMITH,
piano; Buddy Christian, banjo; Bill Benford, bass; Jazz Carson, drums.

Columbia 14107D Santa Claus Blues—KEEP YOUR TEMPER[1]

June 12, 1929
Clarence Williams' Jug Band—Ed Allen, cornet; Cecil Scott, clarinet;
Ikey Robinson, flute; SMITH, piano; Clarence Williams, jug.

Philips LP 7521 (England) What If We Do

December 1929
Seven Gallon Jug Band—Ed Allen, cornet; Cecil Scott, clarinet; SMITH,
piano; Ikey Robinson, banjo and vocal; Clarence Williams, leader, jug,
and vocal.

Columbia test record number W149690–2 Wipe It Off

July 8, 1933
Clarence Williams Washboard Band—Cecil Scott, clarinet; SMITH,
piano; Ikey Robinson, banjo; Floyd Casey, washboard; Clarence Williams, jug; Clarence Todd, kazoo and vocal; Eva Taylor, vocal.

Columbia 2806, Philips LP 7521 (England) Shim Sham Shimmy Dance—
High Society

[1] Currently available on Columbia's HARLEM JAZZ ODYSSEY.

Parlophone 1680 (England), Philips LP 7521 (England) Chizzlin' Sam

Columbia 2863, Philips LP 7521 (England) Organ Grinder Blues—
You Ain't Too Old

May 7, 1934
Mezz Mezzrow and His Orchestra—Max Kaminsky, Reunald Jones, Chelsea Qualey, trumpets; Floyd O'Brien, trombone and arranger; Mezz Mezzrow, clarinet, alto saxophone, and arranger; Benny Carter, alto saxophone; Bud Freeman, tenor saxophone; SMITH, piano; John Kirby, bass; Chick Webb, drums.

Victor 25019, Bluebird 10250, Label "X" LP 3015 Apologies—
Sendin' the Vipers

Victor 25202, Bluebird 10251, Label "X" LP 3015 Old-Fashioned Love—
35th and Calumet

April 2/3, 1935
Willie Smith and His Cubs—Ed Allen, trumpet; Cecil Scott, clarinet and tenor saxophone; SMITH, piano; Willie Williams, washboard.

Decca 7073 There's Gonna Be the Devil to Pay—What Can I Do?

Decca 7074, 1144 Streamline Gal—HARLEM JOYS

May 22, 1935
Willie Smith and His Cubs—Same as above.

Decca 7086 Breeze—Sittin' at the Table

Decca 7090 ECHO OF SPRING—Swing Brother Swing

March 12, 1936
Mezz Mezzrow and His Swing Band—Frank Newton, trumpet; Mezz Mezzrow, clarinet; Bud Freeman, tenor saxophone; SMITH, piano and vocal; Al Casey, guitar; Wellman Braud, bass; George Stafford, drums; Lucille Stewart, vocal.

Bluebird 6319 Mutiny in the Parlor—The Panic Is On

Bluebird 6320 A Melody from the Sky—Lost

Bluebird 6321 I'se a Muggin'—Parts I and II

April 13, 1937

Willie Smith and His Cubs—Dave Nelson, trumpet; Buster Bailey, clarinet; Robert Carroll, tenor saxophone; SMITH, piano; Jimmy McLin, guitar; Ellsworth Reynolds, bass; Eric Henry, drums.

Decca 1291

> The Swampland Is Calling Me—
> I CAN SEE YOU ALL OVER THE PLACE (Boy in the Boat)

Decca 1308 More Than That—I'M ALL OUT OF BREATH

July 14, 1937

Willie Smith and His Cubs—Frank Newton, trumpet; Buster Bailey, clarinet; Pete Brown, alto saxophone; SMITH, piano; Jimmy McLin, guitar; John Kirby, bass; O'Neill Spencer, drums and vocal.

Decca 1366 Knock Wood—Peace, Brother, Peace

Decca 1380 Get Acquainted with Yourself—
> THE OLD STAMPING GROUND

September 15, 1937

Willie Smith and His Cubs—Same as above.

Decca 1503 Achin' Hearted Blues—Honeymoon on a Dime

Decca 1957 Blues Why Don't You Let Me Alone—
> I've Got to Think It Over

November 11, 1937

Milt Herth Trio—Herth, electric organ; SMITH, piano; O'Neill Spencer, drums and vocal.

Decca 1553 The Dipsy Doodle—That's a Plenty

January 7, 1938

Milt Herth Trio—Same as above.

Decca 1612 *Bei Mir Bist Du Schon*—Big Dipper

January 10, 1938

Willie (the Lion) Smith piano solos accompanied by traps.

Decca 2269 PASSIONETTE—MORNING AIR

February 11, 1938
Milt Herth Trio—Same as above.

Decca 1699 Lost in the Shuffle—Josephine

Decca 1736 The Campbells Are Swinging

March 17, 1938
Milt Herth Trio—Same as above.

Decca 1727 Sissy

Decca 1736 Popcorn Man

April 7, 1938
Milt Herth Trio—Same as above.

Decca 1727 Jazz Me Blues

Decca 1816 The Toy Trumpet

Decca 1966 Copenhagen

April 28, 1938
Milt Herth Quartet—Teddy Bunn added to Trio on guitar.

Decca 1800 Looney Little Tooney—Flat Foot Floogie

Decca 1816 Three Blind Mice

May 17, 1938
Milt Herth Quartet—Same as above.

Decca 1868 Shoot the Likker to Me, John Boy—Egyptian Ella

July 5, 1938
Milt Herth Quartet—Same as above.

Decca 2087 Minuet in Jazz

Decca 2227 Goblins in the Steeple

July 22, 1938
Milt Herth Quartet—Same as above.

Decca 1966 La De Doody Do

Decca 2087 Home Cookin' Mama with the Fryin' Pan

November 30, 1938
Milt Herth Quartet—Same as above.

Decca 2227 Jump Jump's Here

Decca 2623 The Spider and the Fly

December 1938
Willie Smith, celeste; Joe Bushkin and Jess Stacy, pianos.

Commodore 520 Three Keyboards

Willie Smith and Joe Bushkin, piano duet.

Commodore 520 The Lion and the Lamb

February 1939
Willie Smith, piano solo "The Lion of the Piano."

Commodore 518, LP 30004 What Is There to Say—Tea for Two

Commodore 519, LP 30004 Stormy Weather

Commodore 519, LP 30003 I'll Follow You

Commodore 521, LP 30003 ECHO OF SPRING—FADING STAR

Commodore 522, LP 30003 RIPPLING WATERS—FINGER BUSTER

Commodore 523, LP 30003 MORNING AIR—PASSIONETTE

Commodore 524, LP 30003 SNEAK AWAY—CONCENTRATING

Commodore 525, LP 30003 The Boy in the Boat

Commodore 525, LP 30004 Between the Devil and the Deep Blue Sea

LP 30004 I Can't Give You Anything but Love

LP 30004 Smoke Gets in Your Eyes

LP 30004 Just One of Those Things

LP 30004 Madelon (Marching Tune—French)

LP 30004 A Pretty Girl Is Like a Melody

LP 30004 Hallelujah!

June 8, 1939
Milt Herth Trio—Herth, electric organ; SMITH, piano; O'Neill Spencer, drums and vocal.

Decca 2572 In an Eighteenth-Century Drawing Room—
The Shoemaker's Holiday

Decca 2632 Everybody Loves My Baby

November 22, 1939
The Haitian Orchestra—Kenneth Roane, trumpet; Sidney Bechet, clarinet and soprano saxophone; SMITH, piano; Olin Alderhold, bass; Leo Warney, drums.

Varsity 8360, Baldwin 1013 Baba Rhumba (Nana)—
Tropical Moon (Diane)

Varsity 8363 Original Haitian Music, Parts I and II

Varsity 8364 Original Haitian Music, Parts III and IV

Varsity 8399 Magic Islands (Merengue)—Mayotte (Merengue)

Varsity 8405 Rosa Rhumba—*Sous les Palmiers* (Merengue)

Baldwin 1012 Ti Ralph—*Merengue De Amour*

February 17, 1940
Willie (the Lion) Smith and His Orchestra—Sidney De Paris, trumpet; Jimmy Lane, Johnny Mullins, Perry Smith, saxophones; SMITH, piano; Bernard Addison, guitar; Dick Fulbright, bass; Puss Johnson, drums; Naomi Price, vocal.

General Tavern Tunes 1712 Peace on You—NOODLIN'

General Tavern Tunes 1713 Won'tcha Do It to Me—RUSHIN'

November 26, 1940
Big Joe Turner, blues vocals accompanied by SMITH, piano.

Decca 7824 Doggin' the Dog—Rainy Day Blues

Decca 7827 Careless Love—Jumpin' Down Blues

September 13, 1941
Sidney Bechet and His New Orleans Feetwarmers—Charlie Shavers, trumpet; Sidney Bechet, clarinet and soprano saxophone; SMITH, piano; Everett Barksdale, guitar; Wellman Braud, bass; Manzie Johnson, drums.

Victor 27600 Limehouse Blues—Texas Moaner Blues

Victor 27904 I'm Coming Virginia—Georgia Cabin

Sidney Bechet Trio—Bechet, SMITH, and Barksdale.

Victor (unissued) Strange Fruit—You're the Limit

October 24, 1941
Sidney Bechet and His New Orleans Feetwarmers—Same as above.

Victor 27707 Rose Room—Lady Be Good

Victor (unissued) Mood Indigo—What Is This Thing Called Swing?

Victor 20–3120 Twelfth Street Rag

September 29, 1944
Max Kaminsky and His Band—Kaminsky, trumpet; Frank Orchard, valve trombone; Rod Cless, clarinet; SMITH, piano; Eddie Condon, guitar; Jack Lesberg, bass; Clarence McGrath, drums.

Brunswick 80124, LP BL58043	Dippermouth Blues
Brunswick 80124	Old-Fashioned Love
Brunswick 80137, LP BL58043	Someday Sweetheart
Brunswick 80137	Wrap Your Troubles in Dreams
LP BL58043	Black and Blue
LP BL58043	Jazz Me Blues
unissued	Home
unissued	Eccentric

NOTE: The above were originally cut as transcriptions for the World Broadcasting System.

(The above date is followed by another recording session for Black and White label on the same day.)

September 29, 1944
The Lion's Jazz Band—Max Kaminsky, trumpet; Frank Orchard, valve trombone; Rod Cless, clarinet; SMITH, piano; Jack Lesberg, bass; Clarence McGrath, drums.

Black and White 6 LET'S MOP IT—
HOW COULD YOU PUT ME DOWN

Black and White 24 Muskrat Ramble—Bugle Call Rag

Paris, France, late 1949
Willie the Lion plays, talks, and sings.

Vogue LP 177 (France), Dial LP 305 (United States) *Reminiscing the Piano Greats*. Contains: Don't You Hit That Lady Dressed in Green (Trad.), Shine (Ford Dabney), Chevy Chase (Eubie Blake), Buddy Bolden's Blues (Jelly Roll Morton), Dark Town Strutters Ball (Shelton Brooks), Oh, You Devil Rag (Dabney), Maple Leaf Rag (Scott Joplin), Don't You Strike Me Again (Bob Hawkins), Pork and Beans (Luckey Roberts), When I Walk with Billy (Trad.), PASSIONETTE.

Vogue 78 r.p.m. single (France) WHAT'S MY NAME, TRAINS AND PLANES

New York City, September 1953
Willie the Lion Smith piano solos.

Blue Circle LP 1500 *Musical Compositions of James P. Johnson*. Contains: Porter's Love Song (To a Chamber Maid), Charleston, Carolina Shout, Daintiness, Caprice Rag, Old-Fashioned Love, The Mule Walk, If I Could Be with You One Hour Tonight, THE LION'S THEME.

Willie (the Lion) Smith and His Orchestra—Henry Goodwin, trumpet; Jimmy Archey, trombone; Cecil Scott, clarinet and tenor saxophone; SMITH, piano; Pops Foster, bass; Keg Purnell, drums; Myra Taylor and Neil Lawrence, vocals.

Blue Circle 500–78, 500–45 When the Saints Go Marching in—
THE LION STEPS OUT

Blue Circle 501–78, 501–45 Stop It, Joe!—WILLIE'S BLUES

Blue Circle 502–78, 502–45 THE ROMP—
WAY DOWN YONDER ON BOURBON STREET

Central Plaza, New York City, May 1954
Jimmy McPartland and His *Jazz Dance* Orchestra—Jimmy McPartland, trumpet; Jimmy Archey, trombone; Pee Wee Russell, clarinet; SMITH, piano; Pops Foster, bass; George Wettling, drums.

Jaguar LP 801 *The Jazz Dance* (Sound Track). Contains: Royal Garden Blues, Ballin' the Jack, When the Saints Go Marching in, Jazz Blues.

1956
Willie (the Lion) Smith talks and plays with Steve Allen.

Coral LP 100 *The Jazz Story*. Contains: Ragtime Reminiscences and Rainy Day Blues (Reissue of Joe Turner Decca 7824–78).

1957
Willie (the Lion) Smith and His Orchestra—Henry Goodwin, trumpet; George Stephenson, trombone; Cecil Scott, clarinet and tenor saxophone; SMITH, piano; Sidney Gross, guitar; Pops Foster, bass; Art Trappier, drums.

Urania LP 1207 *Willie the Lion Smith*. Contains: ECHO OF SPRING, Muskrat Ramble, Sophisticated Lady, FINGER BUSTER, Fidgety Feet, Struttin' with Some Barbecue, Ain't Misbehavin', Dardanella, Perdido, THROUGH FOR THE DAY.

November 8, 1957
Willie (the Lion) Smith talks and plays with Wendell Marshall, bass; Osie Johnson, drums.

Dot LP 3094 *The Lion Roars*. Contains: THE LION ROARS; WILLIE'S BLUES; Ragtime Medley (Blame It on the Blues); Carolina Shout; PORTRAIT OF THE DUKE; LION'S BOOGIE WOOGIE; Squeeze Me; BRING ON THE BAND; CONTRARY MOTION; ECHO OF SPRING; FINGER BUSTER; ZIG ZAG; ROLL 'EM, ROCK 'EM, AND WEEP.

January 28, 1958
Rex Stewart and His Orchestra—Stewart, cornet; George Stevenson, trombone; Haywood Henry, clarinet and baritone saxophone; George Kelly, tenor saxophone; SMITH, piano; Leonard Gaskin, bass; Arthur Trappier, drums.

Felsted LP 7001 (English) *Rendezvous with Rex*. Contains: Tillie's Twist, Pretty Ditty, Tell Me More.

March 18, 1958
Willie (the Lion) Smith piano solos.

Good Time Jazz LP 12035, Vogue LP 12256 (France) *Luckey and the Lion, Harlem Piano*. Contains: MORNING AIR, RELAXIN', RIPPLING

WATERS, Between the Devil and the Deep Blue Sea, TANGO LA CAPRICE, CONCENTRATING. Other tracks by Luckey Roberts.

May 1958
Willie (the Lion) Smith talks, plays, and sings.

Grand Award LP 33–368 *The Legend of Willie (the Lion) Smith.* Contains: Ain't Misbehavin'; Tea for Two; Maple Leaf Rag; Darktown Strutters Ball; St. Louis Blues; Charleston; ECHO OF SPRING; Ballin' the Jack; ROCK 'EM, ROLL 'EM, AND WEEP; S-h-i-n-e.

Late July, 1958
Willie (the Lion) Smith and other musicians at live concert presentation at Oakdale Music Tent, Wallingford, Conn.
Willie Smith Trio—SMITH, piano; Milt Hinton, bass; Don Lamond, drums.
Concert Jazz Orchestra—Don Elliott, Buck Clayton, trumpets; Tyree Glenn, trombone; Dick Hyman, clarinet; SMITH, piano; Milt Hinton, bass; Don Lamond, drums.

Metrojazz LP 2–E1009 *The Seven Ages of Jazz.* Contains: Maple Leaf Rag and SNEAK AWAY by the trio; Tiger Rag and Dippermouth Blues by the orchestra.

Englewood, New Jersey, August 16, 1961
Lucille Hegamin, vocalist, accompanied by Willie Smith's Band—Henry Goodwin, trumpet; Cecil Scott, clarinet and alto saxophone; SMITH, piano; Gene Brooks, drums.

Prestige-Bluesville LP 1052 *Songs We Taught Your Mother.* Contains: Arkansas Blues; Mississippi Blues; You'll Want My Love; Corrine, Corrina.

INDEX

Stride piano, 257; defined, 85
Sullivan, John L., 46
Swing era, 218, 221–22; peak, 243

Tanguay, Eva, 111
Tatum, Art, xi, 85, 204
Taylor, Charlie, 40
Teagarden, Jack, 171
Television: Lion, 284; Negroes in, 207 ff, 241
Theaters, 113; Negro, 197–98
Thomas, Lucy, 93
Thornhill, Claude, 171
Thornton, Caroline, ix
Tin Pan Alley, 134
T.O.B.A. (Theater Owner's Booking Association), 105, 127, 198, 290
Training, 252
Trial horse, 40, 40 n, 98
Tucker, Sophie, 111, 292
Tunney, Gene, 20, 173; -Dempsey fight, 174
Tunstall, Fred, 35
Turner, Joe, xi
Tutt & Whitney Smart Set revues, 42, 58
Twain, Mark, 6

Uncle Tomism, 288
Underworld, 28–29, 193–94

Van Vechten, Carl, 136, 137; Nigger Heaven, 136
Variety, 136
Vaudeville: road companies, 113 ff; "spotters," 120; pre-World War I, 58–59

Vaughan, Sam, vii

Walker, James J., 153, 172
Waller, Thomas "Fats," xi, xiv, 56 n, 63, 83, 85, 89, 98, 99, 150, 154, 157, 194, 206; "Ain't Misbehavin'," 138–39; characteristics, 228–30; composer, 258; death, 256, 257; friends, 230–31; parties (society), 225–33
Walton, Maurice & Florence, 110
Warner, Charlie, 21
Waterman, Guy, 83, 188
Waters, Ethel, 35, 67, 93, 94, 123, 134, 137, 183, 258, 289; on Harlem, 110–11
Wellstood, Dick, 253–54, 277
White, George, Scandals, 137, 138
White, Leon, 41
White, Stanford, 108, 132
Whiteman, Paul, 68, 171, 227
Wilkins, Barron, 49, 55, 88, 99, 135, 145, 183
Wilkins, Leroy, 88 ff
Williams, Bert, 56, 94, 95–96, 102
Williams, Clarence, 124–26, 208–11, 247, 258; jug band recordings, 218
Williams, Ethel, 94
Willie the Lion Smith. See Lion, the
Wilson, John "Jack the Bear," 55–56, 85
World War I, 38, 70, 72–79; Black Devils, 74–75
Wright, Lillian, 35, 36, 37

Ziegfeld, Flo, 42
Ziegfeld Follies, 61, 95, 102, 168
Zwillman, Abner "Longie," 21

318 MUSIC ON MY MIND

F24